Jesun

F. Gerald Downing

JESUS
and the Threat of
FREEDOM

SCM PRESS LTD

232

British Library Cataloguing in Publication Data

Downing, F. Gerald
Jesus and the threat of freedom
1. Jesus Christ
I. Title
232   BT202

ISBN 0–334–00764–X

20023060

First published 1987
by SCM Press Ltd
26–30 Tottenham Road, London N1

Typeset by the Spartan Press Ltd
Lymington, Hants
and printed in Great Britain by
Richard Clay Ltd, Bungay, Suffolk

Contents

Acknowledgments

Stimuli for the writing of this book came from many direc-
tions. I cannot hope to name them all.

There is Diana, with her love for God who loves us and
creates us in love, and with her loving interest in and care for
our whole environment and all its inhabitants.

Among many whose words, spoken or written, underly this
book, I must pick out Jeremy Seabrook, for his critical
perception of our present condition.

I refer in this essay to the works of a range of modern biblical
and other scholars. A number of them are picked out in the
Select Bibliography. I have not, however, in what follows
quoted more than a handful of words from any copyright
authors, and such few brief quotations are ascribed in the text
and notes.

The translations from ancient Greek and Roman authors
are (for better or worse) my own; but I record my gratitude to
the Loeb Classical Library (Harvard University Press and
Heinemann), in whose volumes many of the passages used
here can be read in wider context, in the original language,
with a translation.

And my thanks are due to the Council, to colleagues and to
the members of The Northern Ordination Course, who allow
me time and afford me stimulus for this and other reflection
and writing.

Pentecost, 1987   F. Gerald Downing
Crumpsall, Manchester.

Introduction

1. *Freedom*

Freedom for my gaoler is my bondage. Freedom for you to make money out of me means my exploitation. Freedom to enjoy what the adverts promise means I am bound to my company's career structure. Freedom for me to own may leave little free time for me to use, or for me to grow, or relate to others.

Many freedoms conflict. Freedom for one group may be bought at great cost to others. Forty years' freedom from war in Europe seems to have been bought at the cost of endless wars on others' territories, testing out our 'conventional' new weapons-systems. Our freedom to enjoy a high standard of consumption of food, and of raw materials for manufacturing industry, gives third world landowners the freedom to absorb still more of the land that once gave the peasants a living. Freedom for the arms trade leaves third world generals free to play soldier and sadist. Freedom for the nuclear power industry leaves governments free to fence off the countryside and conscript still more scientists. It leaves the clouds from Chernobyl free to wander half the northern hemisphere. A liberty based on nuclear power leaves a few elderly politicians free to make suicide pacts on behalf of the rest of us. People in the first century knew that freedoms conflicted. Writers such as Paul in the New Testament knew it (Gal. 5).[1]

Human beings and human societies – especially male human beings and male-led societies – seem very good at grabbing freedoms that destroy the liberties of others. They are actually also quite skilled at seizing freedoms that severely curtail their own – taking little liberties at the cost of massive enslavement. The scientific and technological advances of the last hundred years have enormously enhanced the available techniques for swapping greater freedoms for less without the exchange even being noticed. It is comfier to watch life on the small screen than it is to live it.

If every bondage can be a kind of freedom, even for the one enslaved, then every freedom can look like a threat, and the liberator may be very unwelcome. I don't want to be free for my neighbour when I have spent years building up defences to ensure my freedom from him.

If the only freedom at stake consisted in having a wide and ever widening range of choices of things to acquire, there might seem to be little to puzzle over. Some people have it, others may win it or (less likely) be given it. The rest must either be conned or policed into continuing to do the work that maintains it, and away from disrupting it. Yet it is not only those on the outside who lack liberty when liberty is restricted to unrestricted purchase of commodities. If the only freedom I enjoy is the freedom to load my hypermarket trolley my freedom even then is very much in question.

In the matter of evaluating liberties, and developing the skills for choosing clear-sightedly and effectively among them, there appears to have been very little progress over the centuries. Even our ability as the rich to enhance rather than decrease our own narrowly selfish freedoms seems little improved and very likely diminished. The slavery of those who thought they were free was very perceptively discussed in the first century; among others, by writers in the New Testament.

We might well, then, look to the past for insight and for encouragement. But we might as readily ask what help could the past offer, when our forbears' wisdom has left us where we are? We certainly cannot take it for granted that the past has anything to offer. And our society may be thought to be so different from any previous ones that even our most successfully emancipated ancestors have nothing useful to tell us. Yet with so precarious a hold on any major freedom, we could do well to look for aid from any quarter. (That is always supposing some greater freedoms are actually desired.)

For Christians and non-Christians alike it is worth noting that the early and pluriform Jesus movement began in an age much concerned with freedom, with enabling freedom, with discerning the threats to liberties in attempts to secure liberty at least for some; and with the possibilities of genuine liberties when the most obvious ones had been taken by force, or guile, or simply lost by careless stupidity. It was an age which had developed quite sophisticated devices of its own for transmuting richer freedoms into poorer ones, and hiding their poverty in specious finery. It is an age that may well turn out to have things to say to our own.[2]

Christians themselves have traditionally deployed the vocabulary of freeing and freedom, they have pointed to aspects of human bondage (Gal. 5), and they have asserted the possibility of effective redemption. Admittedly, Christian liberty has sometimes been seen as an alternative to secular and this-worldly freedoms, even as justifying their curtailment. This present book, however, is written with the convictions that original Christian insights (into 'freedom' and much else) were both 'religious' and 'secular', as well as both 'personal' and 'political', and that on all counts they still have much to offer. Anyone who maintains any kind of specifically Christian commitment is invited to re-examine here some of what still stands in the movement's earliest extant documents, the New Testament writings. People with other convictions may also find things of interest, and even of value.

2. *Some of Freedom's Friends*

On an errand to the market for some fish in a first-century east Mediterranean city, jostling with slaves and wives of workmen and children coming home from school and leisured gentlemen on their way to meet their friends at the baths, your attention is distracted by an eccentric character who doesn't seem to be buying or selling anything. Dressed in a simple cloak, leaning on a stick, looking as though he's not got a penny to his name, not even a change of shirt or a bag for food, he seems to be claiming to be some kind of physician. 'If you think you're in good health,' he shouts, 'don't bother to stop. I'm only here for the ones who are ready to admit they're a bit sickly. Or more than a bit.' You've heard his kind before. They tell you you're sick with worry about your property, about whether your clothes are in fashion, about whether the fishmonger will have anything in tomorrow that you can afford. One day's worry at a time is enough. They'll set you free, cure you of your cares.

We ourselves have very likely heard something of this before, perhaps from Matthew's gospel. But the man in the market place is not a Christian. He is a 'dogged philosopher', a follower of Diogenes, who was native of Sinope on the Black Sea, but lived most of his adult life in Corinth, in the fourth century BCE. The speaker is a Cynic. 'Cynic' means 'doggish', and is said to have come from an insult thrown at Diogenes which he then disarmingly accepted. 'I bark at anything that threatens human living. I'm the best watch-dog you could hope to have.'[3]

Our speaker is 'cynical' in the way he is suspicious of your motives and the good face you put on; he's not 'cynical' in our sense of 'unscrupulous'. Far from it. He is 'a free man under Father Zeus, afraid of none of the great lords'. A Christian might have said, 'no longer a slave, but a son – and if you're a son, you're God's heir'. If you took the trouble to listen to each, 'unpacking' what they said, you might find rather different meanings. Or they might be quite similar. That is an issue that will concern us in what follows. Here it is enough to point out that they would have sounded similar to many hearers.

Our gospel records come from the setting of the Greek-speaking towns where what these Christians said would very often have sounded like what the Cynics said. We need to try to understand it in this setting if we are to understand it at all, and certainly if we want to try to press back to Jesus the Jew as the one from whom it is said to have stemmed.

The Christian and the Cynic would both in fact have sounded 'political'. It was popular preachers like our Cynic who did their best to free people to be more fully and richly human, in the time of Christ. They'd been doing it, sometimes more of them, sometimes fewer, for the last four centuries. Some of the first Christians would have looked like them and often talked like them. I shall argue that the overlap of their concerns, Christian and Cynic, is illuminating – but also potentially enlivening, and liberating – for our social and 'political' lives as well as for our individual living.

There were many ways of being 'political' in the first century (as there are in our day). Some people talk as though only those willing to use force are 'political', and suggest that if Jesus (or his followers; or both) repudiated the Zealot way of armed revolution, or if the Cynics did not adopt it, they were renouncing politics. But you could be involved in imperial administration, or a local town council, you could bribe officials, you could discuss Plato's and Aristotle's political theories; and you could raise ordinary people's critical awareness of society and the world around. All these are genuinely political, and this last, 'consciousness raising', could quite readily appear as subversive, as politically important. It was then, and it may be today.

3. *Then and Now – Chasm or Connections?*

However, I have already drawn attention to an issue that is widely seen as problematic. Is there sufficient in common between our society and that of the first-century east Mediterranean, sufficient for Jesus and others from there to speak usefully to us about any aspects of our lives, political or other? Some would insist that society then and there is so foreign to us and ours that what people said then cannot even be understood, let alone be informative today. The first chapter of this book addresses itself to that question.

In Chapter I we begin by considering, briefly, some of the theoretical problems that are raised. Mainly I shall try to picture the kinds of freedom and the areas of freedom about which people in general were reflecting and expressing concern all those centuries ago, in their everyday lives. It seems inherently probable that the first Greek-speaking Christians, (the people for whom the New Testament documents were written) grew up sharing these general attitudes and aspirations. More evidence to support

this assertion will appear in Chapter III. I shall try to allow both
similarities and differences to appear, as compared with our own
diverse society. I shall then try to allow each reader to judge
whether the similarities are genuine, and enabling; or whether
any real differences that may emerge are such as to preclude our
understanding and so still more our using what was said then –
and lived.

The second chapter consists in a portrait of modern Britain,
France and America, looking with other eyes than just my own, to
press still further the question of whether issues at stake in the
first century do really reappear in our own. The issues on which I
shall there concentrate attention are of course also the ones to
which I hope the remainder of the book will speak.

The third chapter, then, looks at the ways these liberties and
slaveries were discerned in the first century, and the practical
strategies suggested for enhancing freedom, both by those who
spoke in the name of the 'dogged' Cynic tradition, and those who
spoke in the name of Jesus the crucified Jew. It invites a re-reading
of some of the New Testament documents in the light of those
contemporary debates about freedom and bondage. It is clear
that Jesus can be interpreted in many different ways today – and
the most popular in the Western world is as a very private
religious figure offering comfort and supporting conventional
morality. There are other possibilities: other-worldly mystic,
prophet of the end-time, freedom-fighter. What is being asked in
this main section of the book is how Jesus seems likely to have
appeared to those who first heard the stories and the teaching of
the first three gospels – and how he must have appeared to those
who went on re-telling this teaching and these tales. When we set
the stories about Jesus the teacher alongside the Cynic material
available to us, we see him in fact presented as radical and
political and disruptive.

The fourth chapter asks whether we can trace the Jesus
presented in this 'Cynic' guise by at least some early Christians
back to a figure in Galilee and Judaea in the late twenties or early
thirties of the first century. And even if we can, are we also able
still to link him closely with the less clearly Cynic figure
proclaimed by Paul and others like him among early Christians?

For many Christians today who are willing and persuaded to engage in this search, we may well seem to have reached the most crucial section of the book. Yet, if our records of Jesus' life and teaching have anything of the historical authenticity we may hope for, it is our practical, active response to his lived teaching that he would demand. For us as Christians, historical and theological reflection can only be a means to an end, albeit a necessary means. The fifth chapter, therefore, suggests some paradigms for considered action in today's 'Western' world.

I

Freedom in the First Century

1. *Access to the First Century – and to Jesus*

Jesus seems to invite us to a new and quite specific kind of freedom, and also to offer to liberate us from many kinds of bondage. This, I hope to show, is the message that many of the first Christians heard and responded to, and is one which it is open to us as well to hear and to respond to. Listening along with those first Christians we, too, can hear Jesus threaten our captivities with the promise of his liberty. And the promise may even be kept.

Yet, as has already been in effect admitted, two thousand years is a long time for a human voice to carry, accurately and intelligibly. And even if we are convinced that it can, and that it has reached us meaningfully, there is still no guarantee that a message framed in the first century has anything at all to say effectively in the twentieth.[1]

Sex, violence and gluttony on film may encourage us to feel we can be at home in the first century. At least it is not too difficult to imagine dressing up and getting drunk and losing our inhibitions. Remembering what it was like, last time you were confined to bed, trying to eat lying on one elbow, may rather spoil the illusion. But the film makers remain confident. Liquor, blood and lechery are lively interests for most of us. Setting them among pillars, rounded arches and leather-kilted soldiery will not leave us at a loss. We can cross the gulf of two thousand years. Of course it helps if the actors speak English (or American, or French, or whatever our native language happens to be).

A little further reflection may dispel the ready illusion. We've simply imagined our twentieth-century selves playing some self-indulgent charade. We've crossed no gulf of time at all. We've not understood what it would have meant to be a lone German prisoner condemned to the amphitheatre, or a patrician boy with the grim weight of countless ancestral death-masks on your pretty shoulders.

It may simply not be possible for us to cross the chasm, and the gap may be far too great for us to hear and understand anything said or done on the far side.

So some would insistently argue. Perhaps at best we could shed our twentieth-century selves and become immersed in some aspect of the first, only then to have to leave it all behind on our return. The better we'd understood, the more foreign it would all turn out to have been.

Others again say it would be better still were we to abandon all pretence of time-travel. If we must read Paul or Plutarch, it should be as though the Greek, or its English rendering came from some contemporary, writing last year, or yesterday, for us to engage with her words just as they stand.

Yet those who say these things – and write them – expect us to read their books and understand them, though they write in other cities and alien societies, with the help of esoteric philosophies of existence or of structure. If we do read, and concentrate on what is foreign to us, and technical, it can be very difficult. It may be hard to tell even whether the terms of last year's debate are used consistently, let alone gauge to what end they are deployed.

It may be difficult, but it does not have to be impossible. With patience we begin to frame hypotheses (guesses). 'If I've got him right, then he's going to say we enjoy being surprised, and he's going to try to surprise me.' And he does both, and it works for me: I am surprised, and enjoyably. Trying to understand a contemporary is rarely if ever a matter of all or nothing, it is much more likely to be a matter of more or less, and the less can often be improved on.

Yet trying to understand (and use) what someone said or wrote in 1986 is not in principle different from trying to comprehend what he said twenty years ago, or sixty; or what his father said in that conversation; or what his father said sixty years before that. And so on backwards. It is a matter of patient checking, getting more or less of the sense. And the more that what was said (or written) was in colloquy with others who were themselves conversing with others again, the more checks we have on whether we are actually understanding.[2]

If the talk is pure abstraction we may be systematically mistaken: coherent, but misled. If the talk includes reference to attitudes and actions, and if it is displayed in narrative we are much better placed to understand. We are then also in a much better position to respond ourselves. One who talked of loving enemies and was pictured acting out love for enemies and telling stories of love for enemies may be able to free us at least to consider allowing our enemies to love us.

This discussion itself is already rather abstract (and, if the reader wants more such, more is listed in the notes). It is much better to look at the evidence (with these critical questions kept in mind). After all, those who say the first century is alien say they say so on the basis of the evidence. If their claim makes any sense, they must have understood something of what was being said, to sense something strange about it. If they'd tried even harder it might have made still better sense, usable sense even. (Of course, it also might not.)

Trying to understand anything involves us; trying to understand people in the past involves looking carefully at ourselves, trying to be aware of the factors in our own make-up that help or hinder comprehension. As I noted in the *Introduction*, we shall have to survey, if briefly, our late twentieth-century situations – our situations – to which some of us may hope and trust the words and deeds of Jesus may be found to speak. But before doing that we must look a little more closely at the first-century scene itself, to find whether what is said in records from the time seems to be understandable. Even if it seems to be, we must still check to tell if that impression is justified. If it is justified, it will almost certainly entail that what was said and done was itself acted out and spoken in yet wider social contexts also not completely alien to our own. But certainly, before we act on what we may suppose we have understood we shall need to be sure that the contexts then and now tally sufficiently for the guidance from back then to be appropriate. Only so could the freedom spoken of and maybe lived then itself be effectively lived now; (always supposing that we are willing to listen and respond).

So we begin by trying to understand better the first-century audience for the stories about Jesus and his teaching as they appear in the synoptic gospels, Matthew Mark and Luke. In that way we may understand the stories better, and their proclamation of Jesus. If we achieve that we are in a better position to move back again to Jesus himself, and, it may be, perceive him more clearly, too.

2. *Freedom and Human Flourishing*

The sources used for this sketch of first-century life and concerns appear for the most part in another recent work of mine, entitled *Strangely Familiar*, and there are references to appropriate sections of it in the notes to this chapter. Specific references are given in the notes to passages actually quoted here. A wider selection of the specifically Cynic material is due to appear in a separate collection, entitled *The Christ and the Cynics*. The sources used are discussed in section 3 of this chapter, and their relevance for this survey is explained and defended. There is a brief account of the main authors in the *Appendix*.

In the first century, as always, people needed air, water, food, and physical good health; and much of the time these needs go without mention. We'll return to them in due course. They are talked about when they are under threat – or when people are contentedly counting their blessings. Famine and ill-health and early death did quite often hold people's attention, but by no means all the time. The basic needs were well enough met enough of the time for people to attend to other concerns, other hopes and fears.[3]

We shall commence at the level of individuals relating to one another as friends and as associates, and in households as parents and children, husbands and wives. We shall move out from there into education and 'culture' in its more restricted sense, in society at large. After that we shall consider slavery, work, and economic relationships in general. That will lead us to a discussion of political structures, and to 'religion' in the wider community; and from there we shall return to a further brief consideration of individuals.

People wanted to be free to spend time at leisure in congenial company. Aristocratic gentlemen wrote elegant essays about friendship, and kinds of compatibility. They wrote carefully contrived epistles to their friends, for other friends to enjoy – and admire. It is hard to know how we should read the letters that have survived. It could have all been a formal game, with the sole aim of cementing social status. But taken at face value the writing suggests a genuine feeling, a willingness to admit vulnerability and dependence, an openness to finding pleasure in shared experience. We shall glance at one or two in what follows. This is a summary from Plutarch (the pagan priest and theologian and author whose stories William Shakespeare later used for some of his plays): 'Making a friend is a matter of careful judgment. But once made, enjoy him – and depend on him, and allow him to be useful to you, too. And then realize you can't expect to have lots of friends like him.' In the Fourth Gospel the language of friendship is used to summarize what Jesus has effected. As God's 'other self' Jesus has made his disciples not servants, but friends (John 15.14–15); and as such he shares with them all that really concerns him.[4]

Ordinary people, too, valued and enjoyed friendship, and especially savoured conversation with friends over a meal. Working people (and slaves, too) saved up so they could belong to clubs of one kind or another, where people could talk together at leisure over a meal (simple though the meal might well be). We even have some of the rules clubs drew up, and the menu: a quarter litre of wine, a small loaf, a few pilchards, just four times a year. On paper the club's aims might well be mutual insurance cover for burial costs, or promoting devotion to some divine being. In practice it was likely to be about enjoying human company. That was how Cicero remembered the meetings he went to for the cult of Cybele, and it is how any meal for enjoyment is described, as a time for friendly conversation. There are other times and occasions for talking together – the marketplace, the open fronts of shops where regular customers might gather, the theatre, the arena, the town hall, the law-court, the lecture-room. But leisure and at least sometimes food and drink with people whose company and talk you could enjoy were a very important part of any reasonable (and realistic) definition of a life worth living. Some if not all Christians in Corinth (1 Cor. 11) were finding the supper of the Lord Jesus a very stimulating social occasion.[5]

In the circles we know best, men and women did not mix freely. Women sometimes had their own separate clubs, and their own nights out. Even at home the only men they met might be 'family'. There are some signs, though, that this segregation was breaking down, during our period. The Christians in Corinth are just one example of women and men, poor and rich, in one mixed gathering.[6]

Husbands and wives, though, expected to enjoy each other's company, to be friends and partners. That was not all: there is a considerable realism in the elaborate marriage contracts which have survived (in Egypt). Marriage created an economic unit, with socially recognized rights and duties (and financial provision for the dissolution of the partnership). Marriages were 'arranged': her father or some other male 'guardian' acted for a woman (and her 'guardian' might be many years junior to his female 'ward'). There is no suggestion that the result was expected to be an 'equal' partnership, (perhaps 'symmetrical' is a better word). Yet there seems every indication of a widely accepted social norm: husbands and wives should enjoy each other, physically, emotionally, and intellectually. They should be 'free for' each other. They should expect nothing less.[7]

(It would be tedious to keep repeating the words 'free', 'freedom', 'liberty', and so forth. But what is being sketched and evidenced here is kinds of 'freedom for' one another that people in the first century seem to have expected.)

Dio Chrysostom (golden-tongued), who came from Prusa in Bythinia (in what is now Turkey), wrote an idealized account of first-century country life. His model is a romantic match between a couple in their teens who've known each other from childhood, and whose parents simply acknowledge the rightness of their choice. This is, thinks Dio, a much better basis for marriage than the financial contract of wealthier townspeople.[8] Dio's tutor in younger days, Musonius Rufus, teaching in Rome, had this to say:

> What was the creator's purpose in originally dividing our human race in two, and providing us with our respective genital organs, so we are male and female? and then in building in a strong desire to share sexual union with each other, mixed with a deep yearning for each other's company, the man for the woman, the woman for the man? Isn't it quite clear that he meant them to come together as a single unit, to live together, and to work hard to share a common livelihood . . .?[9]

'At the beginning of the creation "God made them male and female," and on that basis a man was to leave his father and mother and the couple were to be united as one flesh: not two individuals any more, but one organism . . .' says Jesus in Mark (10.6–8). 'Conversation, character, and comradeship', says Plutarch, are the stuff of a wife's relationship with her husband: not at all that of obedient servant; a husband's role is to learn empathy, not to play lord and master. His is, for Plutarch, still the leading role, but his task is to lead into partnership, to please and delight his wife, relaxed enough to enjoy a joke together.[10]

It is almost impossible to tell how well the ideal worked out in practice (and I shall not repeat this point every time). It is, anyway, the ideals that this survey is mainly attempting to display. Announced ideals are significant for the freedoms people value. Epitaphs on tomb-stones may not tell the truth; but they indicate what people feel ought to have been true. On contemporary gravestones 'ordinary' husbands (rich enough to mark a grave, but not to erect any elaborate tomb) talk of their dead wives as friends and partners, not as obedient servants. When Dio talks of tension in a household, it is not in terms of wifely 'insubordination' (still less of wife-battering), but of bickering. Seneca discovers a surprising new value in himself when he finds he is valued by his wife.[11]

Stories of the time simply take it for granted that girls will have received the same primary education as boys (though it was unusual for girls to go any further). But for many people their 'culture' will have been absorbed mainly through conversation with their peers, and through listening to public speakers and performers. Among the wealthier there was a strong feeling, as we have noted, that from puberty women should be segregated. But even then, in the family, there might well be cultured conversation, and access to books, too, for its women. Pliny the younger (so called to distinguish him from his adopting uncle of the same name) was a busy and respected aristocratic government official. He writes of his young wife to her aunt who has brought her up:

> She is very perceptive, and a very careful manager; and her love for me at the same time displays her purity. In addition she is taking an interest in literature, an interest that itself sprang initially from her love for me. She has copies of things I've written, reads them, learns them off by heart, even . . . When I read my work to friends, she settles herself close by, behind a curtain (!), and listens out especially for any praise they offer. She sings my verses, to her own settings, accompanying herself on her lyre, without benefit of music master, inspired only by love, always the best teacher.

It is, as said, an 'asymmetric' relationship: but it is clearly a relationship, and at many levels. Paul (or some later editor) may want Christian wives to postpone discussing what is said at meetings until they are back at home with their husbands (1 Cor. 14.34–36). But he knows they are going to want to – and they seem to have been used to responding on the spot to the intellectual stimulus offered.[12]

Among less wealthy people, without the resources for women's quarters, or for womenfolk to be released from economically productive activity, there will have been very similar access to contemporary oral culture for women and men alike.

We must suppose, unless clear indications to the contrary can be found, that at any rate the ideal marriage involved a mutual intellectual as well as emotional enrichment, along with its economic and social functions.

Pliny's Calpurnia, to their great sorrow, never brought to full term any of the children she carried. Musonius, we have noted, allowed that procreation was an important, though not the only or even the most important reason for marriage. Couples wanted children, and not only or always for economic reasons. In some areas social and economic pressures did mean that boys were much more sought after than were girls; daughters might well be 'exposed' – left for any chance passer-by to bring up for whatever purpose they pleased: or to die. But in many instances daughters were as cherished as were sons. Pliny writes of a friend's dead daughter,

> I never saw a girl so cheerful and lovable, someone who so much deserved to live . . . she was so affectionate with her nurses, attendants and teachers; she tackled her books so eagerly and intelligently, her play with restraint and care. She bore her terminal illness with calm patience and a very real courage.

Mark's gospel gives us two tales of daughters restored to health, one of a son. Musonius insists that girls can profit as much as boys from any education worthy of the name. There were no roles in wider society in which girls could 'use' a wider education; Musonius does not seem to have to argue whether or not they could cope with it. (Later, and perhaps already as early as this, the rabbis recognized that girls are mature intellectually earlier than boys.)[13]

Children were not just potential adults, to be tolerated until old enough to earn (though that could be true, too). Children could be appreciated for themselves. Childless and austere Epictetus asks, 'Who is not tempted by attractive, lively children, to join their play and crawl on all fours, and talk baby-talk?' and none of his hearers seem to have queried his question. Of a minority who doubted the value of the family and the bother of rearing children he asked, 'Who on earth follows your advice when he sees his child fallen down and crying on the ground? I guess that even if your own mother and father had known you were going to say such things, they'd still not have followed your kind of advice, and exposed you!' Plutarch (albeit in a very carefully composed 'consolation' to his wife) paints a moving picture of their newly dead daughter, full of careful observation of the toddler's behaviour. But it was not only a Platonist such as Plutarch who watched his child's growth with fascination. A century earlier Cicero had stressed the value for adults of observing the whole range of children's activity, as they try to stand, come to recognize their nurses, play with others, join in games, listen to stories, share what they are enjoying, and freely explore their environment.[14]

Parents care for and about their children, and find them absorbing – or are expected to. And the actual care is not simply the mother's job, not even in a family too poor to have servants. Epictetus pictures as commonplace a father getting his child off to school in the morning. Jesus, too, expects a male parent himself to respond to a hungry child. On the other hand death created many single-parent families, with mother (or aunt) quite explicitly expected to provide fatherly as well as motherly care. The respective roles are fairly clearly defined, but they overlap considerably, and (as today) most people simply had to be free to exchange them.[15]

These are only some of the 'individual' and 'personal' freedoms sought by some people in the first century. Others and these people themselves almost certainly looked for other and conflicting freedoms. I consider later in the chapter some of the problems they faced. What we have seen so far is evidence of a quite common concern to be 'free for' other people, in a way that demands that they should be allowed to be 'free for' us. Some may have seen others as living tools, children as empty containers to be filled (if need be by force), and adults as self-contained rational minds inconveniently embodied. Yet it is the former, humane and 'personalist' complex of ideals that has come down to us much more powerfully in our records of the first century.

Having considered people's hopes of being free to relate one-to-one, or in small groups of friends or family, we move out a little to consider their appropriation of common culture, their patterns of wider socialization, their freedoms in society at large.

Our initial impression of a humane and 'personalist' concern is reinforced. Cicero asks whether it has escaped our notice how great an interest children take in the world around, delighting in some piece of knowledge – and the chance to share it, oblivious to hunger and thirst once their curiosity has been aroused, their attention captured. Even punishment, he says, will not deter them. It is the child's interest, insists Quintilian, that should be the spur to learning. Corporal punishment is entirely out of place. It is up to the educator to ensure that the child enjoys study, and certainly never comes to hate it. It is not that the child should never be corrected, but basically ought on balance always to be affirmed. The teaching relation, Epictetus avers, must be one of trust and affection – for daughters as well as for sons. The test, Philo points out, is whether the pupil can produce original work (and the teacher avoid congratulating himself). There is no pretence, however, that this is easily achieved, and Epictetus has a nice little pen-portrait of the disgruntled undergraduate:

> I wonder what they are thinking back at home? expecting me to be doing well, I bet. Saying, 'He'll come back knowing everything there is to know.' Sure, I came wanting to do well at everything, learn all there was to learn. But it's a hard grind. No one's sent me anything from home for ages, and the baths (= recreational facilities?) here are lousy and my digs are rotten. And so are the classes.[16]

Several anecdotes take it for granted that children of plebeian families will receive at least a primary education (girls and boys alike, I have already pointed out). Teachers were poorly paid. Parents (mothers and fathers alike) too poor to buy even cheap education are nonetheless thought likely to have sufficient education themselves to be able to share it. How realistic this ideal is, it is hard to say. But there is in these circles no suggestion that the elements of a 'liberal' education would be wasted on the poor. Literally (in Latin) that meant the education fitted for someone legally free. But bright slaves in a large household might also be educated, to serve as steward or secretary; and others were likely to pick up a lot of what was being discussed and recited around them. Epictetus (himself a highly educated freed slave) readily imagines a servant such as he was dealing with his master's dilettante doubts about the validity of sense-experience (see below).[17]

Adults as well as children are expected to be motivated by the subject in hand, by a desire to explore, to enrich their experience, to create. Music, mathematics, astronomy, geography, biology, history, political theory, romantic fiction, bawdy comedy – all were worth attention, for their own sake, and because others were interested in them, too. Other people were intriguing. Of course, understanding them might give you freedom to manipulate them, allow you a heady power over them (and we return to that kind of possibility later); but our writers seem to display a concern for genuine persuasion that starts where a hearer is and takes him to a conclusion he can himself authentically affirm. And recent scholarship has discerned just such an intention in Jesus' parables (as we shall note again in Chapters III and IV). It is by no means beneath you to attempt to communicate with people who have enjoyed less of an education than you have, insists Quintilian. Dio is flattered to find that other people are making money out of better or worse transcripts of his speeches, selling them in the market, in competition with popular song-sheets. (It is here, of course, that it becomes clear that even among our 'aristocratic' writers we are in touch with a much wider audience.) People expect to be free for this kind of intellectual stimulus and enrichment.[18]

So much has been written, and yet there is still so much to be found out, so many hypotheses to be elaborated, and tested for their coherence – and for their fit with external reality. Dio pictures the crowds that gather when a trained physician discourses on physiology or a student of astronomy describes the latest theories. Our sources display a frequent refusal to rest satisfied with past 'authority', whether in 'pure' thought or empirical explanation. Pliny the elder died on an expedition to see at first hand what was happening in the erruption of Vesuvius which overwhelmed Pompeii and Herculaneum. Quintilian asks, 'Who doesn't ask about the causes of natural phenomena? not even ordinary countryfolk are uninterested.' Epictetus almost loses his temper with people who disparage sense experience. A house slave, says he (having been one himself) would soon sort them out. They'd quickly find they could tell the difference between bath oil and anchovy sauce . . .[19]

When a block is reached in an individual adult's path through this shared exploration of the human world, the only valid help will be Socratic. Socrates, Plutarch reminds us, actually did not 'teach' at all. He teased out people's perplexities, he acted as a midwife to ideas waiting to be born, but not as yet fully formed. At most he proposed instances, parables, paradigms, allowing others to reach their own conclusions.[20]

This humane and 'person-centred' view of learning and culture extends on into an appraisal of social, political and economic reality. Ideally there would be no slavery. What possible justification can there be for the institution? asks Dio. It can only ever have got under way through war or kidnapping, through injustice. Societies that refuse slavery are held up for admiration by Pliny senior, and by Philo. Slaves are fellow humans, insist Dio and Seneca. Zeus is our common father, your slave is your brother, argued Epictetus. Call no man 'Master', insists Jesus in Matthew (23.10). Though Seneca risked ridicule for sharing meals and meal-time conversation with his slaves, Pliny junior expected admiration for his determination to allow all well-behaved slaves to die free, with the dignity of a will which their master would take it on himself to execute, and he allows himself to grieve a little. 'I don't care what I've said about the Law concerning mourning for slaves. My slave Tabi was a man of worth', says Rabban Gamaliel in a tale told later. And slaves, as we have seen, could belong along with freemen and freedmen to religious and to burial societies. Each year the Saturnalia, the festival of Cronos at the winter solstice, had masters waiting on their servants (I don't think we know in how many households), re-inforcing the myth of a Golden Age where no one was slave, and no one exploited, as the model of how things ought really to be. It was a myth of a returning 'Golden Age' that appealed especially to Cynic radicals. It has also attracted attention among Jews.[21]

That no one should face the risk of being master is less clearly said in this context; that power corrupts at the highest level was forcefully pointed out, as we shall note a little further on.[22]

Ideally everyone – every family unit, at least – should be economically self-supporting. That did not entail solitary self-sufficiency, for a division of labour would allow each to contribute to the common good, and best distribute what each really needed; and only such co-operation could sustain the kind of production and leisure that might allow people to share each other's company and together enjoy a rich communal culture of the kind outlined above.[23]

It has to be admitted that this last ideal seems to be openly spelled out in 'practical' economic detail only by a few of our authors. It is most clearly stated by Dio, addressing the emperor Trajan in the seventh, the 'Euboean' discourse. People should be allowed to own such land as they could reasonably work, and no one should be forced into jobs that really are demeaning (though no genuinely useful job should be seen as demeaning, either). Land and employment ought not to be distributed in a way that forces people into towns, to beggary, and to exploitation, often sexual. It is probably significant that Dionysius of Halicarnassus' popular history of Rome allows the debate over land distribution and the economic system that deprived peasants of lands once held to range on from episode to episode. Cicero is uneasy; Seneca, with his own vast wealth, could not imagine how vast estates could ever have been honestly gained, from the time of the Golden Age when all was common property. Jesus' story of the workers hired throughout the day and all paid the same wage also suggests an awareness of the problem. Freedom from poverty and exploitation was an issue that people would at least discuss at all levels of society.[24]

Cicero notes that it goes without argument that a prime call on any administration is the ensuring that basic needs are met for all. State doles and the 'patronage' system ought to suffice. Philo, also wealthy, offers for admiration the scriptural demand (as he reads it) that any remaining poor should have their needs met, not as a matter of optional or even legal charity, but as a right, as integral to their human dignity as children of the same divine father.[25]

In no human grouping should any be made to feel outsiders. You've been debating long enough, says Dio to the fully enfranchised citizens of Tarsus. You benefit economically from the linen workers in the city, and when other trade is not so good you make noises about granting them full citizen's rights – but you never get round to doing it. That's just not good enough. An economic community, many agreed, should be as mutually beneficial to those who have a part in it, as are limbs of a body to one another. It cannot be right to have two cities in one, a rich one and a poor one.[26]

Diogenes the Cynic, exiled from his own home-town, resident alien in Athens, was credited with coining the term 'cosmopolitan', citizen of the world. The ideal is often quoted in our period, the insistence on human unity across barriers of status and race, barbarian or Greek, bond or free. The outsider can be the one who holds up a mirror to you, calling you back to a fuller humanity. Even the hated Samaritan can be an example to Jews.[27]

Although there are some theoretical – and practical – anarchist tendencies at this time, most of our thinkers presuppose a minimum of social organization and so of leadership. But it must be leadership for the people, even if few suppose it can be leadership by the people. It must also be government with the people's consent, their active co-operation. Nothing less than this can be effective in the long term, and nothing less than this is worth having. With this in view, the distinctions that are by this time classical, between aristocracy and oligarchy, monarchy and tyranny, democracy and anarchy, are firmly maintained. The favoured one of each pair involves the clear maintenance of law, as minimum structure of civic relationships that allow people to know where they are, with plenty of room created and maintained for variety and a sense of freedom. Whether created statute law or tested customary law is to be preferred is debated. But it should be maintained in a way that does not favour the rich against the poor, the influential exercising their authority against the marginal, 'lording it' over them. So said Jesus, among others (Mark 10.42–43).[28]

The highest ideal at the time is a 'democracy' of people mature enough not to fall victim to anarchy, oligarchy or tyranny. But contemporary preference is for ideals that seem realizable. Utopianism is not the ideal solution. Some measure of real present freedom, some practical enhancement of present freedom is worth more than a distant promise. 'A little while back', wrote Philo, 'when some actors were staging a tragedy of Euripides, and reached the lines,

The name of freedom is worth all the world,
If you have just a little, value it a lot,

I saw the entire audience [in Alexandria] get to their feet and cheer loud enough to drown the actors.' Pliny junior wrote to a friend taking up the governorship of Greece (Achaia), 'to rob them of freedom's name and appearance, all they now have left, would be a cruel and harsh barbarity'. Above everything else, people want to be free, comments Dio.[29]

And that freedom must include freedom from war and freedom from the threat of war and, insist some, freedom from any willingness to use war as an instrument of policy. The liberty sought explicitly entails the freedom to live at peace, with disputes (should any arise) settled by negotiation, and never an easy recourse to armed force. Those who take the sword will die by it. The image of the heroic warrior could be happily ignored, and that of the athlete was much preferred. The Greek east long stood out against the Roman delight in gladiatorial combat (which itself sickened some of our Roman writers). Lucian tells us that when the Athenians were considering building an arena for gladiatorial shows, it was enough for the Cynic philosopher Demonax to ask, 'Along with closing down the temple of mercy?' for the project to be dropped.[30]

Death itself, of course, was accepted as inevitable. In a frequent image, life was a fixed-term loan. But it should be possible to live your span in good health, at least good enough not to be distracted from sharing in the common enjoyment of life. That was part of the ideal, even for the most ascetic. Ill-health bad enough seriously to curtail your social and cultural existence was a signal to surrender the loan, and die with dignity.[31]

You hoped to live without fear and die without fear. (How that might be possible I consider in due course.) For most of those whose thoughts we've been glancing at, it involved the trust that we live within a fatherly divine care, invited to share in celebrating a festival of life. Then you could feel really free to be yourself in relation with others, in a freedom divinely given and guaranteed, not to be tampered with by anyone, least of all by God. There might be yet more living to be enjoyed after this death, but no ground for complaint at the idea that this is all, for this, freely enjoyed, is already wealth beyond counting.[32]

It was important to be able to engage in myth-making, spinning metaphysical webs to tie together the bits and pieces of experience, remaining free to see your myths as just pictures you've painted for yourself or borrowed, but also free to entertain them as possible pointers to how things really are. We find impressive examples in Dio and in Plutarch, both 'popular' and 'popularizing' writers.[33]

3. *Taking Stock*

It is time for an interim stock-taking. The foregoing sketch of first-century ideals is meant to engage the twentieth-century reader, and arouse some sense of fellow-feeling. The reader may find she or he shares at least some of the hopes and aspirations touched on, or, at the very least, is aware that others around us do. Whether the reader's sympathies will have been engaged at all extensively the writer has, of course, no means of judging. The attempt will continue in the next chapter, but from the side of current impressions of our own century.

The account given is also meant to be historically accurate. The evidence on which it is based is, as already noted, set in context in the *Appendix*. That the writings used do go back to the first century or thereabouts is generally accepted.

As importantly, the selection is intended to be genuinely representative of views that then obtained. There is no suggestion that everyone thought the same way, and the point has in fact been made from time to time that these expressions of hope and conviction are parts of ongoing debates. Some, perhaps many, saw things differently. What may validly be concluded is that these were live issues, and the positions presented here were genuine options. It has been noted from time to time already that these options were not restricted to the aristocratic circles to which most of the writers drawn on belonged, but were views in general currency, ideas that would attract and hold popular audiences. The evidence that this is so is best presented cumulatively, and more is forthcoming when we concentrate specifically on the Cynic and Christian evidences.

As has already been asserted, it is inherently probable that the first Greek-speaking Christians had grown up sharing the largely oral popular versions of this culture which we know of mainly, of course, from these literary remains (amplified only by products of the visual and plastic arts). Evidence to support this deduction will, as already promised, be forthcoming in later chapters.

Hoping, then, that the reader will have found some initial points of contact with a number of historically authentic strands in first-century east Mediterranean reflective human living, we shall resume our brief survey.

The debates about human freedom and human flourishing which we have been overhearing were not simply arm-chair nor lecture-theatre theorizing. There were real threats to be faced, there were powerful forces in opposition. Some of these we now consider. If we find we share not only some or many of the aims, but also a range of similar problems, then the practical advice for living that reaches us in the name of Jesus (and maybe others from the first century) may seem still more worth attending to.

4. *Threats to Freedom*

We move in reverse order, from myth and metaphysics, through politics and economics, to culture, and thence to individual relationships.

One major threat to human freedom and human flourishing discerned in the first century by many of the authors already introduced was 'superstition', the fear of offending a tetchy and vindictive divine being. The proportion of people in today's Western world sharing such a crippling anxiety is probably less. The proportion among those claiming to be 'religious' who see religion in these terms may still be quite high (witness the response in Britain to a fire in York Minster). Certainly many who express religious convictions seem committed to a paranoid tribal deity who backs loyalists against republicans (or vice-versa) in Northern Ireland, or Iranians against Iraqis (or vice-versa), or promises 'rapture' to favoured Americans when at last he gets round to igniting the atomic holocaust for the rest of us.

Film viewers in the United States, and in much of the rest of the world where it sells its films will still entertain the idea of demonic possession. Though other supposed 'powers' may not be so clearly 'personalized' they may still be impersonally 'hypostatized', 'reified', as 'market forces' and the like; and as such they may be honoured with more or less conviction as benign. The factors thus being given mythic expression are often important, and need articulation. The threats to human freedom and integrity when these forces are treated as autonomous and uncontrollable are as real today as they were perceived to be two thousand years ago.[34]

Other fears are perhaps livelier than they were then. Our leaders claim we only live at all in living by fear, fear instilled by our weapons, fear our enemies must feel they instill in us to still their own. There were voices just as loud in the first century in their insistence on maintaining peace by threats of destruction: only then the threats were not quite so obviously suicidal, the arsenals not so clearly a danger to their owners. Lesser fears of 'civil' disturbance (riots in Brixton, in Miami, in Alexandria, in Caesarea, in Prusa) were as urgent then as now: the politics of the poor, those who feared they had nothing to lose. The fears now are similar enough, as is their threat to any real freedom.[35]

Death remains physically identical. Its social interpretation seems to cover a similar range. 'I wasn't, I am not, I care not' on a gravestone in the first century would represent the view of many today. A refusal to come to terms with it, a refusal to talk about it, may mean that a still deeper fear and loneliness undermines for us the culmination of our days; as may the fascination with death glamourized and sanitized on television screens, and courted on the roads. Others' deaths offer far more entertainment today than they did even in ancient Rome.[36]

Our concern for health is similar, as is our attitude to our doctors. The objective dangers to health in the first sixty years of life are less (it is itself a much longer span than the average for those surviving childhood in the first century). We may nevertheless spend as much time grappling with impaired health. The effect on us, on our ability to operate as responsible people, of the threat or onset of ill-health is often as debilitating. 'When the doctor calls,' urges Epictetus, 'don't be scared. And don't let yourself be overjoyed if he tells you you're doing well . . . Don't try to wheedle him into saying you're getting better, don't flatter his self-importance. Just pay his bill.' 'The doctors with the most following', notes Philo, 'are the ones who don't tell their patients the truth. They know it will only depress them, and not help them get better.' And then as now the best thing about a new drug was its newness, as Pliny senior observes, sardonically.[37]

We have, as already noted, less of a tendency to blame ill-health, including mental illness, on divine or quasi-divine visitation; though people still do. Such an explanation was not the only one, and demons might not even be considered, back then, either. 'We normally call it madness, we say people are not themselves, or that they've lost their wits', comments Plutarch.[38]

Responsible participatory democracy is as hard to achieve now as it seemed then. Our Western systems of government are much closer in style to the patronal style of the early Roman empire than might appear. Economic power is in the hands of unelected oligarchies in commercial companies, just as then wealth and power accumulated in the hands of a few, who shared it out in ways that seemed most likely to perpetuate their position and chosen self-image. It was a very wasteful form of distribution, one which demanded a massive foundation of poverty, with the constant risk of a tilt into raging desperation. We are just rather better equipped with doles and lotteries and displays of mindless affluence on television to make the excluded believe they belong, this must all be preserved for one day it could be theirs. And there is always the threat of becoming poorer than Portugal, or Mexico . . . or never being as rich as three-fifths of US citizens.

Representatives in city halls and (in our day) in central government can only do what seems to them best, and claim they have a mandate from the occasional election. Government still depends on consent, but popular consent is little more actively accorded or withheld than it was two thousand years ago. A very similar sense of powerlessness prevails. Leaders laud their own strong leadership, *Führerschaft*. A town council in Bythinia overspends, and Pliny comes in as the central government auditor. The culverting of a town drain in Amastis awaits permission from Rome. The powers of the security services are still stronger than when Epictetus remarked, 'A soldier sits down beside you: but he's in plain clothes. He begins criticizing Caesar, and you think that the fact that he's begun the blackguarding has given you a guarantee of his good faith. So you speak your mind, too. Then off you go – in chains.' But we know we belong to the free world, and we can say what we like, quite loudly, and we treasure the extra consumer goods that reward our fidelity. None of the recently promised socialist utopias has done any better, and most have done worse. Then as now, we feel we have to be realistic, and thankful for the small mercies accorded us. We are constantly reminded of how much smaller they might be, if we did not allow the rich to get richer still.[39]

Reforming social legislation is welcome, so long as it does not touch (and preferably distracts attention from) the customary bias of the law in favour of the property rights of those who have much at stake. Now, even more than then, the rich have much readier access to the courts than have the poor. Pleading then was still in many cases a rich man's sport, done for the fun of it at a client's request to his or her patron (and as long as the solidarity of the rich was not endangered). 'Justice' is far costlier now in much of the Western world.[40]

Nonetheless, the theoretical justification of minimal law as a framework for freedom is as much canvassed today as two thousand years ago. The anarchy that allows the physically powerful to take over oppression from the economically powerful is no gain for the oppressed.[41]

Yet the will and ability and the techniques for maintaining sectional interests also seem very similar across the time-gap. Then as now a black skin marked you as inferior – and threatening. A different language, a different accent, a different trade, a different schooling and upbringing could all count as justifications for excluding others from a share in your large or small privileges. It might well not be in their own best interests to include them. Disturb the whole system, says Cicero (and the moral majority and the white electorate in South Africa), and no one is better off. Make us poor enough, say the really poor, still, and we might as well give up altogether, we have nothing to lose. Freedom for the rich to be richer and to get even richer still today leaves the poor free to starve.[42]

We are far from being free in our Western 'democracies' from patterns of economic and social exploitation that leave individuals not simply with very little choice, but with their lives lived for them by others. Others are constantly making decisions for all of us, and not just for the poor. By unpredictable whim or by all too predictable rule they take control. In offices and shops and factories and homes, women and men, adults and children continue to be for much of the time extensions of others around them. The fact that this is not legal servitude, and that 'wage-slavery' is an unfashionable term, and domestic bondage a joke, serves only to disguise the pressures, and even exacerbate them. As Epictetus pointed out, there are strategies for dealing with slave-masters. It can be much harder when society demands that you pretend to a freedom you do not experience. We are not so free as to have nothing to learn from others' strategies for interim liberations.

Just as real then as now, and just as restricting, is the half-concealed prejudice of many self-declared liberals. Philo, who will admire the Essenes and others for not having slaves, will also talk of slaves' depraved characters, their low resistance to base self-indulgence; and so will an early Christian bishop. See what a mess an emancipated slave makes of his life! says one (ignoring the corruption of free 'high' society). See what a mess the ex-colonies have made of their independence! gloats another today. It is easy to ignore both the successes of some erstwhile colonies, and equally the corrupt and violent path of west Europeans and north Americans to their present occasionally elective oligarchies.[43]

Doles still get paid out to the poor, job creation schemes are cooked up, public works for public relations, palliatives for the plight of the impoverished in a system that needs them. That the poor should have economic 'rights' accorded them, that the rich have any duty beyond the occasional stirring of compassion, is as contentious. A re-distribution of real wealth, of power, of the control of the means of production is as much a dream now as it was two thousand years ago. Rome, Italy, and the major cities of the Empire as readily 'exported their proletariats' as our Western economies do. Within the cities everything had to have its price, as Dio noted, and the poor exploited the poor in tacit support of the system that degraded them. Then as now taxation hit them the hardest. The rich who see themselves as the thinking heart of the body politic still stress the organic model of inter-dependence, and most of the time the poor are as readily conned. When control snaps it is other poor groups, or ones very little better off, who are the likeliest targets for the ineffective fury of the oppressed, whether in Birmingham, England, or Birmingham, Alabama.

The basic human impulse to have someone to exploit in practice and to look down on, together with the social structures and the patterns of child-rearing that reinforce such drives remain very much the same, and are still as firmly entrenched (among women as well as men) despite equal opportunity laws. Epictetus asks how we can expect girls to fulfil their potential when from twelve or younger society tells them to be pretty play-things for men. It is a curious irony that a British women's magazine taking as its title Diogenes' coinage, 'Cosmopolitan', draws its main revenue from socially conservative industries perpetuating just that kind of restrictive role (alongside its editorial contradiction). The barriers to any effective 'world citizenship' for any woman or man, however willing they think themselves or are, do not seem to have changed much in character or strength.[44]

Yet among all these dehumanizing pressures, people do still hope to relate to others as people. A frequently canvassed reason for the high divorce rate in the United States for the past thirty years and in Britain for the past fifteen is the high expectation people have of that very relationship. It is quickly abandoned if the ideal is not realized. 'He wasn't just a husband,' said a young widow, 'he was a friend.' People have not been entirely seduced into the roles of 'buyer' and 'consumer' and 'producer' and 'processor'; they expect to relate as persons, and positively.

And still the problems for partnership within marriage remain. Plutarch's humane counsel to bride and groom would most likely infuriate even the mildest feminist today (who might prefer an open declaration of war). Yet the kind of opinion expressed in the more realistic secular 'marriage advice' pamphlets of this decade can make Plutarch look daringly liberal. It is the woman's task, in today's advice, to make the marriage – by a ready compliance (which of course her husband should graciously acknowledge).[45]

Some recent currents in adult (and younger people's) education are once more Socratic. Slogans such as 'The pedagogy of the oppressed', 'conscientization', 'person-centred learning', and the like, are very close to the humane traditions of the first century. The risk of escaping from the tyranny of the experts into a prison of one's own subjectivity remains as real. The amount of information and insight available is clearly enormously increased, and with that the range of choice of interest and skill and power over one's own life is enhanced. Yet techniques for critical appraisal and assimilation remain a problem.

There is still pressure on girls to accept a narrower range of interests than boys are offered, and every encouragement for the children of the rich and the not so rich to corner learning as a commodity and source of economic power. Thus defined in terms of economic power, learning is made to appear irrelevant to all but a few of the hispanics, the blacks, the poor. Then only a manageable and minimum necessary tally of recruits is drawn in from below to support without disturbing the holders of power and their ideologies.

The humane potential in learning is easily lost or endangered. 'Further Education' is a luxury commodity in the United States, and a soft target for public savings in Britain. The threat implicit in 'conscientization' is clearly recognized, and the critical study of society is actively discouraged; as it was in the first century. And learning, and skill in communication still allow us to manipulate others, though rather more effectively.[46]

The threats to any human flourishing, to any enriched human freedom in the first century seem frequently paralleled in the late twentieth century. The hopes that many entertained then, to be free to relate to other people in a varied and engaging world appear in very similar form today. Popular strategies for realizing those hopes then, and early Christian variations on such themes were worked out in a world that often looks familiar, even if at other times we do have to acknowledge aspects that are alien. It is always possible that more study, perhaps from a variety of available sociological stances, might distance us further. They might as readily bring us closer. There does for the moment seem to be sufficient similarity to allow some writing from that first century to face us in our time with the promise – and the threat – of an enhanced freedom.

(The 'pure' scholar may prefer to skip Chapter II, which is not obviously about the New Testament. I hope he or she will not, unless it is very quickly obvious that she or he is fully aware of the factors in our world there briefly reviewed, and their bearing on our understanding of what was being said by the early Christians and others in their day.)

There is a brief account of the non-biblical sources used here, in the *Appendix*.

II

Freedoms Under Threat in the Late Twentieth Century

1. *Where We Are*

People in the first-century eastern Mediterranean world can be understood by us, I have been suggesting, and can talk intelligibly about topics that concern us, major human freedoms among them. But even for those of us who start with some kind of traditional Christian commitment it is important to assess this intelligibility and relevance in detail. It is important for the honesty of our own living and reflection. It is significant in any attempt to share or simply debate our insights with others. And academic integrity as such is of more than 'merely academic' interest.

It might still not seem especially urgent. If people around us judge that all is well with our modern Western world, and humans flourish freely and securely, there is little of practical moment at stake. What ancient Christians have debated and what modern ones may repeat and reinterpret on issues of freedom and flourishing may not seem particularly pressing – even to Christians. Perhaps 'liberation theology' will have a ready audience in the dictatorships of Latin America. But in North America and Western Europe we have arrived at freedom, and need only to defend it against external threats. Or so it may be supposed.

In this present chapter I shall argue to the contrary, calling a representative group of witnesses to support my case. The opportunities for humans to flourish freely are limited and precarious, and the outlook is bleak. The threats to our major liberties discerned in the first-century debate menace us today, in our Western world. The fulfilment of the hopes we may well share with those of old time is far from guaranteed. The issues are live and urgent.[1]

That still does not in itself show that what we may read and understand about human freedom and flourishing in the first century has any practical importance today, even for Christians. That is for the reader to judge, in assessing the chapters that follow this one, and that comprise the main contribution of this book.

2. *Poverty and Oppression, US – UK*

A dominant set of supposedly attainable ideals for today's world is presented by the advertisers, the treacherous clerks of the cult of consumption. Freedom is packaged for sale in spray-cans of hair lacquer and deodorant, in the heavier metal of auto-mobiles, in bottles and packets of socially approved drugs. Those who buy are eternally young and lithe and good company – or at least, very attractive to the lithe and the young, and reality is an interminable soap opera set in plastic opulence, all available on credit.

So much for the fond faith. The reality is other. For the millions in the wealthy West who are excluded by age or by poverty or by gender or by commitment to dependants, the reality is quite clearly other. (I return a little later to those apparently more favoured.)

To live in relative and involuntary poverty in Reagan's America, or Thatcher's Britain, or Chirac's and Mitterrand's France, when freedom and human flourishing are defined in terms that exclude you, is destructive for the human spirit. The extremes of 'relative' poverty impose on the victims the role of non-member, of scape-goat. You serve solely as a dire warning to encourage the rest. Like the damned in Augustine's hell, you are needed to enliven the jaded pleasure of those meant to be enjoying paradise. ('A little bit of heaven on earth' – British Prime Minister

Margaret Thatcher, on her government's programme, 5 June 1986.)[2] For yourself you are nothing, for you have nothing to spend, and only spending is perfect freedom.

Your poverty may be 'merely' relative, and you may have the use of more consumer durables than a doctor or lawyer of a hundred years ago in New England, or of today in mainland China. But relative poverty brought home to you by every hoarding, newspaper and radio and television programme, by every visit to your neighbourhood shopping centre, and by every innocent and not so innocent display by others' children – and their parents – tells you you do not belong where life is being lived.

And this relative poverty has its absolutes. Those it includes are most likely ill fed and too hot in summer for comfort and too cold in winter for safety. Ill-fed and ill-clothed and ill-sheltered, they are most likely ill. Physically and psychologically they are more likely to be ill, and less likely to have their sickness tended.

In what follows my own eyes are aided by others, mainly by Michael Harrington for the United States, and Jeremy Seabrook for Great Britain, together with an occasional reference to John Ardagh for France. I also depend on the British daily newspaper, *The Guardian*, and the monthly journal *New Internationalist*. The chief concern of this chapter is to consider how things are for the poor, for the insecurely rich and for those in at least apparently safe possession of admired and envied wealth. Practical reflections on the implicit and explicit analyses wait until Chapter V.

There has been an increased internationalization of trade. Britain's economic supremacy was declining a century ago, overtaken by Germany and the United States. Now the heavy industries of all the Western countries, the United States included, are faced with competition from the Pacific basin, in iron and steel production, ship-building, the manufacture of automobiles, and so forth. And the 'new necessities', the multifarious electronic devices, are also mainly made there. When Britain and France had empires, they could export their poverty by imperial taxation and trade preference; and the imbalance between imports and exports was not so serious. The United States could hide its poverty within an 'internal' commercial empire, in Appalachia and the deep south. It was possible to imagine that domestic poverty could be overcome by increased production and some fine adjustments to the structures of distribution. But there was nothing wrong with the system. All could be made well, without any dramatic change anywhere.

(The economy of the first-century Mediterranean world was already complex. The massive trade imbalance between Rome and the remainder of Italy on the one hand, and, on the other, all the rest, was met by imperial taxation. But it was exacerbated by the cheap-labour economies of the provinces, themselves stimulated by central demand. There, too, those well-off could get wealthier, the poor poorer, with fewer and fewer in between. The costs of military defence – often 'offensive' defence – did not help.)

The situation to which Harrington recalls attention in the United States is one where the older 'blue collar aristocracy' – steel workers, builders of automobiles, operators of expensive mining machinery, have been shaken out of their security. Some will certainly have returned to favour with their bank managers. But even for them, the heavily mortgaged house, the other credit commitments, the health insurance, all the tokens of well-being now line up as potentially destructive hazards. And for many past forty the house in the area where no one wants to move to, the frightening cost now of travelling what was once the attractive distance from where work was done, the school running down with the children facing dead-end jobs if anything at all, can engender a shattering despair. The freedom you enjoyed (and took for granted) has either vanished or become very insecure.

Britain's industrial cities have faced the same kind of crisis. Workers had been lured into believing that things could only get better. They could have their place in a nation of home-owners, houses furnished as lavishly as the sets of the soap operas and situation comedies. There was no need to keep money in hand. Everyone had a right to a holiday in the sun, and a car that would hold its place in the fast lane, and other elaborate toys that would make children happy. Science would ensure an improving health service, cheaply staffed by an endless supply of doctors and nurses and ancillaries from abroad. The children of those who worked with their hands would go through university into teaching, free from financial cares, respected by all. Children were no longer to be bound by the cramping traditions of family employment – or its lack.

French heavy industries felt the shock later than the British. Despite initial reservations, the Common Market had served France well. Now the north east has suffered the same kinds of cut-back, with the same injury to people's self-confidence, even when new jobs are arranged. Much of France still prospers, second homes spring up all over the countryside: and the disparities of wealth remain the most extreme in Europe. The necessary pool of the unemployed prepared to do the least popular jobs for the lowest wages is provided by legal and illegal immigrants (as in Britain and the United States). They are also, in France in particular, the scape-goats for the resentment of those only marginally better off.

'Structural' unemployment belies the promise that anyone who wants to can join the ranks of the securely rich and really live. Yet the message that 'This is the only way for humans to flourish' is hammered home if anything even more insistently. The chasm between those who receive the blessings and those who have no chance to widens. It relentlessly engulfs the rejects from among the blessed, and inexorably entombs them with those already trapped.

Some of the rejected poor in our Western nations, are of course, really poor, in absolute terms, as well as relatively poor in social terms. They are poor enough to be frequently or consistently in poor physical health with its expected psychological concomitants. They are weak enough to be the easiest prey for neighbours a little stronger, a little more ruthless than themselves, in the despairing attempt to seize a little of the only life that is agreed to be worth living.

The door was once modernized with a cheap sheet of hardboard. That now hangs buckled and sagging. The lock has been replaced twice, once after the only key was lost, once after a break-in. The door-jamb still bears the scars. The door itself stays open through the day, to let the children in and out. Today it is warmer outside. There is no electricity for the telly, or for light, or for cooking or heating. Someone robbed the coinmeter, and it's the householder's responsibility to safeguard and insure. Denise was in no state to do either. With three children and a fourth baby on the way she has no energy and no strength. Her most recent man has found someone much more attractive. She sits and smokes a cigarette, half listening to the little radio that nestles on the stained kitchen work-surface, surrounded by old loaf-wrappers and biscuit packets and a few small cans of food.

Her social worker has tried, really quite patiently, to explain how to budget her social security money and child allowances, but the child allowance books have been held as security by the local money-lender since the final effort Denise made to raise the money to hold her man. The children all have colds, the youngest is coughing and listless. Denise has few options, and none of them attractive. Talk of the good life in a free society for her is a hollow sham.

The neighbours have long given up trying to help Denise and others like her who move in and out of the run-down houses along their refuse-strewn road. They can just keep their own heads above water, there is no lee-way for generosity, and every expectation of being conned if they offer kindness. The lonely old lady bolted and barred in the next house gave the children sweets when they first came, until they did what Denise told them, and took her purse. Now she only goes out once a week, when the still-friendly milkman is on his round, and otherwise opens the door to occasional expected official visitors, her doctor on his promised monthly visit once a quarter, and the gas man and the electricity meter-reader. Once or twice a year her son arrives from the south, and carefully parks his new car half a mile away and wears old clothes.

The only other neighbours who even thought to welcome Denise and her children have returned to keeping themselves to themselves. Her children's thieving they expected and could cope with; her children's perpetual ill-health is too great a risk. Fred, the husband, is off work with an industrial injury which his firm's insurance company has been refusing to acknowledge for seven years; Jackie, his wife has a tendency to bronchitis, but her earnings from the supermarket are essential. Without her slim wage-packet the carefully balanced diet, the cheap new shoes for the children, the licence fee for black and white television reception, all would be lost – even the fifty pence a week they defiantly contribute to their local Methodist church. No, ill-health must be kept at bay: Denise's children out, and their own in (unless Jackie can find the energy to take them along with Fred to the one park the council is still caring for, three miles away). Lose the little freedoms that Jackie's job enables, and the family would have nothing to share, as well as less for themselves.

It is a constant complaint among my older friends that poverty of this sort makes friendship into a luxury they feel they cannot afford. That is a measure of its cruelty and barbarity. It has made simple friendliness too costly for many people to sustain. To have put so clear a price on friendship, and then to have priced it out of the reach of many must count as a remarkable success for the system under which we live. This is the ethos to which the faith of the first Christians and of Jesus must speak, if it is to be heard at all.

The most recent available official figures for Great Britain show 2.8 million people living below the official poverty line, 4.8 on or around it. As many again are so close to it as to lack any safety margin if some disaster strikes: such as illness or accident, or the loss of a job. That amounts to a quarter or more of the population, around fifteen million, with a very high proportion of children (even higher than the proportion of the elderly).

These are redundant people in British society; and so in France and in the United States. Many others, of course, are securely comfortable.

As in Britain and in France, so in the United States, the proportion of the gross national product absorbed by the most wealthy fifth increases, while the proportion allotted to the poorest fifth falls. Even taxation is adjusted, so that the proportion taken from the poor goes up, and that levied on the rich declines. After some successes in the anti-poverty campaigns of the Kennedy and Nixon years, the field has been progressively surrendered.[3]

Harrington, as has been noted, distinguishes in the American scene between the traditional poor and the newly insecure. Inherited poverty is accompanied by self-destructiveness: violence in the family, addiction to alcohol and other drugs, and assaults on the nearest and weakest. As poverty is increased under Reagan, its productivity is signalled by the booming crime-rate. You always had a better chance of being mugged, shot, raped, your home burgled and vandalized, if you were black or hispanic, unemployed, poorly paid and walking to and from work, or just the hope of it, at the wrong time of day, or simply too dependent on public transport. The likelihood of any or all of these has merely increased, and with them the difficulty of maintaining sufficient physical and psychic resilience to relate to other people, to allow your well-being to depend on them. The American dream has a nightmare quality about it for those condemned to live in the great conurbations. Freedom means freedom to be all kinds of victim.

Harrington's estimate for those living in poverty in the United States is between forty and fifty million.

It has become harder to help the most desperately poor, the people sleeping where the stale air is pumped from the tower blocks, the young workers still looking for jobs and living in bed-sits ('single room occupancy'), harder than it was twenty years ago. There are more people, many are younger, often still strong, and angrier; more are mentally ill, having been 'returned to the community', where there is none. There is no sign of the happy cameraderie of 'clochards' that Ardagh still claimed recently to find in Paris. Here when an epileptic is 'relocated' there is no one now to notice if he doesn't appear, so he dies. Now if someone faints in the street of an American city he will most likely lose his shoes, if nothing more.

There are families, too, living in cars, in abandoned and decayed motel chalets, in 'trailer camps' (caravan sites) or in single rooms if they can find them. Women and men, they have had jobs, poorly paid, even well-paid, but the work has run out, the firm has collapsed. They are people looking for paid employment, often ill, encumbered with ill-fed and sickly children. This is in the wealthiest among the nations of our planet.

This poverty creates a battleground of the poor against the poor (which is always in the interests of the wealthier). The chicanos, the Mexican immigrants, mostly illegal, are ready to undercut the wages of the poorest citizens; and are then at the mercy of any employer's threat to denounce them.

The worst sufferers are the women, and among them the women who are also black. In Britain as well as the United States there is the myth of the woman who spawns children so as to live easily off welfare benefits. Apart from the fact that the benefits fall so far short of comfort they don't even reach sufficiency, there is the fact that single parenthood is almost always the decision of the one who leaves, and that is most often the man. (The French provide far more generous support for the '*famille nombreuse*' apparently without having to face this suspicion let alone the actuality.) In a country where people's humanity is violated, the violence is passed down the line until it reaches the lowest rung, which is where the women are, with their dependent children.

Dio of Prusa found the same victims in the first century, just as the prophets and legislators of old Israel had done centuries before, and as did James.

3. Poverty and Oppression Worldwide

There are many more victims still among the countries being 'developed' to supply fruit and grain and meat and minerals and a defence of the possessors against any threat of change. There are 16 million refugees (mostly across borders bequeathed by colonial powers). There are 462 million people so ill-fed they are starving, and almost twice as many again so under-nourished as to be unfit for the work they need to do, poorly resistant to disease, disqualified from any full enjoyment of social life. A higher than natural proportion of these are women, suffering from chronic anaemia, yet in many cultures the main stay of subsistence and even of cash-crop farming. The infant mortality rate in the thirty-eight poorest countries is around twenty percent, with the women bound to bear more children to ensure workers for the family and support in old age if it is reached.

(The proportion of very rich people in the first century was tiny, with a great gap between them and the still quite small group below them, symbolized by the property qualifications for senators and equites in Rome, separated by a great gap from the mass of ordinary people. As a guess, the proportions for the population of the planet today must be very similar. There are a few enormously rich, even in the poorest countries; quite a few well off, especially in the wealthiest countries, but they are still a very small percentage of the whole. And then there are the rest.)

Food production in the thirty-eight countries with the lowest per capita income is lower in the mid eighties than it was in 1970; less than a fifth of the population of these countries can find pure drinking water.

Maybe not many of the problems are the deliberate creation of people in countries like Great Britain or the United States or France, maybe not even the foreseen consequences of decisions taken for other reasons; not all are even direct but unpredicted consequences of the system we live in. We did not invent malaria or bilharzia. Perhaps it is not our fault if people saved from smallpox or cholera still need food. It is more profitable, of course, to supply drugs to deal with water-borne diseases, than to supply pure water. Even ancient Rome managed things better.

The system from which even the poor in our wealthy countries benefit in some measure is the system which seems to ensure plentiful continuing victims in the rest of the world.

We create markets for our goods, most happily taking over existing demands and destroying the livelihood of local producers. What we supply has to be paid for, by the export of minerals or cash crops, or the ill-paid work of local people (preferably of docile women). Very little surplus is shared locally, and the sharing is very localized. A wealthy native elite may be created, but the wider 'spin-off' is minimal, if it occurs at all. This is a 'free' market.

The cash crops take over from land producing food for local consumption, which has then either to be imported or foregone. There may be a profitable balance for the local employees of the large international agribusiness, there may be a deficit for the country as a whole, and starvation for those deprived of their right to work their land. Quite like New Testament times.

The local elite is far from secure in its enjoyment of its prosperity. It must be surrounded by a loyal military caste, whose loyalty is well rewarded. This cost in weaponry and pay must be met by more exports, in deals greatly encouraged by France, the United States, and Britain. This increased strength may well look threatening to the elites of neighbouring countries, with envied resources of land, and minerals and labour. So the market for arms grows very nicely. 'Freely', one might say.

The country supplying the expertise and the transport and the machinery and investing a little in the local infrastructure further to secure its base has very likely a monopoly. If the local elite gets too grasping, the agribusiness, the chemical conglomerate, the mineral company, can up roots and go elsewhere, knowing that none of its competitors is going to want to encourage the greedy. Mostly the vassal state accepts that it will have to produce more and more even to continue receiving just the same as came its way ten years ago.

So the poor actually get poorer in a world economy that could easily feed everyone. They get poorer as the good news of the culture of consumption is spread more and more vividly, in the cities of the wealthy. But these poor are needed to encourage those on the fringes to cling on as cheap labour. If there is any hint of their threatening the wealthy instead of competing with others still poorer, the most cost-effective remedies are bullets and systematic torture. The weapons supplier will readily instruct in the use of both. (The CIA manual on destabilizing Nicaragua through terror is only the most blatant recent example.)

So the misery of the poor in the wealthy countries is passed down the line, and intensified. The goals of the rich are seen more and more clearly, the costs are born by the poor more and more dearly, while the chance of achieving this paradise (or even of escaping the hell it sits on) recedes more and more nearly into pure make-believe.

There is no need to romanticize the prior condition of subsistence farmers and hunters the world round in order to see that the quality of their life has been impoverished. For most human beings in their relationships with one another in the context of a living world that is our only present home, life is worse than it was for their grandparents. The possibilities of enjoying life, of living it freely and fully, have diminished and continue to diminish. That is how things are for millions upon millions of our fellow humans. In fact, it is the lot of the majority to be worse off than their parents, and see only further deterioration ahead, if the present system is maintained.[6]

4. *Bound to Fail?*

The system under which we live manifestly fails to deliver what it presents as goods to most of our contemporaries. If it is the freedom to consume, most people have little or none, and certainly less than was the case thirty years ago. If it is freedom of choice, theirs is disappearing. If it is any other freedom, they are waiting and dying before it reaches them.

It could of course be argued (and is by some) that this is all the necessary suffering that precedes the bliss that their grandchildren will enjoy. If they do not pay the full price, utopia will never be attained by anyone, and their pain will still have been in vain. If they hang on, their grandchildren will bless them. That, clearly, leaves a trio of questions at least. Why should they suffer for those not yet born? What in the ethos of consumerist hedonism encourages anyone to altruism, or even to enjoyment at third hand? And where is the guarantee that the promise will be kept? If present day consumerism depends on a pool of miserably poor people to supply the cheapest labour for the securely rich, what value has anyone's assurance that this part of the system can be changed without the rest having to alter, too? But third, and perhaps most important, is the question still unanswered: is Western consumerism a good thing even for those it favours? We need to reflect on how well or poorly freedom and flourishing go for us now, and our neighbours, who are (relatively) very rich, and even (relatively) secure.

Since the first issue is not worth pondering unless we can find a positive answer to both of the other two, we can safely leave it for the moment. If the poor are not even suffering for the good of their descendants, there is little left other than to continue deception and repression. And since a reassurance on the attainment of a global sharing is worthless unless what is attained is actually worth having, we do best to concentrate on the third question. It is on this third one, anyway, that we are going to try to listen to the dogged pagan Cynics, to early Christians, and to Jesus the Christ. We must consider, though still only briefly, the quality of life for those actually and currently receiving the larger portion of the supposed benefits of the system.

We are now, of course, talking about quite a small number of people, whether in France, Britain, or the United States. As Harrington says, it is easy to overlook the 'dirty little secret' that a great many Americans who are not poor are still far from wealthy enough to enjoy all that the ethos of the times tells them they should be enjoying.[4] A promise to reduce taxes on income is directed towards those who already have most, in the conviction that they feel they cannot yet spend quite enough. It works well in all three countries.

It is nonetheless possible to pick out areas of the life of this wealthy minority where the advertised blessings are being enjoyed, and where they are blessings that might be included in many accounts of human freedom and flourishing, not least in our New Testament documents: love, joy, peace, at least, and even a spot of long-suffering.

As a prime instance, genuine friendships clearly occur among wealthy people, friendships that last because the range and the depth of shared interests grow. Time spent together is not simply affirmation of the past. No simple cost-benefit analysis is imposed, emotional, financial, political. Marriages among such people can last in much the same proportion as among many if not all other sectors of the population. Children can grow up enjoying their widening experience and their acquisition of psycho-physical skills, including those involved in ordering and appraising experience. Such children growing to adulthood are likely to be healthier than most, even allowing for wealth-related diseases. At very least there is no clear evidence to suggest that riches preclude human flourishing, or necessarily inhibit the freedoms under discussion.

In terms of 'culture' in the narrower sense, wealth in today's world can provide the context for a very rich human flourishing, so rich that though one might imagine many alternative recipes, one could hardly imagine anyone organizing their time and attention so as to sustain much further enrichment: the quality as well as the depth of someone's appreciation may go on increasing, but the tally of their waking hours remains in the same range as everyone else's. Wealth, then, may allow its possessor to attend theatres, concert halls, ballet, and opera, to tour art galleries and museums, to own pictures and statues and other prized art-objects, to have time for novels and poetry in books possessed, to play a musical instrument for their own enjoyment, to walk the countryside, to engage in sports (including those involving expensive equipment or locations or both), and savour many different kinds of food and drink. It is, further, possible to combine some such inventory of pursuits with a part in one's country's politics and political theorizing, and even with church attendance and theological and other reflection.

It seems that some people do find it possible to enjoy these kinds of cultural richness while also working in a well-paid profession. (Their wealth does not have to have come from inheritance or a casino.) The intellectual stimulus of law or surgery, business management or financial dealings can marry with a wide, even a very wide range of other interests.

The conclusion that such cultural flourishing does occur is based, confessedly, on no one's systematic investigation. It is based on incidental observation and anecdotal evidence in part, but mostly on noting the published price-tags on much of this culture in our Western countries. Culture at a high price sells well, and that must be to more than just the inheritors of wealth.

Of course we have to allow for other 'cultural' factors, in a wider sense of the term. My frequent appearance in the stalls at Covent Garden as clearly suggests I have arrived socially as would a frequent attendance at the Bolshoi Ballet in Moscow. There may be an element of ostentatious consumption in the devotion of the most ardent lover of opera. Educating your palate to discriminate among wines may be as demanding an occupation as learning to distinguish among moths. That it is costly may well be an important reason for choosing wine, as may also the fact that the cost makes it necessarily a minority pursuit. Moths fly openly past almost anyone. (Wine may taste nicer, and relax my inhibitions more. Moths are visually richer.) There is almost certainly a non-aesthetic 'cultural factor' in many people's choice of interests to cultivate. Its social cachet is often at least as important a factor in the following a pursuit attracts as is any intrinsic interest its devotees find in it, and owning elaborate equipment as interesting as the activity itself.

Yet we must allow that financial wealth in our society does make available a genuine human flourishing, and some wealthy people avail themselves of the possibilities. Wealth certainly does not seem to entail relational or intellectual or aesthetic sterility. The range of people's freedoms, both to choose and to enjoy, can be enhanced. So far the answer to the question we are considering might be a tentative 'Yes'. The quality of life lived by some wealthy people in our society does look attractive, judged by quite a wide range of criteria. It is attractive enough to warrant sharing, if it can be shared, (and sustained in the sharing).

Yet a crucial issue remains to be considered. We are imagining opening to more and more people the freedoms and the flourishing at present restricted to just a few. Are the freedoms and the flourishing we may be right in discerning sufficiently attractive in themselves to generate and sustain interest within a consumerist society that values in terms of price, and ranks in terms of scarcity? If that remains the dominant ethos, and if it is thought to be (and even worse, is) the only mechanism by which the ever increasing wealth is to be produced for sharing, must it not necessarily conflict with the values we are hoping to share?

A picture may have a high price on it at least in part because many people who have enjoyed looking at many different pictures have found this one well worth lengthy and discriminating attention. It could simply have a high price-tag, attached by auctioneers' hype. If it is put on public display it is looked at by many more because of the fame of the price-tag. A very good copy may receive very little attention, though the potential stimulus may be indistinguishable. (That is, unless it is by a forger whose work is now also a sound investment.) Limited edition prints cannot (by definition cannot) be distributed by the million. The ethos of a consumer society must by logical necessity oppose the widespread sharing of anything that it highly values.

Fashions in music and dress for the young are no exception to this rule, only constituting a variant on it. Here value, still highly priced, is attached to initial scarcity combined with novelty. It is important to be identified with a group that is itself constantly distinguished from others, in dress and in music. It is actually quite pleasing to be imitated, but only when we are moving on to the next sound, the next style. Again, this approach to culture can be financially very rewarding for those able to manipulate it. It is not impossible in fact to imagine the generation of similar variations on rhythmic and melodic themes, and kinds of apparel and fabrics without any commercial impetus. However, so long as 'having acquired it first with others following, admiringly' continues to be integral and important in the enjoyment of the sounds and the clothes, it is an enjoyment which it is logically impossible to share.

If this analysis is valid, then it seems that rather than 'consumerism' just happening not to have delivered the goods very widely yet, it in fact concentrates our attention on 'positional' goods which cannot be shared. They cannot be shared as things of value, for much if not all their value lies precisely in their not being shared.[5]

Alternatives sources for values to adopt would seem worth investigating, and one such source is the early Christian gospel tradition, as proclaimed in the early days. To that we shall shortly turn.

Issues of physically limited resources, of minerals, land for growing food, space, and so on, are deliberately left unargued. Even were resources sufficient, as food is said at present to be, though its distribution is not, the idea of a universal consumer society would seem to be self-contradictory.

People can be friends, people can give and receive love in all kinds of circumstances. Friendship can happen where the poor are competing for physically scarce resources, in the simply contrived poverty of a concentration camp, or the more complicatedly contrived poverty of the African Sahel. The evidence available to me would suggest, as already noted, that truly loving relationships can also emerge and be sustained among those who must be counted rich and even very rich, competing for goods made good by being competed for. Yet it would seem that in logic (whatever the practice) the problems in the latter case are even more profound.

In extremes of poverty, sharing my crust with my friend may deprive her of her only friend, of the only point of eating the crust anyway. Yet while consciousness remains, the awareness of love given and the gift of acceptance may outweigh any loss. The value in the sharing does not necessarily self-destruct.

The logic of consumerism, on the other hand, seems to conflict inherently with the mutual sharing of love. The artist who gives her prolific and exciting paintings away as tokens of affection thereby deprives them of value. Even if the recipients wanted to sell, no one would buy. They are mere tokens, they have no intrinsic worth. They might as well be photos cut from a colour supplement.

Love says to the beloved, I want the best for you. Consumerism presses the addition, 'the best I can afford'. Love gives and waits vulnerably to receive, for any forcing of a return would make it at best gratitude, and at worst the settlement of the account. But the last thing that love wants is the first thing that the consumer ethos demands. How can what I give be shown to have been worth giving if it doesn't show a good return? How else can I value what I have received, unless I assess it as a wise investment?

To repeat, this is not to suggest that it is impossible for the rich to have a share in true freedom. They can by splitting themselves in two. They may readily spend parts of their lives evaluating everything in cash terms, and other parts insisting, 'Where everything has its price, nothing has any value.' But the present argument does try to make clear that there is a very real conflict. Shall I send a really valuable gift which is very beautiful, and risk putting the intended recipient under an obligation? Do we care enough for each other for me to send a poem of mine, and risk looking mean – and ungrateful for his last gift, or censorious?

The more there is of life that is dominated by a consumer ethos, the less there is of life left free for human persons to relate as such with others.

There are many other dilemmas that confront us besides. The competition for scarce resources, the conflicts inherent in pressing for 'positional' goods, the race to exploit before you are exploited create a world society brimming with antagonism and hostility, willing to risk the entire environment to ensure power supplies for immediate growth in consumption, willing to destroy everything to deter competitors from risking destroying everything. (If we need this much to deter each other, are we sane enough to be deterred?)

I hope I have paraded sufficient brief reminders of how things seem to be, at least to suggest that everything is not clearly set fine for a goodly future in which all could (let alone assuredly will) be brought some day to share. The ethos of Western society contains inherent and destructive problems of self-contradiction.

Among alternative sets of values, those debated in the New Testament collection (as well as by pagan radicals in the ancient Mediterranean world) may have no greater claim to general attention than any others. They do not seem to have attracted a particularly successful following over the past two millennia. But the problems which I have suggested are inherent in a consumer ethos (problems which others have discerned and displayed more clearly than I have) do at least seem to be the kinds of issues to which these early Christian and pagan moralists addressed themselves. This book expects Christian readers (if it draws any at all), and they are assumed to be willing to attend to reappraisals of original Christian insights. So it is to these, often shared with the pagan world around, that we now turn.

In this next chapter (III) we shall be considering the use early Christians made of their traditions of Jesus' teaching and other activities. What Jesus himself may have meant by any of these sayings and other deeds ascribed to him (supposing the ascriptions are at all valid) is another issue, to be considered, though briefly, in the chapter following (IV). In what follows now, we shall note how the early Christian proclamation of its traditions of Jesus is likely to have sounded to the majority of people in the Hellenistic towns whose views of life were at least in part formed by what the Cynics used to do and say. Both would have been disturbing; but a great many more similarities emerge, which may help us understand the force of what those early Christians were saying and doing.

III

Christian and Cynic Radicalism

1. *Appearance and Authority*

We commence where the initial impact of the itinerant Christian preachers would have begun, with their dress and their public and observable behaviour, including their manner of addressing those around them. These early Christians would have looked and sounded most like Cynics; and then, as we shall see, the content of what they said would have further re-inforced this impression, for their appearance and behaviour itself already conveyed much of the same sharp and powerful message.[1]

Christian evangelists, like Cynic moralists, deliberately flouted convention in their dress. Their appearance was an acted parable of their hostility to the life-style the majority affected or at least aspired to. At the risk of an inverted pride, they adopted an ostentatious penury.

It has been suggested, however, that the early Christians actually aimed to display their poverty quite distinctively. Thus, while Mark allows the staff that many Cynics carried (Mark 6.8), Matthew 10.10 and Luke 9.3 forbid it; and all three evangelists refuse the distinctive begging-satchel (compare also Luke 10.4, Q).[2]

Yet it would be wrong to imagine that Cynics were expected to arrive uniformly unkempt. Most wore their cloak doubled, with no tunic under (though probably with a loin cloth). But we have Herakles, as the Cynics' model, in his lion-skin, (e.g. Dio 1.61), and a contemporary of Demonax sporting a bear's pelt (Lucian,

Demonax 19). Mark's tradition, followed by Matthew, has Jesus' immediate predecessor, John, clothed in camel hair with a leather belt. Jesus himself is spoken of as wearing a cloak (Mark 5.27, etc.), as are his followers in other contexts (Matt. 5.40; Luke 22.36). When Dio describes his own readily recognizable appearance he mentions neither staff nor satchel (for, like Paul, he seems to have preferred to work to support himself (33.14; 72.2). Diogenes himself, according to Diogenes Laertius, only began to use a staff in old age (6.22–23). The initial impression the early Christian missionaries would most likely still have suggested is that they were some kind of Cynics.

If the Christians were at all distinguishing themselves in any way from the Cynics by their dress and other equipment, they were nonetheless even more significantly defining themselves in terms of this model. They intended, perhaps, to appear as a particularly radical and severe sort of Cynic. However, if we start with Musonius, rather than some of the other suggested passages, there is rather less of a difference. 'Wearing only one shirt (*chitōn*) is better than needing two, and wearing just a cloak (*himation*) without a shirt at all is better still. Going barefoot, if you can, is better than wearing sandals (*hupodedesthai*) (19, cf. 16). The forgoing of staff and wallet does not even need to be mentioned.

Cynics were not alone in enacting parables, but they were particularly likely to do so. It was partly a matter of consistency: the message was meant to be acted on. That, too, was a commonplace, but one especially stressed in Cynic practical 'philosophy'. A merely verbal commitment to the Cynic rejection of any publicly esteemed life style was easy enough. 'Someone wanted to do philosophy under Diogenes. He gave him a tunny-fish to carry, and told him to follow him [through the crowded market]. For shame [at the servile task] the would-be disciple threw it down and left. Some time later Diogenes met him. "Our friendship was broken by a tunny-fish coming between us," he said' (Diog. Laert. 6.36).[3]

The Christian invitation to accept baptism would very likely have had a similar impact. In a culture where physical cleanliness was valued highly and punctiliously maintained, to admit you needed for any reason to be given a bath would be difficult. But you were also agreeing that none of your own people's rites of purification were effective. You were making, as it were, a clean break. As Epictetus notes, 'When someone is convinced and has made their choice and been baptized, then they're a Jew in reality as well as in name. We, though, are "pseudo-baptists", like make-believe Jews, out of tune with the reason we lay claim to, miles away from using the things we talk about' (II 9.20). (Whether Epictetus is actually talking of Jewish proselyte baptism, or the Christian sacrament, does not affect this assessment of its significance in the eyes of an outside observer at the time.)[4]

Baptism is once for all. The persistent spurning of social conventions about dress is a still more disturbing declaration of opposition to the norms that the conventional clothes symbolize. Its significance emerges in the contrary insistence by a later Christian writer that his group cannot be held to be subversive, for 'they follow local custom in food and dress and the rest of life,' (Diognetus 5.5. If we want wider evidence for this point, we may compare Paul on men's and women's hair-styles; but also Epictetus, III 1; Musonius 21). Appearance is very significant.

The message dress conveys is expressed verbally in Jesus' ironic comment on the Baptist's appearance. 'What did you go out into the wilderness to see? a reed shaken by the wind? No? Well, what did you go to see? a man in soft clothes? You find people got up like that [in fine clothes, living in luxury] in royal courts' (Matt. 11.7–8, and Luke, Q). The palace is only an elaborate wardrobe, peopled by coat-hangers. Or, as Crates is made to say, 'A Diogenes-style cloak is despised, but it doesn't let you down, and its wearer is more to be trusted than someone in the fine clothes of Carthage' (Crates ep. 13). 'Take a look at me,' says Epictetus's ideal Cynic. 'I've no home, no city, no property, no slave . . . no governor's tiny mansion; just earth and sky and one worn cloak' (III 22.47), and he pours scorn on the speaker who needs smart clothes and an auditorium (III 23.35). Demonax mocks an aristocrat making a display of the purple band on his toga: 'A sheep wore this before you had it – and was still only a sheep for all that' (Lucian, *Demonax* 41). James chides the fawning subservience won by the bright clothes and gold ring of the chance visitor (2.2). The medium must tally with the message, and the message is one of defiance of society as it is currently based and organized. Even Seneca, toying ineffectively with Cynic radicalism, writes, 'Believe me, your words will be more impressive if you sleep on a pallet and wear rags . . . I at any rate listen quite differently to what our (Cynic) friend Demetrius has to say, when I've seen him lying down to sleep with nothing over him – and not even some straw beneath him, either' (*Letters* 20.9).[5]

The accumulation of wealth as such is constantly attacked, as we shall consider in a little detail below. But here it is wealth expressed in dress and granting or eliciting authority for one person over another that is being challenged by the Cynic and the Christian life-style.[6]

That kind of external, imposed authority of power, where one person's freedom is parasitic on another's, is totally rejected. 'You know full well that those who consider themselves to be in charge of the various nations lord it over them, and their great men make their authority felt. It is not to be like that among you' (Mark 10.42). 'So, then, who has any authority over me?' asks Epictetus. 'Has a Philip, an Alexander, a Perdiccas, or any "Great King"? Where could they get authority over me from?' (III 24.70). 'You invited me, insisting it was not to be ruled over, but to rule over others, yourself included. But I have to say, I've never learned how to rule over other people ('Socrates' ep. 1).[7]

Luke's version (or Luke's editing) of Jesus' saying on authority brings in the term 'benefactor' (22.25–26). That is how people in authority want to be seen, exercising power for the good of the compliant; they may even believe it themselves. One of the most popular Diogenes stories, found in the Letters, and in Cicero, Dio, Plutarch, and Epictetus, has Alexander come up to Diogenes when he is sunbathing. He stands over him and offers, 'Ask me any boon you like.' 'Stand out of my sunlight', snaps back Diogenes (Diog. Laert. 6.38). Benefaction is immediately unmasked as a very lightly disguised assertion of power, a reading that emerges particularly clearly in the version in Letter 33 of 'Diogenes'. The one who gets between you and the divine sun is arrogating divine authority. (It is worth noting that the 'hymn' of

Philippians 2.5–11 seems to draw an explicit contrast between Jesus' refusal to treat divine power as a prize, and the traditional mythic portrayals of Alexander's triumphant conquests.)[8]

Other portrayals of royal power in the gospel tradition are as subversive. Mark's Herod in his banqueting hall, also expansively offering a benefaction, finds he is simply the tool of another's vindictive hatred (6.21–28). In his sexual affairs the lawless ruler shows he cannot even rule himself. We later hear of pagan Cynics rebuking Titus in much the same way, for his affair with the Jewish princess Bernike. One critic received a flogging, the next was executed (Dio Cassius, *Roman History* LXV 15.3–5). In Luke's tradition Jesus dismisses Herod Antipas as 'that fox' (13.32). For expressing his opinion of Caesar, Epictetus would expect to be arrested (IV 13.5).[9]

The true Cynic insists he has no master other than God (however 'God' is understood in the theologies of different Cynics). ' "I'll show you I'm your master!" "Oh?" says Epictetus. "How can you be? Zeus has set me free. Do you really think he's going to allow a son of his to be enslaved?" ' (I 19.9, et passim). The Cynic can serve his God (as we shall see presently), but it is freely and voluntarily, not in response to any imposed dominion. Matthew's community is reminded that though others may like to be called 'Rabbi' (my great teacher), 'None of you is to be called Rabbi, for you have just one teacher, and all of you are brothers. And don't any of you let yourself be called "Father" [sc. as a title] on this earth. You have one Father, the heavenly one. And don't any of you let yourself be called "the expert" (*kathēgētēs*, "professor"). There's only one expert, and that's Christ' (23.7–10). In the Markan tradition (which Matthew softens) Jesus himself refuses the honorific 'Good master' (10.17–18). Even after his rehabilitation, Dio insists, 'The true king, by nature kind and unassuming . . . is called Father of his subjects, but not just as a title. What he does shows he is a father to them. However, he takes no pleasure at all in being addressed as "master" (*despotēs*), not by free people, no, not even by his slaves' (1.22).[10]

Like Epictetus, Matthew's Jesus insists that those who are sons of the divine king are themselves free (17.24–27), and the image recurs time and again in Cynic writing: 'Free under Father Zeus, and afraid of none of the great Lords' (Diog. ep. 34).

It is probably in this sense that Mark's 'render to Caesar' passage (12.14–17) would have been understood. Just as in Jewish tradition, what belongs to God is not less than everything, so too among Cynics 'all things belong to the gods' (Diog. Laert. 6.72; 'Crates' ep. 26, 27; etc.). 'So, to a Cynic, what is Caesar, or a Proconsul, or anyone else – apart from the one who has sent him out into the world, the one he serves – Zeus?' (Epictetus III 22.56). If service to Caesar nonetheless comes within the bracket of serving God who has absolute priority, then but only then are Caesar's orders to be met, as Epictetus goes on to allow (III 22.107). Caesar rules in effect in the realm of the unimportant. What matters is what matters to God, and that cannot be defined by Caesar, let alone be claimed by him. What matters, as what matters to God, must come first. Devotion to God always has priority (Mark 12.29).[11]

The Cynic, like the Christian, can offer unforced service. 'I am among you like a servant', says Jesus in Luke (22.27); 'the Son of Man himself did not come to receive service but to give it', says Jesus in Mark, 'and to give his life as a ransom to set the masses free' (10.45 – that being how the words would have sounded in the context here being described). 'Tell me,' asks Epictetus, 'was there ever someone that Diogenes did not befriend? wasn't he a gentle (*sic*) friend to all his fellow humans, gladly taking on himself this painful toil and physical hardship for the common good? And he offered his friendship as a servant of Zeus ought, caringly, for sure, but entirely subject to God . . . This is how freedom is enabled' (III 24.64–67).[12]

In an intriguing parallel with the story of the footwashing (John 13.2–17), Dio has Diogenes say to Alexander, 'Won't you throw off what you're wearing, put on a slave's tunic, and serve your betters?' (4.66). 'In what is thought of as the Golden Age', asserts Seneca, 'leading was a dutiful service, not an exercise of royal prerogative. No one attempted a trial of strength against those who first enabled him to gain power over them' (*Letter* 90.5).

There are obviously different nuances to be discerned, but also a great deal of common ground. These Christians and these Cynics make explicit their objections to the way political power is based and exercised, and adopt a dress and life-style that is a standing challenge to the society that conforms. It will have been at least as striking as that of any punk, hippy or Rastafarian, but apparently rather more effectively disturbing.

(Only once do we find a suggestion of any Cynic proposing armed rebellion against the existing power structures: Peregrinus, in Lucian's very hostile account (19). The fact that the Cynics by and large eschewed such plans in no way lessened their political importance at the time. Similarly, the fact that the early Christians did not ally themselves with the Zealots of the Jewish Revolt in no way diminishes the political character of the early Christian critique of society and its leaders.)

2. *Practice and Precept*

As was pointed out a little earlier, the importance of words and actions tallying is a commonplace at the time. But it is particularly important for Cynics and for Christians, who both proclaim an ethical 'way', rather than an intellectual exploration. Diogenes Laertius wondered whether Cynicism could really warrant the title 'philosophy', and was not rather 'as some maintain, just a way of life' (6.103). Luke is content to have Paul so style Christianity: 'I serve God in accordance with the way, which others call a school' (Acts 24.14). Musonius insists that philosophy (as he sees it) 'is nothing other than knowing about living . . . Particular clarity and forcefulness in speech . . . I don't rate all that highly' (III and IV).[13]

Cynic tradition has Diogenes claim that even his teacher Antisthenes did not himself live up to his own teaching (Dio 8.2). Diogenes is the real founder of the dogged Cynic way, intent on living out the theory in practice, and working out the theory in life, (Crates ep. 8, etc.). We need to be constantly checking to tell whether 'our deeds harmonize with our actions' (Anarcharsis ep. 2).

So in the little that the Christian tradition preserves as typical of John Baptist is included the insistent demand that those who have accepted his invitation to a changed life should produce results, 'yield fruit'. The tree that produces nothing is ready for felling and the fire (Luke 3.7–9,Q). Matthew in fact has Jesus echo John's own words, as well (7.19). The 'fruit' image is used by various teachers in the Cynic sphere. Epictetus warns, 'Take care that people don't know who you are. Do your philosophy on your own for a while. This is how fruit is produced: the seed has to be buried deep for a time, hidden away and allowed to grow slowly, so it can come to maturity. Take care, my friend, you've grown up too lushly, you'll be nipped by the frost – or it's already happened – right down at your roots' (IV 8.35–39). Seneca notes, 'We praise a vine if it loads its shoots down with fruit . . . and we praise a fellow human being for the fruitfulness appropriate to us humans . . . our soul, and reason brought to perfection in it' (*Letter* 41.7–8).

The Roman imperial government could, without much worry, allow wide-ranging discussions of political theory by intellectuals among themselves. Critics could readily disguise current references by setting the debate in earlier centuries and perhaps in foreign countries. On the other hand, a movement that stressed action, and pressed for a life-style different from that which maintained the even tenour and efficient running of things, was dangerous. 'Innovation' and 'rebellion' are almost synonymous. Energetic conservation of the old is fine. Critical discussion of it can be tolerated. Alternative life-styles put into practice are a threat.[14]

The Christians told of a founder and leader who had insisted on action. 'There's no good tree bearing useless fruit; but neither can a tree be useless if it bears good fruit. You can recognize each kind of tree by the fruit it bears. People don't find figs on a thorn tree, nor do they gather grapes from a bramble-bush' (Luke 6.43–45, Q). 'Evil no more gives birth to good', Seneca points out, 'than an olive tree produces figs' (*Letter* 87.25). 'Hegesias asked for the loan of something Diogenes had penned. Diogenes replied, "You're acting the idiot, Hegesias. You choose real figs, not pen-and-ink ones. Why written rules rather than real training?"' (Diog. Laert. 6.48). 'Why,' asks Jesus in the Q tradition, 'do you repeatedly address me as "Lord, Lord" – and not do what I tell you?' (Luke 6.47). 'Diogenes described himself as the kind of hound much praised, but which none of its admirers dared take out hunting' (Diog. Laert. 6.33). 'Do what the words say', urges James, 'Don't fool yourselves. Hearing on its own is not enough' (1.22). 'Test your words by your deeds', challenges Seneca (*Letter* 20.1).

The strands of early Christian tradition being examined here do not much use the catchword 'free' or 'freedom' (and that does afford one of an important but limited number of contrasts with the contemporary Cynic tradition: we may note Matthew 17.26, and James 1.25; 2.12). But it would have been quite clear that what was being talked about was kinds of freedom: the possibility of change, of adopting a new life-style not bound by conventional restrictions determining in advance the roles people must play out. The kinds and quality of the freedom in question will emerge more fully in what follows, and the vacuity of change in the abstract is nowhere commended. It is this that constitutes the 'repentance' John and Jesus are both said to have proclaimed.[15]

Mark includes the tradition that people were shocked at Jesus keeping bad company (2.16–17). Jesus replies that it's the sick who need the doctor. Rather more defensively, Antisthenes answers a similar protest with, 'Physicians can attend the sick without catching the fever' (Diog. Laert. 6.6). But the physician model is used frequently throughout the Cynic material expressing the conviction that people could change or be changed, and also the determination to enable change.

Of course, the physician model could suggest simply restoring people to the kind of 'social health' approved by wider society, an essentially conservative medicine. It should already be clear that what the Cynics and the Christians discerned was a sick society. They were rejecting accepted definitions of well-being, and offering instead their own quite different understanding of social and personal health. To those who wanted the new and rejected the old they offered the assurance that the change was entirely possible. 'Repent and accept the good news', says Jesus in Mark (1.15; after John's 'baptism of repentance', 1.4). 'A man needs someone to show him clearly that he's not doing what he wants and is doing what he doesn't want to do. As soon as you show someone this, of his own accord he'll refrain completely',

promised Epictetus, somewhat optimistically (II 26.4), but
Musonius had offered much the same assurance before him (10,
and 9). 'I don't despair even over the most hardened case',
claims Seneca. 'There's nothing that determined effort and
attentive and assiduous treatment won't overcome' (*Letter* 50.5,
etc.). And, of course, the 'call of a disciple' stories, to which we
shall return, make just this point in narrative form.

3. *Teacher and Taught*

There are teachers among Cynics and among Christians, and
they are accorded authority. But the authority is intrinsic, it is
based in the effective practice of the theory. The temptation to
rely on the reverence accorded to the social role of teacher is
rejected. We have already noted Jesus in Mark refusing any such
respect (10.17–18). Epictetus presses the self-effacing example of
Socrates: when people asked to be introduced to a philosopher,
he would take them to someone else (*Encheiridion* 46; in fact,
much the same is said of Antisthenes, Diog. Laert. 6.2, 5). So
Epictetus insists:

> Never say you are a philosopher. By and large it's best not even
> to discuss your philosophical reflections with ordinary people.
> Just you yourself do what follows from them . . . Sheep don't
> bring their fodder to their shepherds to show how much they
> have eaten; they digest the food internally, and produce wool
> and milk on the outside. So, instead of trying to explain
> your philosophical reflections to ordinary people, first digest
> them properly yourself, and then let the deeds that result speak
> for themselves (*Encheiridion* 46).

The danger is recognized that followers of the Cynic way may
suppose the shabby appearance itself is enough. 'You say what
makes a Cynic is his wretched satchel, his staff, and his big
mouth.' That is not so, insists Epictetus. It is the witness of the
rich quality of the life lived with this minimal support, free,
fulfilled, undisappointed (III 22.45–50; cf. IV 8). So the special
Matthaean material in particular rebukes every kind of action
done for display, the constant temptation of the activist to 'bad

faith', (Matt. 6.1–18; 23.5, etc.) 'Demonax declared war', notes
Lucian with some satisfaction, 'especially on people who did
philosophy for show, and not in a search for truth' (*Demonax* 48).
No pretence must infringe the freedom of the onlooker or hearer.
Attraction or dissuasion must both be authentic.[16]

The willingness to come to another as teacher is itself important:
so Jesus is shown coming to John, and accepting John's baptism. It
is only on this basis that a teacher can seem fit to receive disciples.
(The force of Mark's account as it stands can be judged by the other
evangelists' attempts to soften it: briefly, in Matthew 3.14–15, but
also in the entire account of John 1.) In the early tradition, the next
generation of leading Christian teachers are shown obeying Jesus'
summons as freely and wholeheartedly as Greek tradition had it
Xenopohon followed Socrates (Diog. Laert. 2.48).[17]

In fact the picture of Jesus as teacher in the synoptic material,
where he travels the countryside and challenges people to some
form of discipleship is only at all closely paralleled for the first
century, in our Cynic sources. These, of course, also provide
analogies for the initiative resting with the would-be disciple (pre-
eminently Diogenes himself: Diog. Laert. 6.21, cf. Hipparchia,
6.96–98; but also Dio *Discourses* 8 and 9). So we have Jesus
coming to John, and the 'Q' sequence, Luke 9.57–62, others
coming to Jesus.[18]

To take communication and learning out of its safe social setting
where it is a commodity styled for the rich and powerful, designed
to reinforce both the structures of authority and the positions of
the current holders, is subversive, and seen to be so. To insist that
the authority of the teacher does not rest in the social recognition
accorded by those already in power, nor in any 'charismatic'
ability to create alternative power-structures is yet more disturbing. The implication seems to be that people already have
considerable resources within themselves and are being set free to
explore and develop them. The teacher is a living parable: but so
too are the taught, themselves, already, even if it takes considerable
effort to help them realize that this is so.

The reticence of the teacher is not simply self-regarding. He is
not just insisting on autonomous isolation for his own self-
culture. That (like Epicurean withdrawal to cultivate one's garden

among congenial friends) would be no threat to anyone. The
Cynic, like the Christian has, as we shall see, a divinely authorized
mission to others, (which does involve a measure of proper self-
concern, in monitoring and securing one's own progress). But the
reticence of the teacher primarily expresses and effects a concern
for the integrity of others. They, too, are not by this being
encouraged into any self-centred autonomy. They are in fact
being drawn out into a much greater openness to others. But they
are being enabled to appropriate the new insights and life-style
for themselves, rather than being moulded into clones of the
leader. The contrast with attempts to ensure an easily manageable mass-culture is clear.

It is worth quoting two of Dio's own self-introductions,
modelling himself on a Cynic portrayal of Socrates:

> I wonder what on earth you came expecting or hoping for,
> looking for someone like me to speak to you. Did you expect
> me to have a nice voice, to be easier to listen to than other
> people . . . like a song-bird? . . . So, whenever you see someone
> who begins by flattering himself on everything he does, and
> courting favour with his dinners and his dress, and minces
> round provocatively, you can be sure he'll flatter you, too . . .
> But when you see some squalid figure, wrapped tight in his
> cloak, walking on his own, a man who always begins by
> rebuking himself, then you need not look for any flattery or
> deceit from him . . . (33.1, and 13–14; and compare the style
> of Jesus' appraisal of John, Luke 7.25–26, Q).

And elsewhere he says,

> Though you have so many enjoyable things to see and hear,
> powerful speakers, delightful writers in verse as well as in
> prose, a peacock-like procession of multifarious sophists,
> borne on wings of fame by a crowd of disciples – yet, despite all
> these counter-attractions, here you are, coming up to me,
> waiting to listen to what I have to say, though I know nothing
> and make no claims to knowledge (sc., like Socrates; Dio 12.5;
> with which, outside of the synoptic tradition, compare particu-
> larly I Cor. 1–2 and 8.1–2).

The Socrates on whom Dio models himself is one who speaks in figures:

> Socrates and Homer . . . were both very effective forgers of similes and parables . . . Socrates often used this method, sometimes admitting he meant it seriously, sometimes making out it was in fun; and all for the sake of being of service to his fellow human beings . . . In conversation with Anytus he'd talk of tanners and shoemakers; but if it was with Lysicles, it would be about lambs and fleeces; if with Lycon, law-suits and informers; but if with Meno the Thessalian, lovers and who they were in love with (Dio 55.9, 11, 22).

Elsewhere Dio brackets together Aesop, Socrates and Diogenes as those who used stories to gain and hold attention, including in with them contemporary Cynics: 'When people think they are going to hear from us the sorts of things that Aesop used to say, or Socrates, or Diogenes, they come up and pester us. They can't leave anyone alone if they are dressed as we are, like birds mobbing any owl they see' (72.13).[19]

It is clear that the synoptic tradition ascribes to Jesus a large number of 'parables', from brief metaphors to short stories. We have seen already how similar some are to those deployed by Cynics (or people closely in touch, such as Seneca), and more will follow, both in this section and in the remainder of the chapter.

Figurative speech, comparisons, similes and metaphors, fables and allegories can be made to start where the hearers are, either drawn from their immediate life (as in the passage but one above, from Dio), or of the kind they are used to enjoying, (as in the last quotation). Some may of course be of both kinds. They may then be used either simply to illustrate or explain a specific point the speaker or writer has in mind, or they may be used much less restrictedly, to free the hearers (or readers) to re-think their attitudes to more or less of life around them. In the latter case the speaker still has a definite intention, but it is to raise questions, rather than answer them, to suggest things are questionable, rather than to impose some other authoritative solution. It is a recognized educational procedure at the time, seen to be in the Socratic tradition. If a Cynic-looking speaker appears and tells 'parables' (or tells of his teacher whose stock-in-trade they were) it is at least likely that this is how he will be understood. He is spurring his hearers to a Cynic rethinking of their lives and their attitudes to the world around.[20]

The medium is itself subversive. It is disturbing to have it suggested that current attitudes are questionable. It is unsettling to suppose that ordinary people, encouraged to reflect, may reach valid conclusions of their own, maybe extending existing sympathies and insights into areas where the formal ethos of the day says they are inappropriate.

It is, on the other hand, also possible for the speaker or writer to start so firmly with his own message that the metaphor or fable is constructed to suit, having no contact, or only fortuitously, with the world and interests of the hearer. In 'allegory' the teacher dominates, even more than in explanatory parable. It is probably nonetheless wrong to attempt to draw too clear a line between any of these. The 'open' parable seems intended to raise issues chosen by the speaker, and it may do so more effectively if he starts where his hearers are, by bringing in some stock characters or situations (and so some appearance at least of 'allegory').

The extent of such 'allegory' in the New Testament parables continues to be debated. The 'Sower' in Mark 4, the 'Tares' and the 'Seine Net' in Matthew 13 have explicit allegorical interpretations attached. Nonetheless, there are so many more left without allegorizing, or with no more than occasional stock figures (kings, stewards) and situations (feasts, accounts), that the ordinary hearer at the time would have been much more likely to take them in the 'open', Socratic way, than as an esoteric code for ideas needing to be learned separately.

Many of the synoptic parables will be brought in under other headings. In what follows we shall consider only a few of those that are not due to appear later.

Luke tells us a story of a kindly and generous man from Samaria (10.29–37). Dio tells us a much longer tale of a kindly and generous man from Euboea (7.1–80). It is not clear whether 'Euboean' had any particular overtones. It may be that an urban audience would have expected a hunter from the wild countryside to be rough and unfriendly: certainly the townsmen in the

story are by and large unsympathetic towards him, and give ready
credence to the suggestion that he is a wrecker, luring ships on to
the rocks. Others think that country people do well for themselves by avoiding all the civic taxes. Dio tells the tale of this
countryman's surprising and costly generosity once to a single
shipwrecked traveller, and on an earlier occasion to two such
unfortunates. He makes it quite clear later in the discourse that he
is hoping his audience (including even possibly the emperor
Trajan) will re-think their attitudes to countryfolk and to the best
use of the countryside, as well as to the problems of urban
unemployment and the wretched exploitation of the poor. Some
of these issues come into the story itself, but many do not. Urban
poverty does not directly, though urban mores seen through the
eyes of an imaginary countryman are good for a laugh. The story
starts with its likely audience, raising 'their' issues of taxation and
the dangers of travel and the chaos of public meetings. It has plot,
development, and tension. It can get people's minds working
today, and was presumably at least as effective when Dio was first
repeating it. People might nonetheless have responded with,
'There's a pretty fable. But the last rustic I met robbed me of a
denarius; and he stank.'

Luke's story ascribed to Jesus is much shorter, though it should
probably be seen as even more carefully and tellingly structured.
We start with the apparent actor, with whom we expect to
identify (as with Dio's initial first person narrator), only to find
ourselves, as it were, the victim (even more than in Dio's tale).
There then appear on stage in succession people who supposedly
stand for security, at least they do in the official belief-system. We
expect some relief from this quarter, but none is forthcoming.
(Dio's 'civil' assembly is very uncivil, the justice it has gathered to
administer is very problematic.) We are left wondering what
positive resolution can possibly emerge. The only character left is
the one we are least happy to identify with: and then that
character deals with 'us' much better than we could reasonably
hope for.

Even if the concluding question, response and admonition in
Luke are part of the original telling, the tale leaves us free to say,
'Quite implausible! No use ever expecting a situation where I

could rely on unfriends to befriend me. No use my ever trying to create a wider neighbourliness. No point even asking whether the present pattern of things has brigandage as a by-product.' But there is at least a chance that we'd have had to face the questions, and we might have been tempted to try out some different answers. If people of the sort for whom Dio framed his story of 'The Good Euboean' heard Luke's 'Good Samaritan', the chances are that they would have 'read it' in some such way. Even if 'Samaritan' lost some of its overtones in the retelling, he would still have stood out as a kind of stranger to the others. Cynics, of course, saw their own urban civilization as corrupting, and expected better (or at least no worse) from outsiders. They were 'world citizens' (*kosmopolitēs*).

At any rate, the two stories have elements of technique in common, and both raise awkward 'political' as well as 'personal' questions.

The situation chosen in Matthew 20.1–15, the workers hired throughout the day, has no clear parallels in the Cynic remains. Again very carefully constructed (avoiding any exact repetition in each successive encounter between the owner and the unemployed) it successfully raises questions about the entire work ethic, much discussed at the time. (The 'work ethic' may have been reinvented after the Protestant Reformation, but it is widely accepted in the first century.) Cynics objected. 'Everything belongs to the Gods, the Gods are friends of the wise, and friends have everything in common. So everything is the common property of the wise' (Diog. Laert. 6.72, again; 'Crates' ep. 26). When a Cynic asks for food he is not asking for a gift, but for what belongs to him. The affront to the contemporary work ethic was considerable, and deliberate (and just as 'theological' in its own way as Matthew's). It is not a simple 'political' objection to 'differentials' in pay..That is only one symptom of the entire ethos that it calls in question. (Dio's *Discourse 7* has a similar breadth of concern, but in the end is less radical, only asking how those excluded can be brought into the system, not questioning the entire system as such.)

The more radical Cynic stance is probably to be seen as part of a sort of 'inaugurated eschatology' (or 'part-restored protology'). It amounts to an attempt to live as though the Golden Age were not lost, or were simply there again for the asking. 'Let us have everything in common, as common as our birth,' wrote Seneca, unguardedly, in an off moment (Letter 95.53, et passim, and 90; but more consistently, Anarcharsis ep. 9).[21]

The imagery in Matthew 13.24–30, (darnel, 'tares') would probably be quite familiar; even so urbane a writer as Seneca, on the fringe of Cynicism, uses it, though in a quite other context:

> Divine seeds are sown in our human bodies. If a good farmer receives them, they spring up like the parent stock, and as good. But if the farmer's a bad one, and provides only barren or waterlogged ground, he kills off the divine seed and raises only weeds, instead of any fruitful plants (*Letter* 73.16).

Closer still to Matthew's parable is this sequence from Diogenes Laertius' account of Antisthenes, already quoted in part:

> On one occasion Antisthenes was reproached for mixing with ne'er do wells. 'Physicians,' he said, 'can attend the sick without catching the fever. But it's very odd,' he added, 'that we weed out darnel [*airas*, not *zizania*] from the wheat, and we weed out those unfit for war; but in city politics the ne'er do wells have no exemption' (6.6).

If the second saying were taken on its own, it might seem to afford a contrast with Matthew's refusal to 'weed' people out. But it would then also be contrary to the previous saying in Diogenes Laertius, and however haphazard his organization of his material may be, it is best to assume that the two sayings did not seem to him to conflict with one another; and they may well have been a complementary pair in the tradition. Antisthenes is then contrasting the rebuke he has received in trying to act as 'physician' to the wicked, with people's toleration of the wickedness he discerns (and expects them to be aware of) in high places. If they want to stand in judgment, they should start at the top.

Even if Matthew's darnel parable has been shaped with the allegorical explanation (13.36–43) in mind, and even if it was always addressed just to a Christian community, and never had wider society in view, Antisthenes' use of the metaphor shows how radical Matthew or his tradition is at this point. Hearers would (even without the explanation) identify the darnel as 'something that should be got rid of', 'the wicked', (or, just possibly, 'wickedness'). Yet here it is suggested that the wicked (or wickedness) can only be isolated at unacceptable cost to what is valued (goodness, or, more likely, 'the good'). Most societies are very reluctant to suppose that 'the wicked' belong to them, that boundaries cannot be drawn with 'us' inside and some rejected 'others' expelled. Matthew's parable (very much in Cynic mode) invites its hearers to be both much more self-critical and much less censorious.

Another parable that is often thought to be allegorical is Mark's wicked tenant farmers (12.1–9). The climax of the narrative, with the owner risking his unprotected son, has seemed implausible in itself, and 'son' more likely a coded reference to the special status accorded to Jesus. However, the fact that the parable itself contains in the narrative no hint of resurrection (and Mark or his community needed to add a text of scripture, 12.10–11, to make good the lack), means that the parable itself can hardly be Mark's own, or the work of some recent predecessor in the community, and we are justified in considering its impact as used in the earliest days of the Jesus movement. 'Socrates openly criticized the junta of thirty dictators, saying they were like wicked cowherds. They'd taken charge of a large herd of healthy animals, and reduced it to a sickly handful' (Dio 43.8); with which one may compare, 'A shepherd's job is to exercise foresight, and safeguard and protect his sheep; not, by Zeus, slaughter, butcher and skin them' (Dio 4.44; cf. Anacharsis ep. 7; and, e.g., Ezekiel 34, of course).[22]

'Herding', of sheep or of cattle, is an entirely conventional model for exercising political authority in Hellenistic, as it is in Jewish writing. Talk of pastoral mis-management in criticism of political leaders is so commonplace among Cynics that Lucian throws the charge back at them (*Runaways* 14: it is they who 'sheer' the sheep). But Mark's story focusses on husbandry, which never seems to provide a metaphor for leadership (compare Philo, *de agricultura* 27–29, where 'ruling' only enters the discussion when the model changes). As hearers we can identify with tenant vine-dressers whereas we would be much less likely to with stock authority figures. We see ourselves in people who have demands made on them, demands they resent. We see our work as our own, and other workers as competitors, enemies. And then we are made to ask, What is the likely outcome of such vicious competitiveness, this refusal of solidarity even with those in a similar situation to our own – especially if we do believe that there is one 'owner' of all, and our greatest resentment has been aimed at those he has sent to remind us that we've not been giving him his due? If we listen to the story carefully, it catches all of us and all of our life, it catches high and low alike, and provides no easy way for passing on the blame. (Mark, unfortunately, puts it into a framework that does just that: punishment has fallen on Judaea and Galilee, the challenge must have been confined to them, and we are let off the hook.)[23]

There are also intriguing resonances again with the Golden Age myth as it appears in our other writers. The earth then, as the property of the gods, was for human kind to enjoy in common; but now it has been misused by people who want their own bits of it just for themselves. The gods have punished this possessiveness with fratricidal conflicts and self-destructive passions and greed (Anarcharsis ep. 9; Seneca 90, 95. Dio 30 [but the latter with no overt reference to Cronos]). Such would have been the most likely 'reading' of the tale of the vicious vintners among people in the Greek cities in the first century.

Even a well-placed Cynic like Dio in his later days will say this sort of thing of rulers:

> If one of your officers disagrees with you [the Emperor] and opposes you, he'll very quickly and properly meet with censure and disgrace and be removed from high office to give way to someone better able to serve your imperial administration. So emperors [kings] themselves, I must suppose, also receive their power from Zeus to act as his stewards (1.44).

I have suggested that an early Christian evangelist, missionary, or itinerant speaker would have looked like some kind of Cynic. The visual values would have been reinforced by his obvious predilection for parabolic utterance. It would also have suggested the most likely 'reading' of what he said, and I have analysed a few instances. But there is much else that would have further strengthened the impression that this was the right way in which to understand the tales he told about his teacher, Jesus, and the remarks he made, and the subversion he preached.

4. *The Bold and the Beastly*

Cynics were notorious for their loud-mouthed uninhibited frankness, '*parrēsia*'. The word itself does not occur in the synoptic tradition as such, and only once in editorial material (Mark 8.32). It is much more frequent in the New Testament epistles, where it is used of our bold and confident approach to God. (In a culture in which attitudes to deity were taken as clearly indicative of attitudes to authority as such, this is itself quite striking.)

(The absence of this almost technical term '*parrēsia*' itself from the early tradition of Jesus' sayings is not particularly significant. The word belongs in 'second order' editorial comment by and large, even in the Cynic material itself, and what we have in the synoptic tradition and James is 'first order': what is said and done, rather than reflection on the manner or the content. It is the uninhibited frankness itself that is significant.)

Christians carried with them the example of John and of Jesus castigating their hearers severely . . . well, in effect, abusing them as all kinds of animals. This was standard Cynic behaviour. 'You viper's brood,' storms John (Luke 3.7, Q; Jesus, Matt. 23.33). 'Although you look like human beings, you are apes at heart,' explodes Diogenes (ep. 28). 'The poor woman . . . has been changed from a human being into a viper', protests Epictetus (I 28.9); 'the man becomes a wolf, or a snake, or a wasp, instead of a human being,' (Epictetus IV 1.127). 'I send you out as sheep among wolves', warns Jesus (Luke 10.3, Q; where 'sheep' is itself by no means complimentary! – Epictetus IV 5.21, et passim). 'You wail like shepherds when a wolf carries off one of the sheep', mocks Epictetus (III 22.35). 'They were like frogs unaware of the water-snake', comments Dio (8.36). 'People living with flatterers are in as bad a way as calves among wolves', warned 'Crates' (6.92).[24]

Cynic boldness is not, of course, confined to using disparaging animal metaphors. It is the willingness to reprimand all and sundry that is distinctive. 'No sooner had I arrived in Elis and was going up by the Gymnasium,' Lucian tells his friend, 'than I heard a Cynic bawling out in a loud harsh voice. It was the standard street-corner stuff about Virtue, along with abuse of all and sundry' (*Peregrinus* 3; cf. *Philosophies for Sale*, 10). Lucian approves of Demonax as an exception to this Cynic rule (*Demonax* 7). Though Seneca may at times be attracted by aspects of Demetrius' message, (and even, we have noted, impressed by his consistent life-style) he cannot commend making an exhibition of oneself: 'Our wise philosopher will not disturb common custom, nor attract popular attention by adopting some novel life-style . . .' (*Letter* 14.14). It is precisely this upsetting that the true Cynic intended, and the early Christians must at least have risked, presumably meaning to. Their models, John and Jesus, take on all comers.

The Cynic's first target is people with a sense of their own superiority. 'Diogenes the Cynic Dog to you so-called Greeks: Be damned to you!' Diogenes is made to write in *Letter* 28. 'You lay claim to everything and actually know nothing at all . . . You're just as ignorant as your ancestors . . . look how many people you have killed and the kind of people they were. Some you killed in wars fought for sheer greed, some on accusations made in peace-time – as you choose to call it. Weren't many hung on crosses, didn't many have their throats cut by the public executioner, and others take poison at his hands?' So Jesus denounces those around him who see themselves as at least in some measure enlightened: 'You've got it coming to you, you Pharisees! You build tombs for the prophets your ancestors killed: you're witnesses and access-ories to their deeds. They did the killing, you build the tombs' (Luke 11.23–12.1, Q; compare Luke 10.12–15, Q).

'And you lawyers, you've got it coming to you! You load people up with burdens it's hard to bear and you don't lift a finger to help carry them.' 'Diogenes heard a couple of lawyers in an argument. He decided against both of them: one had undoubtedly stolen something, but the other was as certainly inventing his loss' (Diog. Laert. 6.54). 'Why do you delude yourself, and put others at risk?' Epictetus asks his fellow philosophers. 'Why do you dress up in someone else's role, and walk around as thieves and robbers with your stolen titles and illicit deeds?' (II 19.28). 'Outwardly you seem to other people to be righteous,' says Jesus in Matthew, 'but inwardly you are full of hypocrisy and lawlessness' (Matt. 23.27–28). And Dio's portrait is similar again: 'These are the sorts of things Diogenes used to say to mock people who were self-important. But it was mainly the sophists that he insulted, for wanting to be looked up to, and to be considered more knowledgable than other people' (6.21). 'You take away the key to knowledge', Jesus charges the lawyers: 'you don't use it to enter yourselves, and yet you get in the way of others trying to get in' (Luke 12.1, Q).[25]

Society then as now depends on most of us acting as though we took at face value the role-playing of those who hold power. Most of us want to trust them; we might otherwise have to take responsible action ourselves. Both may laugh in private at each other's gullibility. But the public disclosure that fools are leading those who must be idiots, villains those who must therefore be rogues, is likely to be somewhat disquieting for all. Cynics and Christians castigate ordinary people as well as the eminent.

Once back within 'the establishment' Dio was less than happy with the performance of some in the 'movement'. 'These Cynics,' he complained in Alexandria, 'con youngsters and sailors and crowds made up of that sort of person, stringing together jokes and gossip and market place back-chat.' What they had to say, he accepts, is authentic; but they direct their scorn at philosophers, and let their hearers themselves off too lightly (32.9). But the mass of the people continue to remember the sayings of Diogenes (72.11). It is to the market place that the Cynic must go; that's where many people spend much of their time (Diogenes ep. 6; compare Lucian, *'Philosophies for Sale'*, 10). Epictetus (like some of the Cynic letter-writers) does not expect a mass popular response, but a Cynic teacher must be able to talk to enquiring individuals and to the many (III 22.26,23,34; cf. 'Crates' ep. 21). So the early Christian stories of Jesus and his followers talk about 'the people', 'the multitudes', 'the crowds', and 'the many'. The target is the same.[26]

A further striking feature of both is their willingness to address women, and include them, and accept the risk of arousing the suspicions of a male-dominated society; we shall consider this aspect again later, but note only for the moment Lucian chiding his populist Cynics with 'an excessive interest in females' (*Runaways* 18); compare Mark 15.40–41; Luke 8.2; Galatians 3.28. In his attitude to women, the poorest free man can identify with the most powerful and the most learned, and so help to keep power where it is. 'Mind corresponds to man, the senses to woman'; 'women are best suited to the indoor life, never straying from home' (Philo, *de opificio* 165, *de specialibus legibus* III 169–70). 'Queen Alexandra provided a demonstration of the stupidity of men who fail to keep supreme power as a male preserve' (Josephus, *Antiquities*, 13.430–431). 'To women falls most of what has to be done in the home, and by and large they don't experience storms and wars and other such perils . . . Yet no one would think women better off than men on that account', notes Dio in passing (3.70–71).[27]

When Christians and Cynics speak to all alike they undermine in some measure the bases of oppression.

Yet it is also important to realize that for our later Cynics as well as for Christians there was an important sense of divine authorization and compulsion accompanying their liberating address to all and sundry. It was at least in part this that spurred on their 'boldness'.

5. *Sought out and Sent out*

'God says, Go, and bear witness to me, for you're well fitted to give your testimony to me', claims Epictetus, and later expands this: 'A true Cynic will not rest satisfied with being well-trained himself. He must realize that he's been sent as God's messenger to his fellow human beings to show them where they're going astray over what is right and what is wrong; but also as a scout . . . For a Cynic really is a scout, sent to reconnoitre and find what's friendly territory, and what's hostile' (I 19.47; III 22.23–25). Dio urges the people of Tarsus, 'You must not refuse to accept that a man who has arrived among you as I have, out of the blue, has come at the bidding of some divine being to talk to you and advise you' (34.4; cf. 12.20). 'I believe I've taken up this task,' he tells the assembly in Alexandria, 'not of my own choice, but by the decision of some divine being [*daimōn*]' (32.12). 'Go: I send you out', says Jesus in the 'Q' tradition (Luke 10.2). 'He summoned the twelve and sent them out in pairs on a mission' (Mark 6.7).[28]

For Dio, at least, this involved a great deal of travel. '[The] deity ordered me keep on doing what I was already engaged in, "till you reach the very ends of the earth"' (13.9, a phrase strongly reminiscent of Acts 1.8). He tells us he then 'roamed everywhere'. 'I visited as many countries as I could . . . sometimes among Greeks, sometimes among barbarians . . . arriving in the Peloponnese, I stayed away from the towns [in this phase] . . . passing my time in the countryside . . .' (1.51). In fact he crossed outside of Roman territory and visited the Getae, across the Danube, against whom Trajan would not much later fight a campaign. There was no restriction to areas of high Greek culture, let alone to areas where Greek was spoken (compare *Discourse* 36). Musonius and Epictetus seem to have travelled only when exiled. But Lucian's Peregrinus 'the one and only rival to Diogenes and Crates' left home to travel far and wide, including Palestine; and later, with ample funds provided by the Christians, he visited Asia Minor, Syria (including Palestine), Greece, Egypt, then through Italy travelled to Rome, (*Peregrinus* 15 16). Lucian's 'Runaways' are also mobile. Cynics, as already noted, claimed to be 'world-citizens'.

There was a great deal of opportunity for travel in the Mediterranean world of the first century (only slaves, and Egyptian peasants seem to have suffered any legal restriction on their mobility; and even slaves could be sent on journeys by their masters). The economy and the imperial administration depended on rapid movement of people and goods and appropriate information. Officials and their couriers, soldiers, merchants, people going to look for work, all expected to move freely. But footloose wanderers on the other hand always seem to worry those in authority, as potentially subversive. In Lucian's attempt to blacken Peregrinus' reputation, the latter's travels figure prominently, as does the mobility of artisan Cynics in *The*

Runaways. At the end of the first century, Luke's Acts clearly first acknowledges in order to be able to rebut similar conclusions that could be drawn from Paul's known journeyings.

6. Trouble for the Trouble-makers

Christians and Cynics knew they must expect trouble. Rejection and suffering were very likely to come their way.

They broke family ties, or refused to undertake them, in a culture which saw the family as the only solid base for a settled society (Cicero, *de officiis* I 17; Diog. Laert. 6.88, 96). 'One should not wed nor raise children', writes 'Diogenes' (*Letter* 47); compare Epictetus (III 22.69), though he himself thinks others should accept these duties. When he passed that advice on to Demonax, the latter said, Certainly, if he could have one of Epictetus' daughters (Lucian, *Demonax* 55). The involvement of women, referred to just above, of course intensified this threat to social stability (Lucian, *Runaways* 18). Even for gentle Musonius, philosophic integrity came before submission to one's father (Musonius 16). Anyone wanting to be a follower of Jesus must 'hate' (well, at least, act as though hating) father and mother, children, brothers and sisters (Luke 14.26–27, Q; with Luke including 'wife'; cf. Mark 10.28–30).[29]

You expect to be rejected by those among whom you grew up. 'A prophet will always be held in honour except in his own homeland and among his own kin' (Mark 6.4). 'All philosophers have been of the opinion,' notes Dio, 'that life was difficult in their own homelands' (47.6). But it is particularly Cynics who expect a rejection amounting to deliberate exile, like that of Diogenes from Sinope. Even when he takes up residence in Corinth, it is visitors who listen to him, not his adopted fellow-townspeople (Dio, 8.10; 9.5); and Dio compares the treatment meted out to him in Prusa with that received by Socrates in Athens (43.8; 47.2; and compare also Demonax 11). Epictetus says it's better to leave, anyway, to break old habits; and then adds, drily, it's also easier than having people say, 'Look, old so-and-so taking up philosophy – and we know the sort of person he is . . .' (III 16.11).[30]

People at home and people you meet will say you are mad (Mark 3.20–21), as Plato is said to have thought Diogenes and as Monimus' master thought him (Diog. Laert. 6.54, 82; Dio 8.36), and as befell Socrates (Diog. Laert 2.43; Socrates *Letter* 6). Epictetus suggests pleading insanity may be your only way out when you have thoroughly annoyed 'some grey-haired old gentleman with gold rings cluttering up his fingers' (I 22.21).[31]

You can also expect to suffer physically, and a violent death is certainly on the cards. 'You are the happy ones, when people hate you and ostracise you and treat your name as something too evil to be mentioned', is Jesus' paradoxical promise in the 'Q' collection (Luke 6.22). 'Often when Socrates argued particularly forcibly in a discussion, people punched him and pulled his hair out; and by and large he was laughed at and despised. But he bore it all patiently (2.21; compare 6.33 and 44, of Diogenes). 'To some Diogenes seemed quite mad, lots despised him as a powerless good-for-nothing. Some abused him and tried insulting him by throwing bones at his feet as you do to dogs. Others, again, would come up and pull at his cloak . . . Yet Diogenes was really like a reigning monarch walking in beggars' rags among his slaves and servants,' claims Dio, also paradoxically (9.8–9; cf. 73.5–7). 'Hunger and exile and ill-repute and things like that don't look at all frightening to a perfect man. For him they're completely unimportant, leaving him as playful as children with their knuckle-bone dice and multi-coloured balls', insisted Dio, of Diogenes (Dio 8.16). Epictetus makes a similar joke of the troubles that lie in store. 'A rather nice part of being a Cynic comes when you have to be beaten like an ass . . .' (III 22.53), and we may compare his description of a Cynic-Stoic, 'show me someone who while he's sick still flourishes, though he's in danger still flourishes, though dying still flourishes, though he's exiled still flourishes . . .' (II 19.24). 'As a leading figure, Demonax fell foul of the mass of the people, and gained no less hatred from them [initially] for his frank speaking and independence (freedom) than his predecessor [Socrates] had done' (Lucian, *Demonax* 11). 'Socrates said, "Follow these instructions, if you are willing to listen to me at all, so that you may live happily, letting yourself look a fool to others. Let anyone who wants to, offer you insult and injury . . . if you want to live happily, a good man in all sincerity, let all and sundry despise you' (Seneca *Letter* 71.7; cf. 18).[32]

As we shall see, neither Cynics nor Christians are commending masochism. It is not pain for some perverse enjoyment's sake; at least, it does not appear to be. It is the simple realism of people who are aware that they will be seen to be attacking the roots of society, and opposition shows that their words and their acted parables have struck home. Not expecting any quick or easy victories, they must take their satisfaction here, where it offers. And though there is much to value in life as it may be lived among people in the world around, that value itself is vulnerable. It may be that death is the only protection for it. (This is, of course, the greatest possible affront to the established order. It must be ridiculed as fanaticism, but also made as humiliating and as agonizing as the torturer's science can devise.)

'Whoever does not shoulder his own cross and follow me cannot be my disciple,' Jesus warns, in 'Q' (Luke 14.26–27). 'Anyone who wants to follow me, they're to deny themselves, take up their cross – and follow me. Anyone who wants to preserve their living self [their soul-self] will lose it . . .' (Mark 8.34–35). 'Concern yourself with how you're to leave this life', urges 'Diogenes' (ep. 39). 'If you want to be crucified, just wait. The cross will come', Epictetus promises. 'And if it seems reasonable to comply, and the circumstances are right, then it's to be carried through, and your integrity maintained' (II 2.20). 'So a woman,' Musonius assures us, 'who's studied philosophy has trained her mind for great things, so she rates death as no evil – nor living as good in itself. So, too, she'll not avoid painful hard work, or ever look for a trouble-free existence' (3).

(The question is sometimes asked, whether such teaching would ever have incurred sufficient official displeasure to warrant the teacher's crucifixion. It would not have surprised first-century hearers to be told of a Cynic teacher being executed, even on a cross.)[33]

That this is not a masochistic fanaticism (or is not meant to be: the charge may need answering on behalf of someone like Ignatius of Antioch) emerges in some of the still more frequent common themes of early Christianity and of Cynicism. The prospect of persecution and death is set in the context of friendship, caring, love and conciliation. It is with these that we begin to see the positive base of the negative protests and denunciations that we have been examining so far.

7. *Friends for Foes*

'Throughout the beating,' Epictetus continues in the passage noted just above, 'you must love the people who are beating you as though you were father or brother to them all' (III 22.53–54). A part of the motive does seem to be self-regarding: you are minimizing the damage to yourself. 'How shall I defend myself against my enemy?' Diogenes is asked, in a free-floating saying. 'By being good and kind to him', he replies (*Gnomologion Vaticanum* 187). 'When someone boxed Cato's ears, he didn't retaliate, he didn't even offer to forgive. He refused to admit that anything had happened. His denial was more high-minded even than forgiveness would have been', Seneca suggests (*de constantia* xiv 3). 'If a philosopher cannot despise a slap or abuses what use is he . . .? 'demands Musonius (10). 'Practice putting up with being abused', advises Epictetus. 'Then you'll be able to go on from that to taking a slap and saying to yourself, "I seem to have got entangled with a statue"' (III 12.10). It is an important freedom for Cynics (and Stoics) that one's attitudes should not be reactive. The initiative remains with me, whether to pay attention, as well as whether to show I do; and if I do pay attention, it is I who decide its mood, not a social code which says I must not lose face, I must retaliate.[34]

But mostly, for Cynics as for Christians, an equal or even more important freedom is the one Epictetus points to in the first passage quoted in the preceding paragraph. It is the freedom to love the unloving and the hostile. 'Love your enemies,' Jesus commands in the 'Q' tradition, 'do good to those who hate you, bless those who curse you, pray for those who abuse you. If anyone slaps you on the cheek, offer the other one as well . . . Love your enemies and do good . . . (Luke 6.27–29, 35; compare also Luke [only] 10.29–37, discussed above). 'Someone told

Diogenes that his friends were conspiring against him. Diogenes replied, "Well now, what's to be done when you have to treat friends and enemies the same?"' (6.68). (The saying is enigmatic, presumably deliberately so; but taken with the tradition's picture of one determined to 'heal', the actual implication must be positive. Friendship is the model for relating even to false friends and other enemies.)

'People offend (sin) against you. You take it without going wild, without harming the offenders. Instead you give them cause to hope for better things. That's the work of a civilized and humane human being', proclaims Musonius (10). A number of Dio's longer addresses are to citizens pursing vendettas against neighbouring towns. 'If the citizens of Mallus have behaved stupidly – and they have! – ' he tells the assembly at Tarsus, 'it's up to you to put anger aside and forgive them the punitive revenge you thought you had a right to; and, instead, work out a solution to this dispute over boundaries' (34.43). 'Never to give way, never to concede a point to a neighbour (or not without feeling humiliated), never to marry getting your own way with allowing others to have theirs as well – that's not manly conduct or strong-minded, it's just ignorant stupidity' (Dio, 40.34, in Prusa). 'We shall never desist from working for the common good,' insists Seneca, 'helping one another, and even our enemies, till our helping hand is stricken with age' (*de otio* I 4).[35]

Seneca cannot have been alone in hoping that this strategy may 'work', that it may 'enhance love and diminish hatred' (Letter 95.53). There is, of course, no guarantee. It may be despised as 'slavish', and those who adopt it may simply be wiped out. On the other hand, it is the only policy for which we may consistently have a hope of success. The consistent vendetta is simply a recipe for mass suicide, even in an age with a relatively simple technology. The loving of enemies, with its close analogy in the forgiving of debts, subverts the structures of exchange at their most primitive and basic level.

'Forgive us our debts,' runs Jesus' prayer in Matthew (Matt. 6.12; Luke 11.4 [sins]; cf. Mark 11.25), 'as we forgive their debts to those in debt to us.' It is worth taking care to contrast some current English theological usage in which we talk of 'forgiving others', forgiveness absolute, as it were. It suggests a much closer identification of the sinner with the sin than the early Christian (and general *koinè* Greek) usage with which we are here concerned. Rather is forgiveness, *'aphesis'*, a putting away, a sundering of sin from sinner. In the one model provided, the remission of a debt, the distinction is quite clear. It is reinforced by the parable Matthew includes, of the freed debtor's failure to free the man in debt to him (Matt. 18.23–35). At the word of forgiveness from whoever is in a position to utter it, a debt as debt no longer exists. It has become gift, instead. We may then be grateful, and go on being grateful (though we are not told we must be). But we are debtors no longer. Sinner and sin are disjoined. So, says Lucian, 'Though Demonax attacked their sins he forgave the sinners'; (*suneginōsken* seems to carry an overtone of 'was understanding with'). 'He thought it proper to follow the example of physicians who heal illnesses without getting cross with the people who are ill' (*Demonax* 7).

(Jesus' parable is as incisive as the others we meet. We admire the generosity of the king; we burn with indignation at the refusal of the man let off to extend the same treatment to a colleague; we vindictively approve the punishment he then receives: and the parable's trap snaps shut on us.)

God is shown treating past sin with a quite irresponsible light-heartedness, on the sole condition that we treat all offences that way, and not just our own. Demonax, Lucian continues, 'considered that it is human to err, divine, or very like the divine, to set right what has gone amiss'. The future matters, the avoidance of fresh failure. For that reason, the drag of past failure is removed. The attitude of Jesus in the tradition, and of the Cynics, contrasts with much Christian heavy-handedness. Constant Christian appeals for forgiveness (rather than change) concentrate attention backwards, and make our past look like a mortgage which God holds over our heads, rather than allowing us now to see our past, failures included, as gift. God's generosity, says James, precludes any kind of reproach (1.5).

Others in the Cynic sphere maintain a similar attitude. 'The immortal gods themselves are not deterred from pouring out unending kindness even to those who are sacrilegious and neglectful towards them', Seneca assures us (*de beneficiis* I 1.9), and Dio says he believes 'God is kindly – I take it, that's what it means to be God – and he treats the folly of the mass of humanity with gentleness' (32.5). 'By and large only humankind among living creatures is an image of God . . . As God is high-minded, beneficent and humane (that's how we conceive him to be), so we must think of human beings' (Musonius 17). 'You slave,' chides Epictetus, 'won't you put up with your own brother? He has Zeus as his forefather, and that amounts to be being born of the same seed, the same heavenly origin' (I 13.3). (Quite what various Cynics meant by 'God' needs discussion, which we shall undertake briefly a little later. For the moment it is sufficient to note that Christians and Cynics would again, at least on first hearing, have sounded very much alike.)

Forgiveness of this kind, ('keeping no score of wrongs', I Cor. 13.5) greatly enhances the freedom of the one whose past is made into gift. I owe no reparations, no interest or capital repayments. Any positive response I or we make can now be freely made as pure gift, not restitution. But you who have magically and totally transformed the debt into gift are also now free to relate to us, or to me, as friend, and are no longer in the role of creditor. You, too, have a new liberty, like the freedom of God.

No social order based on private property could survive on this basis. But then neither Christians nor Cynics thought it should. However, we return to questions of property a little later. For the moment we continue to pursue the more general themes of sins and sinners.

This Christian and Cynic approach to wrong-doing is not confined to an individual's dealing with wrongs done to her or him. It goes along with a refusal to stand in judgment. It should be clear beyond question by now that such an abstention from censoriousness does not mean that 'anything goes'. The standards are high. In fact the refusal to condemn others is at the heart of the very exacting ethic that Cynics and Christians proposed.[36]

'Don't stand in judgment, and you'll not stand in the dock. Don't condemn, and you'll not be condemned, release and you'll find release', says Jesus in 'Q' (Luke 6.37–38). Maintain a system of censoriousness, and you will find yourself caught up in it: 'the measure you use will be used for you' (v.38). 'Judgment will be merciless to those who've shown no mercy', says James (2.12; cf. 4.10–12). 'So Diogenes used to marvel at the literary scholars investigating the ills of Odysseus and ignoring their own, the orators fussing over justice, but never practising it, the avaricious crying out against money while inordinately fond of it' (Diog. Laert. 6.29). 'How can we accuse dictators,' asks Musonius, 'when we remain worse than they are? We have the same impulses as they have, just without the same opportunities to indulge them' (23). Epictetus picks out signs that someone is making progress: 'He condemns no one, praises no one, blames no one, accuses no one, and says nothing about himself to suggest that he's all that important or knowledgable. When anything gets in his way or hinders him, it's only himself that he blames' (*Encheiridion* 48.2).

So Jesus in this tradition teaches, 'Why take note of the speck in your brother's eye, but ignore the log in your own? . . . you hypocrite, first throw away the log from your own eye, and then you'll see clearly to take the speck out for your brother' (Luke 6.41–42, Q). 'And you,' asks Seneca, 'are you at liberty to examine others' wickednesses and pass judgment on anyone . . .? You take note of others' pimples when you yourselves are a mass of sores . . . It's like someone covered with revolting scabs laughing at the odd mole or wart on someone of real beauty' (*de vita beata* 27.4). Musonius warns, 'Don't try telling people what they should do when they know full well you yourself do what you shouldn't' (32). 'The Cynic's directing force is to be purer than the sun.' Epictetus insists, 'If it isn't, he'll be censuring others while he himself is involved in some wickedness of his own' (III 22.93). 'The judge in your case is in just as much danger as you are', he assures us (Epictetus II v 29).

To repeat, the sins, the failures, the wickedness are sternly rebuked, censured. But the criticism (as we have already noted) is first to be directed at the critic's own actions. And still no person is judged (however severely the sin may be); no one is condemned.

The gospel material does not spell out any implications for penal policy in the political community. Epictetus and Dio make it clear that they realize that what they say does have clear implications for punishment in society. They are against it (Epictetus I 12.21–22; 17.5–6; Dio 12.41; 31.25, etc.). That does not at all seem to imply that society neither needs nor deserves protection from wrong-doers. It implies that society's base should be changed so as to be less productive of wrong-doing.

8. *Persons and Property*

Things are for sharing, they are for relating to other people with, not defences around oneself or against being a person at all oneself. 'If someone takes your cloak from you, let him have your shirt as well. Give to everyone who begs of you, and if someone takes away your belongings, don't ask for them back', commands Jesus in the 'Q' tradition (Luke 6.29–30). So Diogenes used to say, 'We should hold out our hands to our friends palm open, not tight-fisted' (6.29). Diogenes in the tradition seems to intend his actions to be 'universalizable', as we have seen, in fact to be paradigmatic. So we may suppose that is how we should take the story of his being asked to return a cloak. 'If it was a gift, it is mine. If it was a loan, I still need it' (6.62). Certainly in the tradition Crates is known as someone who gave all his property away (Diogenes ep. 9; Diog. Laert. 6.87). 'How much more splendid than consuming lots of goods, to do good to lots of people.' Musonius judged, 'How much better to spend money on people than on bits of wood and stone' (19). 'What we have now is enough for us', explains the peasant in Dio's Euboean story; 'but you take whatever you want of it' (7.42; and note the following).[37]

We have already noted one major Cynic reason for sharing property; when we give to the wise we return what is already theirs, held in common with the gods as their friends, (Crates Letters 26, 27). Still leaving for later discussion how 'God' or 'gods' are understood, this sharing and generosity are discussed in explicitly 'theological' terms. This has already emerged in the discussion of forgiveness, where Musonius' saying, 'As God is high-minded, beneficient and humane (that's how we conceive him to be), so we must think of human beings – as his own image, so long as they live according to nature, and are eager to' (17) has already been quoted in part. 'The whole human race,' Dio affirms, 'is held in high regard – and equal high regard – by God who gave it birth' (7.138). And Jesus in the early tradition demands that we should be generous as our Father in heaven is (Luke 6.35–36; Matt;, 'perfect') and so be 'sons of the most high.' 'The immortal Gods themselves,' Seneca believed, as we have already seen, 'are not deterred from pouring out unending kindness even to those who are sacrilegious and neglectful towards them' (*de beneficiis* I 1.9); just as for Jesus God is generous to the ungrateful and the wicked (Luke 6.36 again). There is a basic shared conviction or at least trust that this is how things really are in the universe. The life of the age of Cronos, the innocence of the garden are there for the living. Greed, selfishness, the preference for ownership over relationship are a perversion, and reality is actually other.[38]

Matthew's commendation of human caring in his picture of 'the great assize' must almost certainly be taken as restricted to Christ's emissaries, 'the least of these his brethren'. Whether or not in Matthew's tradition such care was urged towards outsiders, Seneca expresses some very similar concerns. Rejecting Epicurus' self-seeking view of friendship (to ensure help for me in time of need) Seneca insists one has friends so that you may have someone whose sick-bed one may sit at, someone one may ransom if he is taken prisoner (*Letter* 9.8). 'You have sworn,' he argues, 'to give your help to people who've been shipwrecked, taken captive, fallen ill, become needy, or who are under threat of execution' (*Letter* 48.8). The kindnesses shown by the hunter to the shipwrecked in Dio's story are similar again (7.56–57, 60–61). And similar again is James' 'religion pure and unblemished' – the care for widows and orphaned children (1.27; cf. 2.16).[39]

This is not at all an altruism that distances the carer from the one cared for. 'If someone doesn't love himself, how can he love another, whether it be stranger or son or brother?' asks Dio (74.5). 'Do you want to win the favour of the Gods?' Seneca enquires. 'Then be good. Anyone who imitates them is offering an entirely adequate worship. Then comes the second question, how to deal with humans . . . our relations with one another are like a stone arch which would collapse if the stones didn't afford support to each other (*Letter* 95.50–51, 53). 'If you would be loved, love,' he counselled earlier (9.6); and, 'my advice is to rate a friend as highly as yourself' (95.63). Jesus' saying at Mark 12.28–34, choosing the *Shema* ' (Deuteronomy 6.4–5, 'Hear, O Israel, the Lord our God is one Lord, and you shall love the Lord your God with all your heart and with all your soul [and with all your mind] and with all your strength') and of Leviticus 19.18, ('You shall love your neighbour as yourself') are as obviously Jewish in origin as is much else in the gospel tradition. The double injunction would still have made good sense to Gentiles (as perhaps others as well as Jesus' followers and very likely Jesus himself realized). 'Human kindness forbids you be arrogant to those around you, or greedy in your relations with them,' Seneca avers, '. . . and its main reason for loving what it finds good for itself is that this will in fact be good for others' (*Letter* 88.30). 'If, however, you are fulfilling the royal law to the letter of "loving your neighbour as yourself," you are doing splendidly', agrees James (2.8).[40]

'Let each one here reflect how he feels towards those who try to do him down', Dio prompts his hearers in one of his 'general' speeches. 'That way he'll have a fair idea how others must feel about him, if that's how he behaves' (17.8). 'Think how you want other people to treat you, and treat them like that yourself', says Jesus in the 'Q' version of 'the Golden Rule' (Luke 6.31). In one form or another it is found widely, but certainly in Cynic contexts as much as elsewhere. 'Take care not to harm others, so others don't harm you', Seneca advises (*Letter* 103.3–4).[41]

It is not that the Cynics or those early Christians at all seem to have thought that they alone lived as humans in relationship with others. It is clear that they expected to be understood, and that their urgings would make sense, and have at least some initial attractiveness. Their contribution to human relationships was in removing hindrances, and in offering assistance in what they took to be the common human endeavour.

9. *The Prize of Poverty*

Poverty should not be forced on others, as we have just seen, and also noted earlier in the brief discussion of some of the parabolic material. But poverty may well be chosen as part of the path to freedom, so Cynics and Christians both urged. Riches could only bar the path to human liberty and flourishing. So riches must be renounced.

When Crates renounced his inheritance he proclaims, '*Kratēs Kratētos Kratēta aphiēsin eleutheron*', 'Crates son of Crates sets Crates free' ('Diogenes' *Letter* 9, again). The name sounds like the verb '*kratein*', to have power over (as in our 'autocrat', 'democrat', and so on). Crates assumes power over his own life, liberates himself from slavery to wealth; (compare also 'Crates' *Letter* 8).[42]

'Where what you really treasure is,' warns Jesus, 'is where your heart is too' (Luke 12.34, Q). And your 'heart' is not simply your emotions (like our 'he set his heart on it'). Your heart is the thinking and willing centre of you as a person. Christians have often allowed the mention of the 'heart' to authorize the kind of concession Seneca makes. Insisting 'no one who doesn't scorn wealth is worthy of God,' our multi-millionaire adds character-istically: 'Of course I don't forbid you own it' (*Letter* 18.13). But this is not the mainstream early Christian or Cynic approach. Where your time and attention is, is where your heart is. You are slave to God or you are slave to wealth. Each is a freedom of a sort; but they exclude each other (Luke 16.13, Q). 'I have been set free by God, I acknowledge his demands, no one else can have me as a slave . . . saying, "Aren't I master of your body?" . . . I regard what God wills as better than what I will. I commit myself to him as his servant and follower', announces Epictetus (IV 7.17, 20).[43]

For Cynics at least, the theology goes further still. 'Socrates used to say that the fewer his needs, the nearer he was to the Gods' (2.27; cf. 'Crates' *Letter* 11). Doing without earthly treasure is a return to the Golden Age, which men shared with the gods (Seneca *Letter* 92.31). If your 'treasure', that which absorbs your time and attention is 'in heaven', you are presumably sharing your life now with God, you are finding your reality there. The sense is similar, even if the phrasing is different.

On poverty as such there is considerable agreement, and the distinction that is sometimes drawn between '*penia*', 'on a low income' in the pagan texts and '*ptōchos*', 'destitute' in the

Christian ones, is not born out by the texts themselves. 'Poverty lives here, evil is debarred', Diogenes suggests as a lucky inscription over someone's house. Poverty would drive away jealousy, hatred, tale-bearing, house-breaking, indigestion, colic, and other serious ills (*Letter* 36). This can of course look utopian. Epictetus found that poverty does not prevent your losing one of your very few possessions, for a thief stole his lamp. It only led him to insist more vigorously that the fewer the things your life is bound up with, the freer you can be (I 18). 'What tyrant or thief or court,' asks Epictetus (in an interesting collocation) 'can frighten anyone who does not care about his body or its possessions?' (I 9.7).

'We should not get rid of poverty, only our [bad] opinion of it', Epictetus urges (III 17.8). 'You know what Diogenes used to say about poverty and death and painful toil? You remember how he used to compare his rich life with the life lived by the Great King' (Epictetus III 22.60). 'Is anyone,' asks Seneca in one of his more resolute moods, 'going to be in two minds about putting up with poverty, to free his mind from madness?' (*Letter* 17.7). 'You are the happy ones, you who are in poverty here and now', Jesus affirms (Luke 6.21; Matthew adds 'in spirit'), and Dio would seem to agree: 'Human flourishing does not come from possessions outside of oneself, from things like gold plate . . .' (3.1 et passim).

The blessedness of this carefree poverty was very much bound up with the conviction that a divine parent was caring for you: yet again, a condition that for Cynics characterized the Golden Age. 'It seems to them,' Lucian mocks, 'that this is the life of Cronos, with honey really pouring into their mouths from the sky' (*Runaways* 17). 'Diogenes used to say very emphatically that human life had been made very easy by the Gods, but we couldn't see it for looking for honeyed cakes and scents and the like' (6.44). Musonius imagines a poor man saying, 'Good God, that's all very well, but I'm a poor man without property. Suppose I have lots of children, where am I going to get food for them all?' and answers him, 'Well, where do the little birds go to get food from to feed their young, though they're much worse off than you are – the swallows and nightingales and larks and blackbirds? . . .

do they store food away in safekeeping?' (15). 'Why not consider the beasts and the birds,' Dio suggests, 'and see how much more painlessly they live than humans do, how much more pleasantly and healthily. They are stronger, and each lives the longest span possible for their kind – despite lacking hands or human intelligence . . . They have one enormous advantage over us to counter-balance any ills they may suffer – they are free of property' (10.16). Very similar to both of these, of course, are some of Jesus' best known words in the 'Q' collection, 'Consider the ravens – they don't sow or reap, they've neither store-houses nor barns; yet God feeds them. Just think how much more you're worth than the birds are. Yet which of you can add a cubit to his span of life by worrying about it?' (Luke 12.24–25). And explicit reference to divine care appears in other Cynic passages: ' "Won't having God as our maker and father and guardian be good enough to release us from grief and fear?" "And what shall I do for food?" ". . . Every one of the dumb beasts is self-sufficient, and suffers no lack of food, nor any other appropriate natural necessity for its kind of life' " (Epictetus I 9.7,9). 'The universe remains in being because it is protected by the care of its ruler' (Seneca, *Letter* 58.28). 'Carefree and happy, the philosophic wise man will laugh at people busy with their riches, and others scurrying around trying to get rich. Why postpone being yourself into the distant future?' (Seneca *Letter* 17.10).[44]

This kind of trust, (with this kind of life style) is perhaps the hardest part of the Jesus tradition for twentieth-century Westerners to take seriously. It is much more difficult than are tales of miracles . . .

It is not entirely impossible for a small number of people in our societies to live maybe as simply as Diogenes in his jar, or Jesus with nowhere to lay his head, but even that for the most part depends on the by-products and cast-offs of others committed to some level of the consumer society. Any attempt by the majority to 'drop out' would clearly be fatal for most. But then it would already in the first century. Cynics and Christians in or near towns would depend on those with a stake in the economy, even if in the countryside ('Diogenes' *Letter* 36) one could live off the land independently of any farmer.

The aim of the exercise is not that of playing Robinson Crusoe, it is rather that of a steady reduction of impersonal needs (typified by Diogenes throwing away his cup when he sees a child drinking out of cupped hands ('Diogenes' *Letter* 6, Diog. Laet. 6.37). This renunciation can only increase our need, and perhaps our willingness, to find our happiness in each other and in God.

(For the pagan Cynics the simple life would clearly include still more enjoyment of the rich intellectual and aesthetic heritage that they already shared. The breadth and depth of the parabolic material ascribed to Jesus in the tradition would suggest a similar appreciation of this kind of wealth, one that is increased by sharing, rather than diminished. There is of course no sign in the Jesus tradition of any awareness of a wider Greek culture. The emphasis is even more on people and on God.)

'Another, whose business it is, provides food and clothing – and your senses, and the concepts you think with', affirms Epictetus (III 12.13). 'For everyone, always and everywhere, there is the Father who cares for them' (Epictetus III 24.16). 'I go about the whole earth, a free man under Father Zeus' ('Diogenes' *Letter* 34). 'In their dreams young children often reach out their arms for absent parents, filled with deeply and intensely felt longing for a father or mother from whom they've been torn away. In just the same way we humans love the Gods who do us good and are our kin', says Dio (12.61). 'Acting as our parent, God has put close to hand whatever is going to be good for us' (Seneca, *Letter* 110.10). 'Is there a father among you,' asks Jesus in 'Q', 'who'll give his son a snake when he asks for a fish, or a scorpion when he asks for an egg? . . . how much more certain is it that your heavenly father will give good things [Luke, holy spirit] to those who ask him?' (Luke 11.9–13). 'All good giving, every perfect present, come down from above, from the Father of lights' (James 1.16). We still have not reached the point for discussing what the various speakers and writers may have meant by 'father' in these contexts. But at least superficially they would have sounded to be making a similar sort of point: we can live in the world as adults at home with a caring parent. The model is quite explicitly contrasted with any that suggests we are here to 'exploit' the earth, let alone one another.[45]

10. *The Wretchedness of the Rich*

'And now, you listen, you wealthy people! Weep and wail over the hard times ahead for you. Your wealth has rotted away, your fine clothes are moth-eaten, your silver and gold have rusted away, and their rust will bear witness against you and consume your flesh like flames . . . The wages you've withheld from the workers reaping your fields are crying out against you, and the outcry of the harvesters has reached the ears of the Lord of Hosts. You have lived in wanton luxury on this earth, fattening up your innards for the day of slaughter' (James 5.1–5). 'Isn't it the rich,' 'James' has asked earlier, 'who oppress you, drag you into court, and blaspheme the fine name that's been pronounced over you?' (2.7). Denunciation of the rich as such (and not just of wealth, which, as we have seen, even Seneca is willing to criticize) is common among the more radical Cynics, and is particularly fierce in this early Christian writer.[46]

'Crates to the wealthy: Go hang yourselves', storms one writer. 'You've got simple lupines and dried figs and water and peasant smocks, and yet you still go trading and cultivate a vast acreage of land; you betray and tyrannize and murder,' (Crates ep. 7; compare Anarcharsis 9). In a piece ascribed to Lucian, but usually taken to be by some other near contemporary, again a Cynic protests:

> All those expensive possessions you have to enrich your lives and to brag about only reach you through other people's wretched suffering. Just consider the cost in labour, in aching limbs, and danger; or, to be more realistic, in blood and death and destruction. There are sailors lost at sea, men suffering terribly to finding the raw materials and working on them. And once they're available, they're fiercely fought over (ps. Lucian, *The Cynic*, 8).

'How hard it is,' declares Jesus, 'for people with property to enter God's kingdom . . . It is easier for a camel to thread its way through a needle's eye than for a rich man to enter God's kingdom' (Mark 10.24–25). 'Alas for you rich,' threatens Jesus in Luke, 'You have had your time of happiness' (6.24, ?Q).[47]

The injustice of accumulated wealth is one major thrust of the critique, though only one. It is clear to the critics that wealth is accumulated at the expense, and often the very bitter expense of others, the poor, to whom it should be returned. The rich would, of course, prefer to see themselves as 'benefactors' (Luke 22.25), 'creating' wealth which then spreads out into the community (like crumbs from the rich man's table!).

Another line of attack we considered earlier: accumulated wealth can give those who hold it an illegitimate power over others, (both because of their need and of their greed). Disparities of wealth severely threaten the well-being and freedom of the dispossessed.

Wealth is seen as inseparable from greed and violence; and wealth as such is seen as destructive of any full human living. Yet in denouncing wealth itself, we meet a positive concern for the rich. The wealthy are themselves enslaved and in dire need of liberation. The attack on wealth is undertaken at least in part on behalf of its prosperous victims, as well as its hungry and dying ones.[48]

Wealth and greed go destructively together, to the hurt of all involved. 'You want something and don't get it' says James, 'and so you murder in your jealousy' (4.1–2). 'We try to restrain homicide, the murder of individuals.' Seneca notes, 'But how about war and the glorious crime of genocide? There's no bounds to our greed, nor to our cruelty' (*Letter* 95.30). Dio would agree: 'Greed is the greatest evil for each person themselves, but it also causes grief to those around them . . . It serves no real interest of the individual or of the community. Quite the opposite, it overthrows and destroys the rich well-being of families and whole city states' (17.7). Epictetus is more radical, as we may have come to expect. 'If it is in my real interest to own a cloak, it's also in my real interest to steal one at the baths. This is the origin of foreign and civil wars, tyrannies, coups' (I 22.14).[49]

(Violence itself is clearly abhorred by the writers just quoted. Jesus insists that the evil man should not be resisted (Matt. 5.39). But what is to be done about violence against others is not discussed, still less what one should do if ever it seemed that patience in one's own case was perpetuating or even encouraging violence against others. And how does one protect the violent against losing their humanity?)

The rich themselves run other risks besides. In the previous section we noted the assertion that wealth absorbs its possessor's living attention, his 'heart', it attacks and corrodes his freedom, his living self. It is from this actual (or at very least, potential) danger that the wealthy should be freed, from slavery to their wealth, from being mastered by 'mammon'. 'Luxurious living harms both your body and your soul', is Musonius' conclusion (20). 'Just as iron is eaten away by rust,' Antisthenes asserts, 'so are envious people eaten up by their own ill-disposition' (6.5). Epictetus's analysis is even closer to that from Jesus in 'Q': 'Where there's "I" and "mine", that's the direction in which the animal is bound to incline. If they're in the living body (the flesh), that's going to dominate; if they're in someone's moral choice, it's that that's dominant' (II 22.19). 'A man gives his attention to increasing his wealth and forgets how to use it . . . the master becomes just a steward', writes Seneca, from some depth of experience (*Letter* 14.18). 'Riches have kept many people from philosophic wisdom. Poverty leaves you safely unhindered' (17.3). As the more knowledgable could have shown him, the latter is unlikely to be true in a situation where gross disparities of wealth obtain. In fact none of those who praise poverty and prize it suppose its gifts come automatically, and certainly not in a culture which despises and fears it and artificially intensifies it.[50]

Wealth does not simply distract. It creates a false consciousness: a false sense of one's own identity, a distorted relationship with other humans, and a distancing from God.

> The daimon of avarice loves gold and silver and lands and cattle and blocks of apartments and all kinds of property . . . regarding the Gods as nothing more than indicators of where to find great treasures . . . watching everyone suspiciously, seeing them as threats, distrusting everyone (Dio 4.91).

'No one is worthy of God unless he despises wealth', concludes Seneca (*Letter* 14.18), and insists:

Our soul knows, I tell you, that wealth does not lie where it can be heaped together. It is the soul itself that we ought to fill, not our money-chests. It is the soul that we may set above all other things, and put, god-like, in possession of the universe (Seneca, *Letter* 92.32–33).

'Anyone who decides to befriend the world has taken up hostilities against God himself', James declares uncompromisingly (4.4). 'You cannot serve God and wealth' (Luke 16.13, Q, again). It is so hard as to be nigh on impossible for the rich to allow themselves to be ruled by God (Mark 10.24–25, again). Only by a miraculous detaching of them from their wealth as well as from any lingering concern for it can their freedom for God be won.[51]

Jesus' dialogue with the rich man finds fascinating parallels in an encounter between Epictetus and an enquirer. With Jesus:

'Good Teacher, what shall I do to inherit eternal life?' . . . 'You know the commandments . . .' 'Master, I've kept them all since I was a boy.' . . . 'There's one thing you still lack. Go and sell all your possessions and give them to the poor, and you will have riches in heaven [in your relationship with God]. And come and follow me.' The enquirer was downcast at this, and went sadly away, for he had a great deal of property (10.17–22).

With Epictetus:

'Where should I start then?' '. . . You have come here to me like a man who thinks he has no real need. What could anyone possibly imagine you lacked? You're rich, you have children, even a wife, still, and lots of slaves. Caesar knows you, you've lots of friends in Rome, and you perform all your recognized duties . . . What do you still lack? . . . You don't know about God, you don't know about being human, you don't know about good, or evil. Well, you may stand being told all this. But if I go on to tell you you don't understand your own self, how will you put up with me and my questions then? Will you stay? Not a chance! You'll go off at once in high dudgeon . . . And that includes all of you whose concern is with property and fields and slaves and positions of power' (Epictetus II 14.18–24).[52]

Family and property, status and power are closely bound together in a society structured round the unequal distribution of wealth. Property involves inheritance, and favours both male primogeniture, and the use of daughters as matrimonial tokens of financial alliance. The Christian and Cynic attack on wealth as a false foundation for human being includes also a rejection of the companion appeal to ancestry, family and race. Crates' model rejection of inherited wealth is also a rejection of any responsibility that went with it, for the maintenance of the life of his native town. 'Diogenes came down particularly heavily on people who had an inflated opinion of themselves for their wealth or family or some such, and wanted to be respected for it. They got a rigorous lambasting from him' (Dio 9.5). 'Don't you start saying among yourselves, "Abraham is our father." I tell you, God can use these stones to produce children for Abraham,' says John Baptist in 'Q' (Luke 3.8; compare Matt. 8.11–12; Luke 13.28–30). 'See, here are my mother and my brothers', announces Jesus in Mark. 'Whoever does God's will is my brother, my sister, my mother' (3.35; compare Luke 14.26–27, Q). 'Dear friend, a Cynic has all humankind for his children, the men as his sons, the women as his daughters . . . He acts as a father, as a brother, as a servant of Zeus, the common parent of us all', explains Epictetus (III 22.81–82). So the Cynic is a world citizen, not a supporter of a sectional economic grouping.[53]

Along with all its other ill-effects, wealth encourages its possessor to fore-close on the future. This is to put your 'heart' somewhere very insecure, ('where moth and rust spoil and thieves break in and steal them': Luke 12.33–34, Q). But it is also to ignore God, to attempt to take the future out of his hands.

And now listen, you who say, 'Today or tomorrow we'll go off to such and such a city and spend a year there in profitable trading.' Yet you don't actually know, even for tomorrow, how your life will go. You're a morning mist, there one moment, gone the next. Instead you should be saying, 'If the

Lord wills, we shall live and do this or that. What you're doing now is boasting in a sham, and all such boasts are wicked' (James 4.13–16).

It is the uncertainty that is foremost in Seneca,

How stupid to plan out the years that lie ahead when you're not even master of tomorrow. What madness to start out with long-term hopes, thinking, 'I'll buy and sell and build, I'll lend money and take back more, and I'll gain positions of honour. And when I'm too old and tired, I'll retire.' Believe me when I tell you everything is unsure, even for the most fortunate (*Letter* 101.4).

Jesus' rich farmer in Luke makes very similar plans; and God disturbs them: 'You fool, this very night your life will be demanded back. Who'll get all this stuff you've been collecting?' (12.20). Dio is similarly cutting: 'You fool! even if everything turns out right, what assurance have you that you'll live to see tomorrow, and not suddenly be torn away from all the good things you expected to enjoy?' (16.8). 'What good does it do anyone,' asks Jesus in Mark, 'to gain the whole world, and lose their true self?' (Mark 8.36–37).[54]

Thus Christians and Cynics alike reject the economic basis of the society in which they find themselves, the lure of wealth. They reject it in favour of life lived attentively in others' company, freed for them, and freed for God. But it is now time to consider a little more closely what these various people may have meant by 'God'.[55]

11. *God of Mercy, God of Grace*

It is certainly possible that some of the references in the Cynic material to 'Zeus', to 'God' or to 'gods' may be no more than rhetorical flourishes, '*nē Dia*', '*me Hercule*', 'by heavens'.[56] Some of the material ascribed to Diogenes in particular sounds sceptical. 'When someone was admiring the votive offerings in Samothrace, Diogenes' comment was, "There would have been far more, if those who did not return in safety had set offerings

up"' (6.59). 'Diogenes saw someone engaged in a ritual lustra-
tion. "You poor bedevilled fool," he said, "don't you realize that
having your way of life wrong is no more going to be helped by
splashing yourself with water than having your grammar wrong
is?"' (6.42). Yet even if this is so, the tradition has him refer to
gods, to their friendship, to their presence, and to prayer to them,
so that early Christian talk could still initially sound quite similar.

Then again the Stoic influence on Seneca, Musonius, Epictetus
and Dio in particular could well mean that 'God' or the gods
designate the impersonal though dynamic pattern that this
tradition discerns in the universe (Diog. Laert. 6.134–140), and
the term 'father', for instance, may be being used equivocally
rather than analogically. It would still be the case that on early
hearing both Christian talk and (Stoic-) Cynic talk would sound
almost as much alike as they do in the other areas we have so far
explored.

Jesus teaches prayer, and prays himself. Dio mentions in an
aside his own habit of daily prayer in the morning (52.1). 'I'm
left,' says Dio, 'with the shortest but most efficacious set of words
that I can utter, the ones I address to the Gods. For the Gods know
what the least human utterance means' (39.8). 'Remember God',
Epictetus urges us. 'Call on him to help you and stand by you' (II
18.29; compare Mark 11.25; James 1.5; 4.2–3; 5.13).

'When you pray,' Jesus instructs his followers, 'say "Father"'
(Luke 11.2, Q?). 'Some people,' Dio notes, 'do not hesitate to
address Zeus as "Father" in their prayers' (36.36). 'For everyone
and for ever and for always there is the Father who cares for
them . . .' was Epictetus' belief. 'Why, to Odysseus it was no
hearsay matter that Zeus is the Father of humankind, for he
always thought of him as Father, and addressed him as Father,
and did everything he did with him in mind as Father' (III 24.16).
Seneca invokes an imaginary Epicurus, 'You seem to want to
worship this being . . . as a parent,' he points out (*de beneficiis* IV
19.3).[57]

Jesus presses the analogy of human paternal care: 'Is there a
father among you who'll give his son a snake when he asks for a
fish . . .?' (Luke 11.11). Dio does, too (as we have already noted,
above): 'In their dreams young children often reach out their

arms to absent parents, filled with deeply and intensely felt longing . . . in just the same way we humans love the Gods who do us good and are our kin, and we feel a deep desire to be with them and enjoy their company in every way possible' (12.61). The kind of parental care pictured in Dio's Euboean story (7) would provide another instance of what he would mean when he called Zeus 'Father' (1.40; 12.75).[58]

If one reads Epictetus, theorizing about a son's duty to his father, the relationship looks to be formal and austere (and foreign to most Westerners; II 10.7). If instead we start with 'Who doesn't find active and attractive children appealing, so that they play with them and crawl on all fours with them and share their baby-talk?' (II 24.18), or Epictetus reprimanding a father for worrying more about his own anxiety than about the daughter whose illness has caused it, or Epictetus considering that a married philosopher might have to nurse the baby, get the older children off to school, and even make their beds (I 11; III 22.71–74), we are then drawn to a rather different picture of what he meant by 'father' when he used the term of and in address to Zeus.

So Epictetus can say,

God has not merely given us these abilities of ours so we may put up with whatever happens without being humiliated or broken by it; as a good king and most truly a Father to us, he's given us these abilities without external constraints, unhampered. He's put them entirely into our hands, without reserving even for himself any power to hinder or restrain (I 6.40–41).

That means, 'I am a free human being and a friend of God, so I may obey him of my own free will' (IV 3.9). The nearest early Christian analogy is in Galatians 4.1–7, and Romans 8.14–17; but compare Jesus' prayer at Gethsemane in Mark, 'Abba, Father, all things are possible to you . . . not what I will, but what you will' (14.36). We are adult children of a caring father; and if we submit, it is freely, under no compulsion. It is worth noting that we are far from any divine undergirding of an authoritarian or hierarchical view of society. 'I go about the whole earth, a free man under father Zeus, afraid of none of the great Lords', writes 'Diogenes' (ep. 34, again).

(While there is no dogmatic monotheism among our Cynic writers, references simply to 'God' preponderate. 'Many people simply combine all the gods into a single force, a single power', notes Dio, 31.11)

The relationship with 'fatherly' deity may involve painful episodes, but in itself it is something very much to be enjoyed, as in effect the total context of human flourishing. 'I thank you, Father, Lord of heaven and earth', says Jesus in 'Q' (Luke 10.21; cf. James 3.9). 'If we had any sense,' asks Epictetus, 'would we be doing anything else, in public or in private, apart from singing praises to God, and reviewing all his kindnesses?' (I 16.16. But enjoyment of God, now and to come, we discuss a little later on.)[59]

In section 9, above, we have already surveyed an important aspect of this sense of being already at home with our divine parent, ('Another, whose business it is, provides food and clothing' Epictetus III 12.13), and in section 7 we considered God's kindness to us in all our failures to respond.[60]

There is an important area of general primitive Christian belief in God's effective care that might, however, seem quite distinctive. In I Corinthians 15.3 Paul quotes an early conviction that 'Christ died for our sins'. In our gospel tradition, Mark 14.24 has Jesus talk of his blood 'shed for many', and earlier he has spoken of the son of man 'giving his life as a ransom for many' (10.45).[61]

Though there is not a great deal of this kind of talk in our early material (there is none in the 'Q' collection), there is besides quite a lot to suggest Jesus is being accorded divine or near divine status. He is a special agent of effective divine care, meant, it would seem, to enable us in some way to improve on our response to God's demands, not just tell us about them; meant to enable us to enjoy the relationship with himself that God intends, not with us just to talk about it or exemplify it.

It is quite clear to me that this not only seems but is distinctive, (and immensely important for the quality of any Christian life-style). However, it is worth noting that here, too, there are traces of some such motifs in some Cynic writing, also; and again these might well have been enough to maintain the impression conveyed by most of the rest of the early proclamation: these Christians are Cynics of a sort, with similar things to say about oppression and liberation. And, again, had the early Christians wanted to insist on making any clear distinction, had they wanted to suggest that even on apparently common ground of word and images they were really quite different from the Cynics they sounded like, they had only to colour more pieces of their tradition with talk of Jesus as God's chief agent for human well-being, salvation, and the result would have been unmistakable. But in fact, as noted, the 'soteriology' and 'christology', the talk of Jesus as Saviour, and as Christ or Lord or Son of God or Son of Man remain relatively unobtrusive, in the traditional materials we are analysing.[62]

'All things have been given to me by my father', claims Jesus in the 'Q' collection (Luke 10.22). 'All things belong to the wise', says Diogenes (6.72). 'God has brought us human beings here to be an audience for him and his works; and not just as audience, but as interpreters, too,' Epictetus believes (I 6.19–20). 'I believe I've not taken up this task of my own choice,' Dio confesses, 'but by the decision of some divine being. For when the Gods are exercising their providential care for us human beings, they provide people who will offer good advice without needing to be asked; and they provide appropriate and useful words for them to speak' (32.12, partly repeated).

'No one knows [who] the son [is] except the Father or [who] the Father [is] except the son and anyone to whom the son chooses to disclose him' (Luke 10.22; Matthew 11.27 lacks the words in [square brackets]). 'Aren't I in fact the one who is pious,' demands 'Heraclitus', 'I who alone know God. You are rash enough to allow that he exists while irreligiously supposing he is what in fact he is not' (ep. 4). 'If anyone has examined attentively the administration of this world and has learned that the greatest and most authoritative and most all-embracing of all social organizations is this one, of humans and Gods . . . why should someone who knows all this not call himself a world citizen? why not a son of God . . . our Father and Maker and Guardian?' (Epictetus I 9.4–6).[63]

'Are you the one we expect,' asks John Baptist, 'or are we to look for someone else?' (compare the earlier 'one greater than I' Luke 3.16, Q). 'Tell John what you see . . .' replies Jesus, tacitly acknowledging the hope (Luke 7.19–22, Q). 'When a strong and fully armed man guards his own palace, he can enjoy his property in peace. Yet if someone stronger attacks . . .' says Jesus in Luke, with the clear implication that such he is (11.20–22, ?Q; compare Mark 3.27). 'Where you're better and stronger than I am, I back down', concedes Epictetus, but adds, 'And where I'm better, you give way to me' (IV 7.36). Dio speaks of 'the hope that we may be able to turn people from wickedness and deceit and wicked desires, and lead them to a love of moral virtue and a yearning for a better life' (4.89-90). There might also seem to a pagan hearer to be some echo of Herakles who 'cleared wild beasts and tyrants from the face of the earth . . . clubbing to death all who attacked him . . . an allegory of cleansing the trackless regions of the soul' (Dio 5 20–21); 'It fell to Herakles to wander round the whole inhabited earth, witnessing the outrageous as well as the law-abiding behaviour of humans, casting out the wickedness he found and cleansing the world of it, and replacing it with the good' (Epictetus III 24.13).[64]

'Something greater than Solomon is here . . . something greater than Jonah is here' (Luke 11.31–32, Q). 'Someone wearing the despised cloak of Diogenes is more to be trusted than someone in the fine clothes of Carthage; his life-style is simple, but much healthier than the Persian king's. His way of living is painfully toilsome, but it's freer than that of Sardanapalus' ('Crates' ep. 13); and note also Peregrinus' disciple, comparing his master with the sun, and with Pheidias' Zeus, as well as with Diogenes, Antisthenes and Socrates (Lucian, *Peregrinus* 4–5).[65]

'I tell you, anyone who acknowledges me in a human setting, the Son of Man will acknowledge among God's angels. But anyone who repudiates me in a human setting, the Son of Man will repudiate among God's angels' (Luke 12.8–9; cf. Mark 8.38, and Matt. 25.31, etc; but also Luke 11.29–32, Q, again). 'Whenever a bad soul happens to meet the souls of philosophers, they flee away from it, realizing that it has sinned greatly in this life . . . [However] there are particularly high honours paid in Hades to good souls . . . They live as leaders over everyone else, in supreme command' ('Diogenes' ep. 39). Dio imagines, 'When someone gets hold of this useful device (reason) and uses it diligently day and night as best they may, they bear their own imprisonment [on earth] cheerfully . . . and when the appointed time comes, they leave easily . . . People like that the Gods sometimes set entirely free from their earthly imprisonment to share their own judicial functions, on the basis of their moral virtue and their wisdom' (30.24). 'Heraclitus' announces, 'I shall be welcomed in the homes of heaven and I shall take my stand as witness against the Ephesians. I shall share full right of citizenship, and that not with fellow humans, but with the Gods' (ep. 5; cf. 9). Claims such as these ascribed to a teacher who otherwise sounded Cynic would not particularly disturb the impression made by the rest of his words and deeds, indeed might fit quite well.[66]

Although the 'Q' material does not narrate Jesus' resurrection to glory, nor use that terminology, its understanding of his place in the judgment to come as well as its continuing response to him as its teacher and 'Lord' make it clear that the 'Q' community shared the faith of other Christians, that Jesus lives and continues to be a central focus of divine activity. This faith is explicit in the evangelists themselves, and in most of the New Testament letters. Yet there is no sign of this faith being read back into Jesus' own teaching, save at Matthew 12.40, Jonah's three days in the whale's belly, the passion predictions in Mark, and the text added on to the vicious vintners. It does not colour other items of the material; nor, for that matter, does it appear in James. Jesus remains Teacher (in Matthew, too: 23.8), and his teaching can be repeated simply as it stands, just as for any other teacher.[67]

Even talk of Jesus as 'deliverer' would fit quite happily into the Cynic picture of him that those listening to the early Christians are likely to have formed. 'The son of man came, not to be served, but to serve, and give his life to set many free,' (Mark 10.45. We have considered already the implications of this passage for Christian views of authority). '*Lutron anti pollōn*', 'a ransom for many' would most likely seem to early pagan hearers to be talking of a mass emancipation, of some unspecified kind. Even less clear, but in the same area, would be the assurance at Mark 14.24, 'this is my blood of the bequest, blood poured out for many'. Some important benefit, integral to the teacher's overall view of things, is expected to arise out of his death.

This sort of possibility, too, is canvassed among Cynic preachers. Musonius, for instance, accepts that the argument may lead this way: 'Someone whose life is useful to many has no right to die unless by dying he can be useful to still more' (29). Epictetus shifts the balance a little: ' "If I preserve my life, I shall be useful to many, but to none at all if I die." "Yes, and if we'd been in Socrates' situation we'd have left prison, even if it had meant going naked through a mouse-hole. And what actual use would that have been then? . . . If being alive was useful at all, wouldn't it have been more useful still to die when we ought and as we ought? Now that Socrates is dead the memory he leaves behind is no less useful, maybe even more useful to his fellow human beings than what he did and said in his lifetime" ' (IV 1.167–169). Without 'dying for' being involved, the ideas of 'freeing' and 'ransoming' also occur. 'Crates' announces, 'We live in perfect peace, freed from every evil by Diogenes of Sinope' (ep. 7), and 'We are for sure already free from wealth, but public opinion has not yet released us from slavery to herself, although, by Herakles! we're doing all we can to escape. Anyway, I shall ransom (*lutrōsomai*) myself from this task-mistress, too' (ep. 8).

Matthew presents us with a further passage in which Jesus seems to offer help as teacher but also, again, more than that: 'Come to me, anyone whose work is hard and whose burdens are heavy, and I'll let you rest. Take my yoke on your shoulders, and learn from me, for I've a gentle and humble heart, and you'll be able to find rest. My yoke is a good one, easy to carry' (11.28–30). (The coherence of these lines with the preceding 'Q' verses suggests they may belong to that collection, despite their absence from Luke.) Epictetus seems to presuppose this kind of offer being made by colleagues of his:

It's deceitful nonsense for someone to announce, 'I'm free from any pain or disturbance. You must recognize, my friends, that while you're in a noisy crowd jostling round worthless fripperies, I alone stand unperturbed!' Are you really not satisfied with having no pains yourself, but must go and advertise it? 'Come to me, anyone whose head is aching, who's got a fever, or who's lame or blind, and see how healthy I am, nothing wrong with me at all!' That's a useless and insensitive thing to say – unless, of course, you are someone like Asclepius, and can show them there and then how they can be restored then and there to good health, and you're only pointing out your own good health with that in mind (IV 8.28–29).

(Physical health is as usual being used as a metaphor for 'moral' health. But physical health itself is important, as becomes clear in what follows.) 'If an accident happens that affects someone's livelihood and he drops from riches to poverty, to powerlessness from being influential, or he suffers some other sad mishap, then he becomes much more amenable to our discipline. Somehow he now manages to put up with what we philosophers have to say and as near as dammit admits he actually needs our consolation and encouragement', notes Dio with ill-concealed satisfaction (27.9). 'Demetrius of Phaleron was not pleased to see Crates approaching. He expected some harsh words, uttered with the usual Cynic frankness (*parrēsia*). But Crates spoke gently with him encouraging him and consoling him in his present situation' (Plutarch, *Moralia* 69CD). 'You don't know how much philosophy helps us at every point. To quote Cicero, how useful it is in the most important things, while touching what seems least to matter. Trust me, and summon philosophic wisdom to advise you', writes Seneca to his friend (*Letter* 17.2–3).[68]

The human situation is such that proclaiming or even parading a set of ideals may seem to be insufficient. More 'help' may be needed, in the form of a human counsellor and friend, as well as the effective assurance that the Cynic ideal is worth risking life for. Talk among Christians of 'freeing' and 'ransom' and 'helping the burdened' could readily be understood along these lines. Yet contemporary with the early Christian proclamation being reviewed here, Paul, for instance, was insisting that through the death and resurrection of Jesus, God had done very much more than this to 'help'. God had altered the entire context of human response both to God and to one's fellow humans; and the gospel writers who put the early traditions into extended narratives worked with a similar conviction. It is most probably already expressed in the Markan tradition's talk of 'ransom' and 'for many'. However, it is clearly not stressed, it is not reiterated, (and there is no hint of it in James). The simpler reading, more in tune with Cynic usage, would still have been easy to maintain, even if, as noted above, there was talk of the Teacher being still alive and focus of divine activity.

And yet, even had there been more emphasis on the human situation being so bad as to need some kind of general restructuring, some special divine initiative, Cynic parallels to such a discernment of underlying human weakness and evil would still have been forthcoming. It is implicit in the severity of the rebukes directed against people in general. It is explicit in 'How long, will human kind go on being so wicked, Hermodorus?' ('Heraclitus' ep. 9), 'your deep-rooted evil' ('Diogenes' ep. 28), 'although perhaps all of us humans, or at least the majority of us, do sin [it still is not "natural"]' (Epictetus I 11.7), 'the wickedness of humankind . . . wickedness is found in almost all' (Dio 74.11), 'in this imperfect humankind there's some kind of evil power – we have a mind so ready for wickedness' (Seneca *Letter* 112.9), '. . . wickedness is so pervasive, is it any wonder that oracles have ceased!' cries the Cynic Didymus in Plutarch (*Moralia* 413C). 'You who are evil', says Jesus, in passing, in the 'Q' tradition (Luke 11.13).[69]

The evil discerned is clearly human. There is no sign that Seneca's 'power that makes for evil' is a personalized or otherwise reified spirit or daimon. The gospel tradition certainly allows for evil daimonions, unclean spirits, which produce insanity. We consider that a little later. These daimonions do not cause human wickedness as such. The Satan, the Adversary, may act as over zealous public prosecutor, and try to provoke rebellion. But in the synoptic tradition (as opposed to the last two evangelists) the choice remains with the human subject, and human wickedness is a human responsibility; (contrast Luke 22.3; John 13.2,7).[70]

When Dio talks about evil daimons (e.g. *Discourse* 4.91–134), he makes it quite clear beforehand that 'each man's own mind is his daimon; the sensible man's is good, the wicked man's is wicked' (4.80, compare 23.12). (A comparison between the eight unclean spirits of Luke 11.23–26 ('Q'), and the three daimons of Dio's fourth discourse together with the 'Libyan Myth' of *Discourse* 5 makes it likely that the gospel passage would probably be read metaphorically; and so, too, the 'Q' Temptation.) Epictetus uses the language figuratively, and then only very occasionally (e.g. IV 4.38; compare Dio 45.1). (Writers like Plutarch, in a Platonic and Orphic tradition, are more ready to accept the underlying dualism of 'real' evil spirits who promote human wickedness. Yet Philo, of course, resists the move, characterizing it as 'superstition', *deisidaimonia, de gigantibus* 16.)[71]

On the other hand, that there should be some divinely given power for good available is much more widely accepted; though, as in the gospel tradition, it is usually seen as focussed on a special teacher or leader. So '[holy] spirit' seems to be available to Jesus at his baptism (Luke 3.16, Q; Mark 1.8, 10, 12), and in his ministry (Luke 11.20–22; 12.10, Q), (and perhaps to the 'prophets' of the Christian community that preserved and used the 'Q' tradition).

'How one can consider any supernatural power (daimon) evil, I just cannot say. And then, if you philosophers suppose a daimon is actually divine, you've made any such conclusion quite impossible', insists Dio (23.9; though not forgetting his note at 4.80, quoted above). Horrified reaction against denigrating (a) holy spirit would make obvious sense in this milieu.

Similarly, then, 'Heraclitus' speaks of the moral benefits of 'the *daimōn*' (ep. 8). And Epictetus wants a listener to say, ' "It wasn't Epictetus who said these things to me. How could he have thought them up? It was some kindly deity speaking through him. Come, let us obey the deity, so we don't remain under his wrath." . . . If he communicates with you through a human voice, are you going to pretend it is only the human being speaking to you, and so ignore the supernatural power?' (III 1.36).

The predominant picture in the gospel tradition of Jesus as God's emissary has him teaching, disturbingly, and acting in character, and disturbingly. This is his service to God and to humankind, the many. There may be more, even very importantly more expected of him, for he has been raised to glory, he is a living Lord. But it is still his teaching as such that forms the bulk of what is repeated.[72]

So in the tradition Jesus is pictured, like any Cynic teacher might be, facing harsh and testing experiences (Luke 4.1–12, Q; compare 9.57–62, Q); but only as what any disciple is encouraged to undergo (Luke 6.20–22, Q; James 1.2–4, 12–13). 'We use the training that works for both body and soul,' claims Musonius, 'accustoming ourselves to cold and heat, to thirst and hunger and to a meagre diet and a hard bed, with abstinence from pleasure, and patience in painful toil,' (6). 'Now's the time for going thirsty – thirst well,' urges Epictetus. 'It's time to go hungry – hunger well' (III 10.8; cf. III 24.17). '[A true Cynic] will challenge each opponent in turn, eagerly contending with hunger and cold, coping with thirst, showing no weakness, not even if he has to undergo a flogging' (Diogenes in Dio 8.16; compare Luke 4.2).

'Hermes took Herakles along a secret path untrodden by human foot till they came to a very high and prominent mountain peak . . . twin peaks, in fact: the Royal Peak, sacred to King Zeus, and the other, the Peak of Tyranny, deriving its name from [the evil deity] Typhon . . . and all the ostentatious luxury designed to present a semblance of glory . . .' (Dio 1.66–67, 79). Diogenes, as we have noted, is constantly confronted by royal power, always succeeding in maintaining his own integrity. Jesus refuses just the kind of royal power Alexander sought (Dio 4.4, Seneca, *de beneficiis* I 13.2); (compare Luke 4.5–6). He also refuses to try to perform some striking action; again in contrast to what is suggested of Alexander, 'in your present state of mind you'll not rise above anyone else at all. You'll never be a real ruler, even if you achieve a high-jump that clears the walls of Babylon and capture it that way . . . not even if you swim the Ocean . . .' (Dio 4.53; cf. 120, and Luke 4.9–11).

In response to this testing Jesus replies with quotations from Jewish scripture that say what a Cynic would be expected to. 'Does a Cynic make an appeal to anyone but Zeus?' demands Epictetus (III 22.56), and makes this commitment, 'I give more weight to God's will than to my own. I shall attach myself to him as his servant and follower, sharing his intentions and aims, willing what he wills' (IV 7.20). 'The Lord your God is the one you're to worship, and you're to serve him alone' says Jesus (Luke 4.8). 'Do you really suppose Homer means that Zeus feeds kings like a nursing mother feeds her child with milk and wine and bread – rather than with knowledge and truth?' (Dio 4.41); 'humankind is not to live just on bread, but by every word from God's lips' (Matt. 4.4; Luke 4.4 has only the first phrase). (For 'tempting God', though, there seems no obvious parallel.)

With a trust so often expressed in the care of the divine Father, one might expect more reference to traditional religious 'means of grace' (in addition to prayer as such, which we have seen is widely commended, though not uncritically). In fact there is a trenchant critique of the religious establishment, both of its personnel and its practices, in both traditions, and again often in similar vein. We noted something of this earlier when we looked at John Baptist, and also at the critique of reliance on family or race.

Both criticize ineffective official guides (especially 'blind' ones) – Luke 6.39–40, 'Q', Epictetus II 12.3; Dio 62.7; Plutarch *Moralia* 439D.

In the gospel tradition the Pharisaic life-style is criticized for its reliance on 'externals', using the technical Stoic-Cynic terminology (Luke 11.39–40): 'moral virtue is complete without reference to externals', says 'Crates' (3). 'Externals are not mine to control. Moral choice is', insists Epictetus (II 5.4, etc.). We shall return to this theme a little later, only recalling for the moment the awareness we have already noted among Cynics of the danger of any reliance on their 'externals', 'the disgusting satchel, the staff, and the big mouth' (Epictetus III 22.50).[73]

There is a similar criticism of the rules about hand-washing, using the same inner-outer contrast, in Mark (7.1–5, 14–23). We may compare, again, Diogenes' jibe, 'Getting your way of life right is no more going to be helped by splashing yourself with water than correcting your grammar is!' (6.42). 'Won't you have a wash?' Epictetus protests. 'Are you meaning to come with us into the temples just as you are? It's against the rules to spit or blow your nose there – and you're going in, a mass of spit and snot! And now you think I'm telling you to visit a beauty parlour! Not on your life! I'm asking you to sort out what is distinctively human in you, your reason, the conclusions it reaches, the results it can have. As for your body, you need do no more than keep it clean enough to be inoffensive' (Epictetus IV 11.32–33). 'The conflict between Jews and Syrians and Egyptians and Romans,' says Epictetus in Rome, apparently assuming that the allusion will be understood, 'isn't over whether the pursuit of holiness should have the highest priority; it's simply over whether pig meat is holy or unholy' (I 22.4). Diogenes was himself believed to have insisted that no animal's flesh was unholy (Diog. Laert. 6.73).

The Markan and Lucan traditions (the former followed by Matthew) have Jesus critical of the way the Sabbath is understood. This, too, is a widely known feature of Judaism, and comes under criticism from others as well as Seneca: 'Let us forbid the lighting of lamps on the Sabbath, since the Gods don't need the light, nor do we humans enjoy soot (*Letter* 95.48; compare Plutarch, *Moralia* 169C).[74]

The disruption of the Temple would also readily match people's expectations of a Cynic teacher. 'Diogenes was dining in a temple, and some rather messy loaves were put on the table. He snatched them up and threw them out. "Nothing unclean," he insisted, "ought to come into a temple"' (6.64). 'He noticed some temple officials leading away for punishment someone who'd stolen a bowl belonging to the sanctuary. "Master thieves leading a petty one", he commented' (6.45). Dio speaks of a philosopher (possibly Musonius) who rebuked the Athenians for holding gladiatorial combats in a place where religious rites also took place – and was forced to leave the city for his pains (Dio 32.121–122; compare Lucian, *Demonax* 57).[75]

Matthew twice has Jesus' actions stem from Hosea's 'It's mercy I want, not sacrifice' (9.7; 12.13); it is probably Matthew's own editorial addition. But Dio would have sympathized: 'I take it you realize that whether someone pours out a libation to the Gods, or just burns some incense, or simply presents himself before them, but does it in the right frame of mind, that's quite enough. Perhaps God requires none of these sorts of things – no images, no sacrifices at all' (31.15). 'Moral virtue is the true sanctity, and any wickedness is the real sacrilege' (3.52). 'It's not the sacrificial victims themselves that afford honour to the Gods . . . it's the right and pious intentions of the offerers', says Seneca (115.5).[76]

Neither the Cynics nor the Jesus of the early tradition are rejecting temples and their ritual out of hand; Jesus wants the Temple to be as stated in the tradition, a place of prayer, and Epictetus similarly says:

> You should come with sacrifice and prayers, after first purifying yourself, and already in the right frame of mind, aware that you are approaching sacred things, sacred things of great antiquity . . . instituted by people long ago to instruct you and to improve the way you live . . . (III 21.14–15).

In the passage quoted above, Dio continues with, 'but such things are not useless, for they do emphasize our devotion and concern towards the gods' (31.15, again).

There are differences in approach between Christians and Cynics (and among each group) but also considerable similarities. Whether deity is clearly one (Christians) or most likely one, or as likely as plural as our experience, trust in God or gods is bound up with human freedom and human flourishing. God does not support the powerful in their domination or exploitation of the weak; nor the possessors against the dispossessed; but neither does God confirm the weak in their weakness. God panders to no one's wish to stay small and comfortable and lazy.

For most if not all our writers 'God' is more than a metaphor for 'nature', for 'things as they happen to be', and God is trusted, as we have seen, as personal. But that trust does very clearly entail a conviction that things as they are can be conducive to human freedom and flourishing, and that nothing less is in tune with how things really are, so nothing less needs to be tolerated – nor should be.

12. *Now and Then*

People can be set free to enjoy each other as God's children and this world as God's world, and God as Father, here and now. We have already taken note of some aspects of this conviction, of its extent, and of the significant ways in which it is shared by Christians and Cynics.

Attention has been drawn to the explicit and implicit evidence that for Cynics this amounted to living in the Golden Age, regained, under the rule of Cronos (or, for Romans, Saturn). For an outsider (such as Lucian), that involved a very large 'as if', it was make-believe, a confidence trick on others and on any Cynic who actually believed it (*Runaways*). But Cynics insisted, it was possible to live at peace with other people, without exploitation or oppression, and to live in the world around without exploitation or oppression. It was possible to 'live according to nature', like the animals, unharmed or unharming – or, at least, with no more harm than animals 'naturally' inflict on one another.

There are various imaginative pictures of this once good life. Virgil had imagined it returning with the advent of Augustus Caesar (*Eclogue* 4). For our purposes, Seneca's *Letter* 90 will serve. It may well not read particularly convincingly (though it could fit some specially favoured parts of today's world). A brief precis is presented here as an indication of an example of an ideal that was quite widely entertained.

In the Golden Age, then, humans were unspoiled, and followed nature. There was leadership, but only by someone whose ability was matched by his (sic) goodness. Before wickedness stole in, and the rule of the good turned to tyranny, there was no need for laws (6). People lived happily without houses, without keys or door-bolts, in caves or thatched shelters. They managed without ransacking the earth for metal ores, living in the style of Diogenes (14), having all their real needs met, content with what is on earth's surface, clothed from animal-skins or soft tree-bark. Civilized needs have enslaved human beings (19). Our wisdom has been side-tracked into inappropriate technologies (passim), when it was meant to allow us to appreciate living in one vast divine temple (29), 'not just aware of the gods, but following them' (34). That was the richest age, for no one was poor:

Then avarice burst into this best of all worlds. Eager to take things off and make them its own, it succeeded in making everything someone else's, reducing immeasurable wealth to straitened need. It was avarice that gave us poverty. Eagerness for more lost us everything (38).

Originally what there was was divided among totally unquarrelsome friends, and the only blood shed was that of wild beasts (41). People lived free of cares, and relaxed (42); 'they still were merciful to the dumb animals, so far was the age removed from the custom of humans killing humans, not in anger or fear, but for entertainment' (45). And in another letter, a little later in his collection, he also adds, significantly, that people's physical health will have been much better, obviating any need for complex medical treatment (95.13–15, 22; among other sources quoted here, note especially the similar selection of themes in Dio's *Discourse 6*, Diogenes).

It should be clear how much of this kind of ideal is sometimes implicit, most often explicit, both in the early Christian proclamation of the teaching and example of Jesus, and in the similar persuasion of those much more whole-heartedly Cynic than was Seneca. But it is also worth noting or recalling the extent to which elements at least of this 'Golden Age' myth had been assimilated in Jewish tradition, to amplify both the picture of primal innocence in Eden and its loss, and of the return to the beginning in the Age to Come. (The point is made at this juncture mainly to stress the wide circulation of these ideas; but it also prepares for part of the argument of the next chapter.) They are to be found in Josephus, *Antiquities* I 60–62, Philo, *de legatione* 11–13, and *de praemiis et poenis* 87–126 (Deuteronomy 28, Leviticus 26, and Isaiah supplemented by Golden Age themes), *Jubilees* 11, *I Enoch* 8, 52, *Sibylline Oracles* I 283–306, III 35–45, 110–116, 155, 367–380, *II Baruch* 73.

For Epictetus the possibility of sharing in God's festival is open all the time. It is there, to be appreciated and enjoyed (a sort of 'fully realized eschatology'), for the span of one's life. That is all (there is nothing to follow save absorption back into the elements, III 13.14–15), but this 'all' is very richly enough. 'Didn't Another bring you in and show you the light, and give you companions to work with, and your senses and your reason? and what was his aim in all this? Didn't he intend you to be mortal, living a short while on earth as a spectator of his providential control, sharing in the festive pageantry?' (IV 1.104). 'What God wants is people who'll join in the festivities and the dancing, people who'll want to clap their hands and invoke the Gods and sing hymns to celebrate the festival' (IV 1.108; IV 4.23–28).

Epictetus uses the analogy of the enjoyment of a celebration of the mysteries, as does Seneca; and it occurs again in Dio (Discourse 12.28–33), where he is imagining human beginnings, where life would have been shared closely with God, 'as in some mystic shrine' (33). This possibility is still open to us, he proposes in *Discourse 30, Charidemus*:

> Our universe is a house, very beautiful, divinely so, built by the Gods themselves . . . Into this universe comes humankind to share the festivities at the invitation of the king of the gods. We are brought in to a banquet, for all of us to enjoy the magnificent feast set out for us . . . We are set alongside tables loaded with all we need, bread and fruit, things cultivated and things growing wild . . . our tables are the meadows, the plains, the valleys, the coastlands . . . There's dancing and every kind of enjoyment . . . What we think of as hard work . . . is nothing worse than what we do at a feast, stretching out a hand to help ourselves . . . (28–32).

In this discourse, at least, Dio expounds an 'inaugurated' eschatology. This life is not all, still more awaits those who deserve it. (The transfer is individual. It does not in this discourse involve humankind as a whole or the universe; but, as will be shown, Dio also has a 'cosmic' eschatology.)

The early Christians told of a teacher who went to parties, and was even accused of being 'a glutton and a drunkard' (Luke 7.33–4, Q). He was able to entertain vast crowds out in the wilderness. He talked of sharing a banquet with God as king (Luke 13.28–29, Q), and told various stories of wedding feasts and the like. He prepared for his death at a meal with his friends, promising he would then abstain until he could share a cup where God's rule was fully effective (Mark 14.25; compare I Cor. 11.26). As we have recalled in some detail, he urged people to trust God's present care for their real needs. God was with them, as a father whose presence and company they could trust and enjoy. It would be very easy for early hearers to take all this as just another variant of the Cynic theme of enjoying the present as already or still the Golden Age. They were already 'blessed', happy (Luke 6.20–23; Matt. 5.3–12), though they could expect much more to come.[77]

In much contemporary New Testament scholarship, the theme of 'the kingdom of God' is seen as important and distinctive, and justifiably so. However, it does not recur all that often in the synoptic tradition itself (it is more often editorial) and occasional talk of 'king' and 'royal rule' would not have sounded much different from talk of Zeus as 'king', and of the Cynic claim to share his 'kingdom' already (e.g. Epictetus III 22.63, 72). There would not have been enough to disturb the general Cynic impression conveyed by the bulk of the Jesus tradition.

A very significant aspect of the new life-style of which the Christians told, and one that may be closely linked to the theme of the kingdom, God's sovereign rule, is constituted by the healing of the sick and the ending of demonic possession. 'The blind receive their sight, the lame walk, lepers are cleansed, the deaf hear, the dead are raised up' (Luke 7.26–28, Q); as well as the poor having the gospel proclaimed to them. 'If it is by the finger (or spirit) of God that I cast out demons, then God's royal rule is effective over you' (Luke 11.20; Matt. 12.28). In addition to these explanatory comments there are a large number of healing and exorcism stories as such (though only one of each in 'Q'; cf. James 5.14–15).[78]

There are no miracle stories in even the most obviously theistic of the Cynic strands. The closest anything comes to it is the assurance 'Heraclitus' gives, 'I shall heal myself . . . none of them [the physicians] is a healer, they are all frauds and quacks' (6). Diogenes in the tradition, and Oenomaus in the second century are particularly sceptical about any supposed divine interventions.

Yet health as such is of great importance in the Cynic scheme of things (much more so than among, say, Epicureans and Stoics). Health is 'the greatest of human blessings' (Dio 38.12). That health can be maintained and still better, improved, following the Cynic way is also an important sign of its validity. The well-being of the Golden Age really can still be appropriated. 'Health and strength of body and soul alike, are appropriate concerns', Diogenes is said to have taught (6.70). 'With exercise, they no longer keep going sick as they used to be, and they acknowledged that they had their health thanks to me, and did not leave me, but continued to follow me wherever I went', writes 'Crates' (20). 'Diogenes offers as final proof,' says Epictetus, 'his body, well compacted and glowing with health' (I 24.8). It may well be in this context that he imagines a contemporary making the self-congratulatory announcement cited above, 'See how healthy I am, not a thing wrong with me', and chides him, 'That's pretty useless and crude, unless, like Asclepius, you explain there and then how your hearers can get themselves well again, then and there . . . That's how to be a Cynic worthy of the sceptre and diadem of Zeus' (IV 8.28–30; cf. 34, 'the sceptre and the kingdom'; and Seneca, *Letter* 78.3–4).

As we noted earlier in this section, good health is an important feature of pictures of the Golden Age, and the motif recurs in most of the late Jewish schemes. The wording of Jesus' answer to John Baptist itself has obvious links only with the canonical Isaiah 35 (and perhaps 29). But the actual picture of health restored would fit clearly into the Cynic picture of living life as originally intended, as Diogenes had showed was possible (cf. Dio, *Discourse* 6, again). Miraculous achievement of physical and mental well-being would, so far as we can tell, have seemed very surprising. The importance placed on that physical well-being itself would be what any Cynic would expect, as part of the return to the Age of Gold.

We have seen in passing that Epictetus has no 'personal', 'final' eschatology for individuals, though Dio and Seneca and 'Heraclitus' have. Epictetus, Dio, Seneca and others accept the idea of the coming Conflagration. The world as we know it is not going to continue indefinitely (Epictetus II 1.8, III 13.4, etc.; Dio 36.47, 40.35–37; Seneca *Letter* 9.16–17; *consolatio ad marciam* 26, and possible some of the language of 'Heraclitus' 6, 8 and 9). That the end may be near is accepted as very likely by, for instance, so sceptical a writer as Pliny senior: 'It is something we can almost see happening: the average size our whole human race attains is decreasing, and very few grow taller than their fathers. It shows that the Conflagration must be near, for the fertility of human semen to be reduced'(!) (*Natural History* 7.73).[79]

(The element of 'judgment' we have already considered in the previous section of this chapter, and the place of the Teacher, Jesus, in the culmination of things.)

The 'futurist' eschatology, and even the sense of urgency in the Christian proclamation would not have seemed out of place to hearers still interpreting the rest of the message in the light of popular Cynic teaching. With so much of the Christian material seeming so like so much of the Cynic teaching, and even this handful of apparently more distinctive Christian themes still finding parallels of a sort, there is no sign that these early Christians were anything other than pleased to sound, look and live like Cynics, sharing many of the same urgent Cynic aims of human freedom and human flourishing in a culture enriched by simplicity.

13. *The People and the Practicalities*

It is in their understanding of people, of the possibilities of humans flourishing in a life lived in openness to one another, at one with the physical world around, that, as we have already seen, these early Christians and contemporary Cynics most clearly share common ground. This is not so merely in words, which both accept are inadequate on their own. The common ground is most obvious in their actual dealings with real people. In particular they are united in taking women seriously, that half of the human race; or, at the very least, they take them more seriously than others seem to. They also both refuse to allow legal servitude to define or shape human relationships. They also both seem to share a similar positive appreciation of children (though this is probably not as distinctive as is the openness to all women and all slaves).

In an age where it is very easy to find disparaging remarks about women, the Cynics stand out from the rest. 'Moral virtue is the same for women as for men', insisted Antisthenes (6.12). 'Women are in no way inferior to men', 'Crates' affirms to 'Hipparchia' (ep.

28). Arguing that men and women should receive the same education, Musonius insisted,

> Women just as much as men have been given the gift of reason, the gift that enables us to relate to one another and decide whether something is good or bad, fine or shameful . . . And not just men, but women, too, have the same inclination towards moral virtue, and the same capacity to acquire it (3).

Society encourages girls from fourteen to see themselves as nothing but bed-fellows for men, and then blames them for not being more, Epictetus points out forcefully (*Encheiridion* 40).[80]

In the gospel tradition we do not have statements of general principle to match these; but the practice seems the same, and, as suggested, must seem still more significant. Mark and Luke simply mention in passing the women who followed Jesus (Mark 15.40–41; Luke 8.1–3); their presence does not have to be explained or excused. Women are seen as valid witnesses to the risen Lord. A woman anoints Jesus' head, a symbolic acknowledgment that the early tradition saw as very significant (Mark 14.3–9) – even if her name then got lost! Other women approach Jesus and are taken seriously (Mark 5.25–34; 7.24–30). Luke has a tale of a woman on her own sitting at Jesus' feet as his disciple (10.38–42). There is little of this kind in the 'Q' collection, however (it has little narrative), though here, too, 'the Queen of the South' is chosen as the ideal disciple questing for wisdom (Luke 11.31). Women's relationships with one another are as likely to be disturbed by Jesus' teaching as men's are (Luke 12.51, Q). Again it seems legitimate to take Galatians 3.28–29 as significant for the early days of the church, as well as Paul's acknowledgment of women as colleagues (Rom. 16, etc.). The Pauline evidence allows us to place some further weight on these incidental hints in the gospel tradition.

A similar argument may hold for the understanding of the relationship of a woman and a man in marriage. Paul's unargued acceptance of mutuality (I Cor. 7.5, 12–16; 11.11–12) suggests this is the community's common view; it is only for restrictions to mutuality that he has to make a case. This is what Jesus' use of Genesis 2.34 in the Markan tradition seems to mean. 'The couples were to be united as one flesh: no longer two individuals, but one organism' (Mark 10.8), with the stress on the relationship (and not economics or procreation, as for instance in Josephus and Philo). It is at least in this sense that the saying would be likely to have been taken in a Cynic context. For we find Musonius arguing,

> What was the Creator's purpose in originally dividing our human race in two, and providing us with our respective genital organs, so we are male and female? and then in building in a strong desire to share sexual union with each other, mixed with a deep yearning for each other's company, the man for the woman, the woman for the man? Isn't it clear that he meant them to come together as a single unit, to live together, and to work hard to share a common livelihood together, and to procreate children and bring them up – and so perpetuate the human race? (14).

Procreation comes into the reckoning, of course, but it is neither sufficient nor even primary:

> The birth of children is not a sufficient basis for marriage . . . In marriage there must first and foremost be a shared life together and a caring relationship of husband and wife together, in sickness and in health, and at all times, since it was with a desire for this, as well as to have children, that they got wed (13).

'The truly good king,' Dio assumes, 'regards his wife not as just a bed-fellow and sexual companion, but as his partner in decision-making and action, and in the whole of his life' (3.122); and we may recall again the account of a romantic love-match in *Discourse* 7. Musonius felt that a philosopher would himself be better off married; Epictetus disagreed, (though if he could find another Hipparchia, it would be different (III 22.76) but accepted, as did Demonax, that marriage counselling was an important part of the Cynic teacher's task (Epictetus III 22.72–73; Lucian, *Demonax* 9).[81]

The early Christian tradition insisted that 'adultery' was an offence against a wife, and not solely against a husband (Luke 16.18, 'Q'; Mark 10.11). In much the same way Musonius objects indignantly to any 'double standard':

> If it doesn't seem shameful or out of place for a master to bed a female slave of his, particularly if she has no other man of her own, let him consider how it would look to him if his wife bedded one of his male slaves ... Yet surely men aren't expected to be morally inferior to women? (12).

Seneca makes a similar point,

> You know full well that a man is lacking in integrity if he demands chastity in his wife while he's corrupting the wives of other men. Just as she should not commit adultery, so you shouldn't have a mistress. And you know this full well. You just don't put it into practice (*Letter* 94.26).

In a slightly later letter he writes, 'What can be more delightful than mattering so much to your wife that you start to matter more to yourself?' (*Letter* 104.5).

On slavery we have to depend on an argument from silence (apart from Galatians 3.28–29 again), albeit a fairly strong one. There are no signs in the early material of any influence of the 'household codes' that appear in the sub-Pauline letters (Col. 3.18–4.1; Eph. 5.21–6.9; I Peter 2.13–3.7), and stress the submission of slaves (as well as of wives and children). But we have seen already that domination and oppression are rejected, and the only service that is accepted is voluntary: though that is highly commended. We have one slave-and-master parable in Luke (17.7–10; cf. perhaps 12.47–48), where the analogy seems to be accepted fairly literally, but nothing of the sort appears elsewhere in other strands. Everyone seems to be approached equally.

The Cynic sources are more explicit. Dio has Diogenes insist very strongly on the inappropriateness of 'making use' of other people (*Discourse* 10), and argues in his own name against slavery, and against any disparaging of those who are slaves and (or) descended from slaves (14 and 15); in 15 he may also be dependent on Antisthenes' arguments about the irrelevance of slave-birth. Epictetus, himself a freed slave, insists that the only important servitude is that voluntarily accepted. Seneca devotes a long letter to insisting on our common humanity (*Letter* 48). Everyone is to be approached in a way that conveys an equal evaluation.

We noted in Chapter I evidence for a quite widespread appreciation of children in their own right. Even if women (free and slave) and slaves (women and men) are distinctively valued among Cynics and Christians, it would probably be misleading to suggest that their open attitude to children was particularly unique. It does, nonetheless, seem to have been consistent with their approach to those others who were especially vulnerable because of physical weakness and legal injustice.

Like Jesus in the Markan tradition (9.33–37; 10.15) Epictetus is willing to teach by children's example (I 24.20), as were Diogenes (Diog Laert. 6.37), and Dio (12.61). Like Jesus (Mark 10.13–14), Epictetus was happy to welcome children (II 24.18). Many of the gospel healing stories are of children, and specifically of girls. Perhaps more significant still is the implication of the Christian material discussed in section 3 of this chapter, the teaching methods encouraged by the early Christians, precisely those to be found among contemporaries with the most open approach to the children around them.[82]

The 'physician', 'healer' metaphor, the open table-fellowship and the teaching on forgiveness and reconciliation have already shown the first Christians sharing the Cynic refusal to exclude anyone from the initial offer (though both groups know that of 'the many called' few choose to respond – Matt. 20.16, 'Diogenes' ep. 12).

Perhaps most significant for both groups is their willingness to allow very 'ordinary' people, not excluding women, to assume kinds of leadership. To invite such people – especially women – into the ranks is an important step. The seriousness with which they are welcomed is tested by the emergence of teachers (or people with some other leadership role) from among them.[83]

Lucian pours scorn on this: 'They were learning to be cobblers or builders' labourers; they were occupied with fullers' vats, or they were carding wool to make it nice and easy for the women', he says in the *Runaways* (12), where he also says they promise to make women into philosophers (18). 'Even if you are quite ordinary – a tanner, fisherman, carpenter, money-changer, there's nothing to stop you annoying other people, so long as you have the cheek, the nerve ... how about boatman or gardener ...?' (*Philosophies for Sale*, 11). In the early Cynic tradition there was Monimus, a servant of a Corinthian banker; when he heard of Diogenes: 'All at once he feigned madness, scattering all the copper and silver coins on the bank counter, until his master dismissed him; then he immediately became Diogenes' disciple' (6.82, again; cf. Mark 2.13–14). On the fringe of Cynicism there was Simon the Cobbler, (Diog. Laert. 2.122) who has been enrolled as a Cynic in the Socratic epistles 12 and 13. Musonius Rufus commends the life of a shepherd or farm labourer; Dio is said to have planted, dug, drawn water for baths and for gardens, and done other odd jobs, as entirely compatible with the Cynic calling (Philostratus, *Lives of the Sophists* 488).

Musonius also comments 'Some people are sure to say that women who spend their time with philosophers are bound to become self-willed and arrogant, deserting their households for the company of [other] men, practising speeches, talking like sophists, when they ought to be at home spinning' (3.) He is not too worried, because that's not how he understands philosophy, anyway. Hipparchia is allowed to defend herself against this apparently standard charge (Diog. Laert 6.98).

Among the early Christians we have carpenter (Mark 6.3), fishermen (1.16–20), tax-collector (2.14), and, in Acts, leather-workers (18.3; cf. I Cor. 4.12; and also Origen, *contra celsum* 3.55). In Acts, also, it is accepted that Peter and John were uneducated and very ordinary (4.13; and cf. John 7.15). 'Where are the sophisticated, the highly literate, the orators?' asks Paul (albeit oratorically, I Cor. 1.20).[84]

Women are not seen teaching in the gospel tradition (unless one includes John 4.39); but then neither are men other than Jesus, save John Baptist very briefly, and the twelve on one limited occasion, (doubled in Luke: Mark 6.11 and parallels, and Luke 10.9). In Acts, the leather-workers Priscilla and Aquila take in

Apollos and both expound the word of God to him (18.26). Romans 16 lists Phoebe, Prisca (again preceding Aquila), Mary who exerted herself 'apostolically', Andronicus and Junia ... notable apostles ... Tryphaena and Tryphosa and beloved Persis, too, women who exerted themselves [i.e. 'apostolically']; Philippians 4 gives us Euodia and Syntyche, 'two women who exerted themselves with me in apostolic evangelism, with Clement also, and the rest of my fellow workers'. Even if the textually suspect I Corinthians 14.34–36 were by Paul and showed him withdrawing women's part in the learning process from a public to a private domestic setting, the evidence remains impressive. As did the Cynics, the Christians approached ordinary people with high expectations.

Neither the Cynic way nor this version of the Christian way became a mass movement, so far as we can tell. But clearly some people at the time did find one or other an entirely practicable approach to living. They offered life-styles that could work.

Both were, of course, entirely impractical from various external points of view. From the stance of revolutionary realists such as the Jewish Zealots of the 60s, this kind of individual 'dropping out' changed nothing. Apart from the one reference by Lucian to Peregrinus fomenting rebellion in Achaea (19), there is no indication of Cynics being persuaded to this kind of action. Attempts to show early Christians involved with Jewish Zealots have been unpersuasive.[85] Military action did change the face of Judaea (just as in Rome it brought a new dynasty to power). The system under which people lived remained the same.

The Cynic approach of Dio, diluted to suit the emperor's taste, seems to have won a hearing from Trajan, and notes of Epictetus' teaching were taken deeply to heart by Marcus Aurelius. There is no sign that either ruler supposed that here was the basis for a practical alternative political programme for human freedom and flourishing. No hard-working Roman or provincial official in charge of the grain supplies was going to be other than grateful for the stimulus provided by trade between centres of population. As we noted above, when Dio got down to practicalities he looked for ways of drawing more of the poor into the system (7.81–152; 34.19–23), rather than change it. Extremes of wealth go on being criticized, but the way life is conducted socially, politically, economically is not challenged. There is a particularly vivid illustration of this in *Discourse* 46, where Dio himself seems to be facing a mob accusing him of profiteering in a food shortage. He is innocent of the charge, for his estates are devoted to luxury cash-crops, not staple foods (*sic*, 46.8), and he has himself been trying to stimulate the local economy with public works (46.9).

Yet it is clear that the Cynic and then also the Christian way could be seen by a commentator such as Lucian as a very real threat to the established order of things.

> You realize what's going to happen very soon. Everyone in the workshops will down tools and away when they realize that all this hard back-breaking grind from morning till night earns them barely enough to live on, while idle frauds of 'philosophers' have unstinted plenty, every dictatorial demand met without them exerting the slightest effort, other than a display of indignation at any refusal; not even a thankyou when people comply. They really do think they're living in the age of Cronos, and honey is pouring into their mouths from the sky (*Runaways* 17).

Lucian may be exaggerating for humorous effect both the likely numbers and the ease (after all, there was the common Cynic tradition of Diogenes begging from statues, to practice being refused, 6.49). But it is clear that many people at the time were held between the lure of sharing in the good times and the fear of slipping into sheer starvation. If both kinds of oppression were removed, the social, economic and political impact would be very considerable. Keeping people enslaved between the carrot and the stick is essential for good government.

The Cynic and the early Christian programmes attempt to subvert the system from within. The prizes are unmasked for the tawdry sham they are, and people become less eager either to compete for them or join in providing them for the free-market lottery to share out. That would make some levels of socially defined poverty less frightening (though starvation remains as fatal). With less human effort and fewer natural resources wasted on providing luxuries for the few, there would be more of what is really needed for the many. An end to the threat of starvation for the mass of the people now for the first time becomes a possibility (though no warranty is issued). With less concentration of wealth there would be less to steal, though generous caring for others is not guaranteed, either. With less to steal there would be less to guard from your own population or from neighbouring populations. You and the greedy rich among you would now be less of a perceived threat or prize.

That would not itself ensure that land-hungry (or simply hungry) peoples may not invade with fire and sword. But there would be less for others to be envious of; and they themselves would not be suffering from such exploitation from 'our' side. With wealth seen in terms of friendship and the sharing of words and music and necessary food together, there would be fewer causes for enmity, and it would be easier to forgive; though still there might be competition for attention, and hostility from some towards the more popular. The stress placed by both traditions on continuing forgiveness and on ways of reconciliation shows that this is no easy utopianism.

It is a fact that Cynicism seems to have appeared the most consistently subversive movement to the Roman authorities in the first and early second centuries. Individual aristocrats can be a threat, but among 'intellectuals' it is Cynic philosophers who are particularly liable to exile or execution, as we have seen. It is the apparently quietist and a-political Epictetus who senses the danger of arrest by a soldier in plain clothes. It is as potentially subversive politically and actually subversive economically that Pliny junior deals with the Christians in Pontus and Bithynia (*Letters* 10.96). The absence of any threat of armed rebellion did little if anything to make such movements any less political, or politically unacceptable.[86]

The Empire depended on the production of wealth and its accumulation by individuals who would then perform onerous civic tasks whose costs could only be recouped, if at all, dishonestly. It depended on the mass of the people believing they were benefitting, and compliantly producing the wealth to be taxed by the state or otherwise drawn off by the wealthy and powerful. (In later centuries the Empire was in fact drawn to more and more desperate measures to combat the kind of insistence on freedom from this treadmill preached in the first century by some Cynics and some Christians.)[87]

Neither Cynics nor Christians, then, had any detailed alternative plans for society, for the control of the means of production and distribution of the simpler requirements they tried to goad and lure people to choose. Neither shows any signs of considering using armed force to bring about a change in people or in structures. Whether it can be possible to change either by their kinds of persuasion is not a question that can be by-passed (and we return to it in the final chapter). That there would be structural changes if this sort of view were coming to be adopted at all widely seems obvious.

Such are the politics of freedom proposed by some Cynics and by some Christians in the first century. They confronted established authority and the aims and ideals of the possessors of wealth and power, challenging them by their dress, their life-style, their ideas. They stressed action over theorizing, learning over teaching. They had little truck with polite convention, sure they had divine backing for their offer of new possibilities for human living, accepting they were likely themselves to get hurt in the attempt to share what they had for sharing. Yet for all their abrasive style, they lived and proclaimed an openness to foe and friend alike, across all barriers of possessiveness and fear. Simplicity was to be the setting where friendships could richly flourish, and the wealthy were to be rescued, as well as the poor: for all are held in the parental care of the God of all things and all people and all time.

I hope that this lengthy chapter will have shown that this is the sort of thing the Jesus tradition was used to say, this is how he and his teaching were presented in the early years by those who used the oral material preserved for us in the synoptic gospels. Of course there would have been differences in presentation (and Johannine and Pauline churches differed still more). There would be differences – important ones – that would distinguish Jesus-Cynics from others (just as there were differences among the others, too.) But this is how the traditions of Jesus' teaching would have been heard, and this seems to be how they were meant to be heard by those who first lived and shared them.

If that is granted, it still leaves other questions. In particular it leaves queries about the 'before' and the 'after'. We must ask the proper historical questions. Do these Christians' proposals go back to Jesus of Nazareth; or ought they perhaps to be seen as a later intrusion of alien and pagan concerns into a tradition about a Jewish prophetic or messianic figure? And we must also ask, though more briefly, what came of this way of being Christian in the years that followed?

(For more or less traditional Christian readers – among them the present writer – the questions are of still more than historical concern.)

IV

Jesus as Cynic

1. General Considerations

The early Christians ascribed stories and teaching to Jesus that must have sounded very like things being said by contemporary Cynics. They were as explosive, socially and politically, if people took them seriously. (Any reader who has not been persuaded of that by the previous chapter, I would suggest should read the even fuller collection of 'parallels' in my *The Christ and the Cynics*.)

This is how this material is likely to have been 'heard' in Antioch or Philippi or Rome. The people who repeated it seem to have been quite content that it should, and most likely fully intended it. We come closest to understanding this early Christian material if we interpret it where it is at home, in this Cynic context. Yet that leaves us, as noted at the end of the previous chapter, with the question, how does this 'Cynic' Christianity relate to any recoverable figure of Jesus 'behind' and before the teacher so presented by these early communities? Can we tell? It will be argued in this chapter that this material (or much of it) does seem very plausibly to take us back to Jesus of Galilee; and that he will have meant it in much the sense we have just been considering.

It is widely agreed that the 'Q', Markan and 'special Matthaean'[1] material in the synoptic gospels belonged to an early stage in the process of tradition among the Greek-speaking Christian communities of western and southern Syria, not far from Galilee, part of the same Roman province. Nonetheless, the 'Jesus tradition' is usually taken to have been largely or entirely 'un-Greek'. It has been taken as emerging from Aramaic and even Hebrew speaking areas of Galilee and Judaea themselves free of any important Hellenistic influences. Even an author such as Martin Hengel who discerns a much more pervasive impact of Hellenism in the Jewish homeland has argued for an adoption of 'forms of thought and expression' in such a way as to 'preserve the traditional religious heritage'. Greek influence on early Christianity has almost always been seen as secondary, arriving with Paul, or the Fourth Gospel, or later still. Anything in the gospel tradition that looks Greek is automatically interpreted as an accretion, and very likely a corruption. So the Johannine tradition, for instance, can only be taken to be early if it can be provided with very 'un-hellenized' antecedents from the Dead Sea Scrolls.

Against the background of this widespread conviction among scholars, the comparative material adduced in the previous chapter (and the additional matter in my *The Christ and the Cynics*) is likely to produce some puzzlement. According to the consensus of otherwise very diverse scholars, such hellenistic Cynic parallels are very unlikely to be relevant, even if they are so much as discussed. It will be important to consider, if briefly, a number of theoretically possible explanatory hypotheses to account for the material here quoted, besides the much larger collection in *The Christ and the Cynics*, just referred to.

1. Perhaps (despite all appearances) the similarities considered in the previous chapter are purely verbal, superficial, and deep down something quite different is being said. Such a case might be presented in detailed and painstaking exegesis. For example, Martin Hengel himself has noted that the closest available parallel with 'let the dead bury their dead' (Luke 9.60) is to be found among Cynics, but still argues that it is distinctive.[2]

To make such a case in a handful of instances might be possible. To have to do it with so much material would surely be self-defeating. In my fuller collection just referred to I have also included the 'Jewish' passages that recent commentators have adduced as most strikingly similar to this early Christian material. Apart from the fact that much of that Jewish material is itself from explicitly hellenized Jewish sources (Philo, Josephus, etc.), it is very rarely as close, and from all the Jewish sources less extensive than from the pagan, Cynic contributions. This latter coincidence which we considered in instance after instance in the previous chapter is too extensive to seem likely to be fortuitous. People cannot have gone on repeating this material without realizing that very many parts sounded clearly Cynic, and the whole like an entirely plausible variant of Cynicism; they cannot have gone on living and speaking it without being content that it should make this impression. At least as used by early Christians to fellow Greek-speakers, the Cynic appearance of the material must be fully intentional and significant.

2. Pagan Cynic tradition includes the figure of the Scythian king, Anarcharis. As a foreign visitor to ancient Athens he could assess hellenistic civilization with eyes unclouded by habit. Cynics refused to allow (at least in theory) that the Greeks had all wisdom.[3] It might then have been just possible for the figure of a Galilaean carpenter to have been adopted (or even invented) to provide a contemporary 'outsider's' critique of life in the Greek cities of the early Empire. But there are none of the signs that we might expect of this being the underlying motive behind such a presentation of a Cynic-sounding Jewish prophet. Jesus is never shown addressing a Greek crowd, still less visiting a Greek town even of the Decapolis, he makes no reference to Greek literary culture, and he really does not address himself to Greeks as such. The concerns and their expression are clearly those of contemporary Cynicism. The places and the people and the institutions are very firmly those of Jewish Palestine.

3. If this odd-seeming conjunction of rural Jewish teacher and Cynic concerns is neither the result of coincidence nor the creation of pagan Cynics, then we are left to examine the possibilities from the side of Jesus' followers, or of Jesus himself. We must certainly consider the possibility that Jesus originally was rather different, or quite different, and it was some of his followers who put him into Cynic dress, as it were.

Perhaps he was originally much more exclusively concerned with God's imminent restoration of his people, Israel. Perhaps he himself had attempted to reinterpret Judaism from within, in more or less polemical dialogue both with traditionalists and also with other radical Jewish would-be reformers of his day. Perhaps he patterned himself on the prophets of old Israel, reasserting aspects of their message. He could even have seen himself as an Essene or a Zealot, maybe. Jesus could have operated along any of these lines, or any combination of them – or some other that was also much more distinctively Jewish.[4] And then after his death his followers, we might imagine, re-interpreted him as a teacher in the Cynic mould, so producing the results indicated in the previous chapter. If Jesus had ordered a life-style that was similarly impoverished and simple, and had said just a few things that were similarly shocking (like 'let the dead bury their dead'), then we might imagine it to have been possible to adopt and adapt most of the entire range of contem-porary Cynic concerns, and put them on his lips. To preserve the illusion that they really were his, they would mostly have been given the Palestinian setting we find, in a semitic-sounding Greek. So the crucified Jewish prophet, teacher or messiah would have been re-packaged as a Cynic.

But why? We are properly reminded from time to time that a rhetorical 'Why?' is far from conclusive.[5] The fact that we may be unable to find a persuasive reason for some procedure does not show that no one in the period being studied could have done. An impossibility or even an unlikelihood for us does not make the suggestion itself impossible or even particularly unlikely for others. Nevertheless, we do know something about the way people's minds worked in the Cynic circles we are considering, and we have some indication of the concerns of the Christians who used the Jesus tradition we have been looking at. There does seem to be nothing at all in the concerns that either group overtly expresses to suggest why a non-Cynic Jesus should have been reconstructed by his followers in Cynic guise.

If the reinterpretation had been done by followers of Jesus who were actually first and foremost Cynic, we meet the difficulty already considered. A Jesus who never addresses the Greek world, never relates to classical Greek culture, and never even relates to Diogenes hardly affords much added impetus to their

Cynic message. If on the other hand the aim of the transmutation had been to enhance the impact of the figure of Jesus himself, there would seem to have been much more effective ways to do that: Paul's, for instance. The less Cynic the material, the more in fact it seems to magnify Jesus' own importance: the miracle stories do, the ascription of titles does. The more Cynic-looking material stresses people's responsibility for their own life-styles. Yet the latter preponderates.[6]

And if Jesus' followers had simply been looking for something – anything – for him to say, it would still have been strange for them to have hit on radical Cynic teaching, and so coherent a selection.

If, then, we suppose two originally separate strands, Cynic and un-Palestinian, Palestinian and un-Cynic, it is hard if not impossible to imagine a relevant reason for anyone deliberately to merge them. However, we have admitted that our failure to guess a satisfactory reason is itself nowhere near conclusive. The further question of 'how' two such separate strands could have come together to produce the material that confronts us in the New Testament must be considered. It is at least as difficult to answer satisfactorily.

4. We find consistent and coherent Cynic-sounding traditions of Jesus in 'Q', in Mark, in special Matthaean and in special Lukan material, as well as often very similar teaching in James. In the form in which we find them there is every indication that these clusters of material have been part of the living tradition of different and geographically scattered communities. (For instance, the baptism and Beelzebul controversies and much else that is clearly similar in 'Q' and in Mark have taken on numerous differences in detail.) So there would have had to have been a widespread agreement to 'Cynicize', or it would have had to have been done very early on, to produce so consistent and coherent a result. There does not seem to have been enough time before the dispersed growth of the Jesus movement for the two strands simply to have drifted together. The result we have considered presupposes a deliberate and authoritative and centrally organized marrying of the two. Only in the career of Jesus himself do we find any indication of such a single and authoritative focus.

The most likely source of the consistently Cynic sounding Jewish Jesus tradition is Jesus himself.[7]

Someone else may be able to put together a coherent hypothesis that deals with all the data, but creates a different explanatory account. It may in fact be possible to spell out feasible steps by which a non-Cynic Jesus had Cynic-style teaching ascribed to him in different centres of the early Christian movement, coherently and consistently. I find it incredible. Another may not.[8]

5. It might be a little less difficult to undertake to show how the socio-economic structures of Roman Palestine elicited from Jesus himself a whole range of responses that closely resembled those worked out in Cynic tradition over the centuries, but without any direct influence from that tradition. Because the social and economic pressures were so similar (if they were!) Jesus would have been responding to the same range of issues. It would then, perhaps, have been fairly easy for early hearers in the Greek cities of south Syria to adjust his social, economic and theological critique to sound increasingly similar to what already stood in Cynic tradition.[9]

At first sight that may look quite attractive, in line with the scholarly orthodoxy which, we have already recalled, prefers to conceive of a context for Jesus little or not at all affected by any strand of Greek thought.

What we in fact find is Cynic-sounding teaching anchored very firmly in Jewish Palestine. Minor factual allusions to places and customs which could readily have been adjusted, remain foreign to their supposed new setting in Syria. There are no signs of the kind of transmutation this socio-economic hypothesis suggests.

What we find demands not just appropriate economic conditions in society, but the living presence of talk along Cynic lines for the originator (or originators) of the tradition to interact with. It really does seem simplest to suppose that wandering Cynics had not by chance missed Palestine (Peregrinus did not avoid it). They would have touched the market places of the Decapolis, and those who mingled there. And, as we shall see, there are other indications of a favourable reception in Galilee in particular, for this kind of practical philosophy. It would seem much the most likely that Jesus produced his version of Jewish-Cynic ideas in reflective (and critical – and Jewish) response to Cynic preaching that had reached his area of Galilee, and was already known among his audience, already in some measure married in with native Jewish thinking, a part of the culture with which he grew up. This is more likely than that he should time and again independently have hit on themes and expressions commonplace among Cynics. Yet that itself is much more likely than that these should later have been 'fathered' on to him, without any foundation in his own ministry.

Whatever the origins, the coincidences displayed in the last chapter (and in my *The Christ and the Cynics*) remain. The Jesus proclaimed will have sounded Cynic. And he is the only one we have access to. However great a 'paradigm shift' it demands, we seem to have to face the strong possibility that Jesus the Jew must also be seen as Jesus the Cynic.

2. *External Evidences*

The main evidence remains the material surveyed in the previous chapter, the close parallels with Cynic preaching; and there is much more in my collection *The Christ and the Cynics*. There is not a great deal of independent evidence relating to Cynic influence in Galilee and Judaea. What there is, is positive.

Our records tell us that quite a number of philosophers who achieved some eminence came from south Syria, sufficiently to suggest a local tradition of philosophical reflection. Among such there was Menippus of Gadara (one of the Ten Towns, and itself situated six miles or so southwest of the lake of Galilee). He was a Cynic satirist, said to have been a pupil of Metrocles in Sinope at the end of the fourth century BCE. In the second century CE there was Oenomaus, from the same town. He may well have won the respect of contemporary rabbis for his trenchant critique of pagan religion (*Midrash Rabbah, Genesis* LXVIII 20 [27]. For further references, see the notes to this chapter.) H. A. Fischel has pointed to Cynic-sounding motifs in later rabbinic material; and though he is probably mistaken in supposing it directly relevent to the first century, it would at least suggest that there is no inherent incompatibility. As much may be said for the explicit and implicit approval of a number of Cynic motifs in Philo of Alexandria.[10]

Much more directly relevant is Josephus' designation of Judas of Galilee as founder of the 'Fourth Philosophy' of the Jews. The Pharisees are said to be akin to the Stoics, the Essenes are made to look Pythagorean, and the Sadducees Epicurean.

> The fourth of the Jewish philosophical schools had Judas of Galilee as its self-appointed leader. At most points this school shares the views of the Pharisees. But they have an unconquerable love of freedom, totally convinced that God alone is their one and only leader and master. They care little about dying all sorts of death themselves, or of letting retribution fall on family and friends, so long as they may avoid calling any human master (*Antiquities* 18.23).

Josephus has a little earlier said, 'Judas assured his followers that the deity would be eager to help them if, with their minds set on great things, they did not shrink from painful effort' [*ponos*: not Feldman's emendation to 'bloodshed', *phonos*] (Ant. 18.5). The picture is quite clearly Cynic.

The reality, of course, may have been quite different, as a brief examination of the other designations shows. It was in fact commonplace to assimilate foreign religious groups to Greek philosophical schools (e.g., Zoroastrians to Stoics, Brahmins to Pythagoreans).

On the one hand Stoicism may in fact have become known and respected among Pharisees, as may be seen from Wisdom of Solomon, from IV Maccabees, and from Josephus himself, with his overtly Stoic defence of a doctrine of providence taken together with his claim to have maintained an allegiance to Pharisaism. On the other hand, nothing has so far turned up in the Dead Sea Scrolls to support his aligning Essenes with Pythagoreans; and for the Sadducees we have no substantial evidence at all.

We must consider carefully, then, Josephus' account of the 'Fourth Philosophy'. He was writing for the Flavian emperors (Life 361) for whom the Cynics in Rome were a particular bugbear. At least one was executed by Titus, who had already personally ordered another one flogged (Dio Cassius LXV 15.3–5). All the major Cynic figures were exiled by Domitian. Josephus says that what led to the Jews becoming sufficiently unsettled for rebellion in the end to be sparked off was the Cynic-like teaching initially promulgated (or early led) by Judas. 'It's impossible to name an evil that did not spring from the actions of these people . . . from them came civil war . . . innovatory change in traditional ways . . . filled our Jewish society with unrest, the seedlings from which grew the ills which in due course fell on the entire community . . .' (*Ant.* 18.6,8–9). It does not seem likely that Josephus would have offered a suggestion that was silly or implausible as so important a factor in his account. Whether he really meant that Judas eighty years earlier had explicitly taught in the Cynic tradition, and if so whether he had any good evidence is a quite other question. What matters is that the suggestion must have seemed credible to the family who led the campaign and came to power through it. It must also have seemed credible to others writing in competition with Josephus (e.g., Justus, *Life* 336–367; others, *Apion* 1.53–56). It is still possible, of course, that he may readily have been understood to be saying no more than 'this group was as much of a nuisance as the Cynics can be elsewhere'.

Judas himself only seems to have led a tax-strike, accompanied by a little supporting action directed against the property of those reluctant to join in. There is no sign here of any armed rebellion (*Ant.* 18.1–10, *War* 2.118). There seems no good reason to identify this Judas with Judas son of Ezechias, (*War* 2.56.) We noted above that the Cynic stress on 'action' is only once said to have involved stirring up armed rebellion (Lucian, *Peregrinus* 19).

Nonetheless, when Josephus desists from blackguarding those who did rebel and allows them positive ideals to affirm, it is consistently in terms he ascribes to the (Cynic) 'Fourth Philosophy', 'liberty', and 'refusing any master other than God alone', (*War* 2.345–349; 4.175–179; 244–251; 5.[365–368], 458–459; 6.350–351; 7.323–324). They are even permitted to suggest that 'the world is a better temple for God' than the one they were defending (5.458). These are not traditional Jewish slogans.

'Freedom' is rare in Jewish scripture. God is sole Lord; but that his sole lordship precludes accepting the authority of any human suzerain is not an accepted scriptural theme, nor that God's sovereignty entails 'secular' freedom. These affirmations sound much more nearly Cynic. The rebels are not content simply to have their traditions permitted by overlords, they want to be openly and politically free to follow them, free of any human master, not beholden even to the most tolerant. This consistent stress on 'freedom' as a value in itself in Josephus' otherwise highly unfavourable picture of the rebels suggests both a genuine historical reminiscence and one that points strongly towards something very like the more radical strands of Cynicism.

Josephus may of course simply be offering a more comprehensible account of the rebels' motives, for his Greaco-Roman readers, than ideas drawn from Jewish scripture would have afforded. The things he allows the rebels to say are, however, strikingly more 'noble', more admirable ideals to die for than the greed, cruelty and megalomania he elsewhere suggests. At other points he explicitly claims that great disparities obtained between the rebels' ideals and their actions. But in these utterances he presents the speakers as meaning what they said. This note of idealism is, then, significant in the light of the otherwise consistently hostile narrative. Perhaps Josephus' awareness of his intended readership was constraining him to allow an actual dominant motive to be expressed, which then looks close to the Cynicism he had already pointed out to us. (That Josephus saw a real threat to the maintenance of Jewish tradition from those who made bold use of Cynic emphases on freedom and independence also appears in the speech attributed to Zambrias, *Ant.* 4.145–149.)

It may also be the case that Josephus sees John Baptist as a Cynic sort of figure, or at least supposes that is how Herod Antipas understood him. John's preaching is summarized (and with approval) in some of the most general terms of Hellenistic ethics ('virtue', 'righteousness', and 'piety'), without any distinctive Cynic note being sounded. But John preaches his ethical message to crowds in a way that seems likely to unsettle (*Ant.* 18.116–119), and that suggests a Cynic model. (It suggests a

Cynic model since there is no obvious Jewish scriptural one for the teacher of ethics as inspiring 'sedition'; nor any other Hellenistic one.) Josephus seems to have no ulterior motive for portraying John in this way: it just is how he appeared to Herod, and, thought Herod, to the crowds.

None of this material in Josephus would be enough on its own to show that there was actual Cynic influence in first-century Jewish Galilee (or Judaea). It could still possibly be explained as nothing but the product of the convention of giving Greek equivalents for quite unrelated foreign schools of thought. However, taken in the light of the Cynic insistence on going everywhere, and of the fact that some eminent Cynics actually originated in the Decapolis near to Galilee, the evidence in Josephus may reasonably be taken to show that the idea of Cynic influence there would at least not have seemed unreasonable at the time.

The main weight of evidence, as has already been insisted, must lie with the synoptic tradition itself, and its Cynic character, which has already been analysed in some detail. The material would have been perceived as Cynic in south Syria in the forties and fifties of the first century CE, not very far from its purported source, not many years earlier.

In the remainder of this chapter we shall go back over some of the material we surveyed in the previous one, but now examine it in the supposed setting of the lifetime of Jesus in Galilee and Judaea. I shall try to suggest that the examples chosen are most plausibly seen as coming from Jesus himself, with much the same Cynic sense as was suggested in the previous chapter they would have had for those who later repeated them and those who listened to them; most likely in response to Cynic preaching that had earlier reached the Galilee where Jesus grew up.

The Cynic parallels for the gospel material have already been displayed, and will only be alluded to in what follows. Solely those items where the argument for an origin with Jesus himself seems particularly cogent will figure in this next section. Assessing whether each 'Cynic' item in the gospel tradition goes back to Jesus would need more detailed argument than can be attempted here. (For instance, the stress on 'interiority', in Matthew only, may be a later addition.) However, all the major strands picked out in Chapter III figure here in the material whose ascription to Jesus is being argued. The kinds of freedom and flourishing proclaimed in his name seem genuinely to have been taught and lived by him himself.

3. *The Cynic Teaching of Jesus the Jew*

(a) *The Teacher*

In the Markan tradition Jesus is clearly a teacher of some sort, one who summons a few among those he meets to follow him as disciples; on one occasion he is said to have sent them out to engage in the same sort of activity as his own. The 'Q' material has no account of Jesus summoning anyone, but there are stories of people volunteering to follow him, and then being presented with his demands, which include homelessness and the renunciation of sacred family obligations. Mark also has people deciding unprompted to follow Jesus. Matthew has Jesus' invitation, 'Come to me . . .' (though this may have been in 'Q'); in Matthew alone we find Jesus claiming to have been sent only to the lost sheep of the house of Israel. Luke has a distinctive story of Peter being called, and one of a woman disciple being taught, as well as notes of other followers who were women. In fact the Fourth Gospel, while differing in detail, retains much the same picture of the master and the disciples.[11]

When Jesus teaches, he does so in his own name. This again seems to be so in all strands of the tradition. He does not speak in the name of a master or a school; but neither does he announce 'thus says the Lord'.

There are no clear models for this kind of teacher-follower relationship in the canonical Jewish scriptures (V.K. Robbins, R. Riesner), nor in any supposed 'prophet-teachers' of more recent times (Reisner's own suggestion). Later rabbinic practice provides no close analogy, either. Yet the role-relations seem to be recognized, and need no explanation.[12]

Much closer analogies are to be found among pagan Cynics and others, as was pointed out in the previous chapter (III 3). It is there that we found stories of the teacher taking the initiative, alongside ones where the would-be follower does. It is among later Cynics, as we have seen, that the teacher moves footloose from place to place; and he simply teaches. The consistent role model for Jesus is unmistakably Cynic. Yet much of the teaching material itself is as clearly Jewish in its foundations. Jesus' own 'teacher' is most clearly reminiscent of Elijah (even if he would also have looked like Herakles to any pagan). The only classical literature cited is from the Jewish canon. The people Jesus defeats in argument are Jews, and the starting point is always Jewish custom or belief.[13]

This is easy to understand if the tradition goes back to Jesus adopting a Cynic style as one readily available, but using it to address fellow Jews in Galilee and Judaea. It is very hard to understand if one supposes that originally Jesus worked with an exclusively Jewish model (quoting prior teachers, waiting in one place for disciples to approach him; or speaking in the name of the Lord, and choosing just a single successor). Why should, and how could anyone, let alone various distinct Christian communities, make such a thorough and consistent change in the picture of the role adopted, while leaving so much of the rest still Jewish?

If the role ascribed to Jesus had been at all exactly that specified for the later communities' own teachers there might have been sufficient motive for re-casting Jesus himself. But the repetition of the tradition presupposes that they by contrast speak in his name, not their own, and continue to invite people to follow him, not themselves. The Cynic role for the Jewish teacher only makes sense if it is in fact the one he himself chose. The fact that he could employ it with at least a modicum of success also suggests it was a recognized role among those he addressed.[14]

And as was pointed out in the previous chapter, to adopt a role outside of the traditional power structures of one's society is subversive; and the role Jesus adopts is one recognized as disruptive. He interferes with family life, seen then as now as the foundation of a settled society. He even involves women. (This is in fact to undermine aspects of Judaism on which it could pride itself in the face of establishment critics: Josephus, *Apion* 2.200). And it all takes place in the backwaters of Palestine.

The style of the teaching ascribed to Jesus appears to tally well with the role adopted, displaying again this distinctive combination of Cynicism and Judaism, and so again demanding a setting in the life of Jesus himself. It is very difficult (not impossible, just very difficult) to imagine the sequence of Mark 10.17–22 being made up later about the honoured Teacher (let alone the risen Lord). 'Why do you call me good?' Jesus asks. The refusal of flattering respect is Cynic (see above p. 93). Matthew finds it far too difficult to accept. Jewish custom seems to identify much more closely respect for the teaching with respect for the teacher. Yet centring as it does on the commandments, the story clearly presupposes a Jewish milieu. Neither the question nor the climax in a quite peremptory command by Jesus would on their own have provided any obvious cue for a later addition of the self-deprecatory preface. It only seems to make credible sense on Jesus' own lips. And Jesus combines a shattering demand with a refusal to play master, to offer himself as some alternative security.

The contemptuous dismissal of those who 'seem to exercise authority' (Mark 10.42), with its perhaps independent parallel in Luke (22.25) is in the same vein. Jewish tradition (and, of course, Stoic) is much readier to see effective power as divinely authorized. (Matthew omits Mark's 'seem'.) Yet the reference to 'Gentiles' demands a Jewish speaker. The disparagement of authority is itself, as we saw earlier, characteristically Cynic. The mix is to be taken as Jesus' own. Again, no other context suggests itself.

We noted before that Jesus the purveyor of parables would have resembled the Cynic picture of Socrates, especially in his choice of scenes from everyday life. Some of the numerous parallels between parabolic material ascribed to Jesus and that found in Cynic sources were set out; more appear in my *The Christ and the Cynics*. Later rabbinic writings contain parables, and quite a few of them are also similar to those in the Jesus tradition. However, if it is correct to see Jesus' parables as an open invitation to his hearers 'to re-think their attitudes to more or less of life around them', rather than to illustrate some ruling laid down; if they mean to raise questions for people to answer, rather than answering them in their stead, then Jesus' use of parables is closer to Cynic than to Jewish tradition as we know it. It is also in keeping with other strands in the picture of him as teacher; and that is again so in all our synoptic sources. Yet the culture and history that is mirrored in some of the most 'open' of the parables (the Spendthrift, the Kind Samaritan, the Lost Coin, the Pounds/Talents, the Wicked Tenants, in particular – see Chapter III) is that of Jewish Palestine. Much else would fit anywhere in south Syria or the rest of the east Mediterranean. If the parables which are most Cynic in mood had been added later to the tradition, we might have expected them to be the least Jewish in detail. Again we find the characteristic mixture that suggests Jesus as its author. We also find a kind of teaching that attempts to liberate people's own insights, and to set them free to see things differently – and do things differently.

The insistence on actions matching words is itself, as was pointed out earlier, a commonplace at the time, and that is so among Jews as well as pagans. In itself it does not distinguish Jesus or his followers from many others. However, so far as our records go, most Jewish discussions of what is to be done are either heavily dependent on scripture (as in the *Midrashim*, and Philo) or are painstakingly systematic (as in the *Mishnah*, and, if to a lesser extent, in the rules of the Qumran community) or they are both (as in Josephus, *Ant.* 4).

In the tradition ascribed to Jesus there is little sign of either. The issue of marriage is related to 'Moses' and to the text of Genesis, though a little untidily. Current customs related to hand-washing and oaths are contrasted with explicit commands in scripture. The question of the Sabbath is answered with help from Samuel/ Kings. One enquirer is referred to the Decalogue, and a question as to the greatest commandment is answered by Jesus with two short passages from Torah. But for the most part, as we noted earlier, Jesus simply states a demand, as in Luke 6.20–49, or the much longer collection in Matthew 5–7. Though in the latter the 'antitheses' of chapter 5 are initially related to scripture, the issue is concluded with Jesus' 'but I say to you'. The formula could be Matthew's own, though many think it is authentic. Its implication is entirely appropriate to the rest of the material, where Jesus issues unsystemized imperatives, with no backing but his own example. Hearers are left to assess each utterance for itself and in relation to all the rest. It is the hearers' responsibility, their freedom. They do not have to buy, or reject, a package. There is no sectarian pretence that their inherited culture is an integrated, monolithic whole. (Matt. 5.17–20 along with James 2.8–11 would on the view taken here appear as uncharacteristic intrusions into the tradition.)

Although the early Cynics are credited with treatises on ethical theory along with much else, they are remembered as those who issued isolated judgments and injunctions, arising out of their own practice. Only occasionally in the popular tradition do they take the trouble to relate what they say to popular culture (Homer, the tragedians) or to other (and systematic) philosophers.

Jesus in the tradition issues his imperatives with Cynic boldness. But the only cultural tradition he does on rare occasions notice, is Jewish. The mixture we have come to expect is repeated yet again, and again we are prodded and drawn to a distinctive freedom.

(b) *Blessed are the Poor*

It is not clear whether Jesus's appearance, and that of his disciples, would have seemed distinctively Cynic in Galilee and Judaea. Both Philo and Josephus note that Essenes travelled light. However, if the 'Q' instructions, Luke 10.4–5, are accepted in preference to Mark 6.8–11, Jesus and his companions went from village to village with even less equipment, even less security than did Essenes. They had no staff, no sandals, and no assurance of finding a ready welcome in the home of a known member.[15]

A double intention behind this severity seems clear in the tradition. Positively there is a trust that the world is a place where God's fatherly care is sufficient. We can see the plants and the birds well enough fed to survive. Negatively there is the refusal to find either security for living or, still less, the point of living, in wealth, in a store of goods. What is left when such wealth is rejected, is God, other people in fairly unstructured relationships, and the plants and birds and beasts, the soil and the air and the water.

To find one's reality so is to be much closer to the Cynics than to the Essenes. The latter found their reality in a highly structured community that itself had considerable resources. It busied itself with the study of the law, and seems to have seen the world around as a workshop. Members produced goods and traded them. Cynics, and Jesus in the tradition were different. Yet Matthew (despite his conviction that Christians have a mission to all nations) preserves a memory that Jesus restricted his teaching to Jewish communities (10.5; 15.24; compare Rom. 15.8), and there is little in any of the synoptic materials to suggest otherwise. Had the Cynic guise and ethos been arbitrarily imported later into the tradition, in the Greek towns of south Syria, one might have expected at least a similar freedom to display Jesus in his 'new' Cynic role addressing such towns' inhabitants. It would be odd to change the dress and leave the milieu unaltered.[16]

We again seem to be led to suppose it was originally Jesus himself who was encouraging fellow Jews to a Cynic freedom to enjoy being God's sons and daughters together in a world that belongs to God.

What is rejected is the consumer society of the first century. The bright clothes of the royal mannequins are not even to be admitted into our daydreams. The conspicuous consumption, the tokens of that kind of success are accorded no value. When the rewards are despised those who have one way or another gained them no longer attract respect. It is not simply that their style of power is refused; they themselves cease to be acknowledged. The system is no longer seen as having God's backing. Wealth is no sign of divine approval, and neither is political power. Once the wealthy and the powerful are no longer seen as 'benefactors' they can only appear as parasites. The structures of society as they stand have no claims on the allegiance of Jesus' followers.

(The implication would seem to be clear from its contradictory in Romans 13.7. For Jesus, nothing is owed – neither respect, nor tax, nor rent. Of course, what is not owed may still be granted as a gift, if that seems from case to case appropriate. Perhaps this is what Paul also meant; for he himself says, 'Owe nothing to anyone, save to love one another', Rom. 13.8.)

Jewish thinkers at the time, so far as we are aware, remained convinced (with Paul, we should note) that 'the existing authorities are ordained by God' (Rom. 13.1). Financial prosperity, too, is in God's gift (II Cor. 9.8), a reward for virtue (unless clearly gained dishonestly). Jesus preaches a Cynic rejection of these twin convictions. Yet, again, some of his most striking sayings on power and on wealth are clearly set in a Jewish framework (Mark 10.17–22, 42–43; 12.13–17, as interpreted in the previous chapter; 'mammon', in Luke 16.13, 'Q', aligned in Matthew with the teaching on treasures).

But (still like the Cynics), Jesus is no ascetic for the sake of asceticism. The tradition has him sharing dinner parties with tax-gatherers and other 'sinners'. As E. P. Sanders, for instance, has persuasively insisted, simply to stress forgiveness and reconciliation for the repentant would be no novelty in first-century Judaism.[17] Rabbinic material, Philo, Josephus, sectarian documents all agree, and Jesus, too, is said to have preached repentance. But, like Antisthenes, Jesus also mixes, and happily, with unreformed sinners. He comes as a physician to social misfits. Sharing parties with them, he repudiates the society that defines itself in terms of its rejection of these, its victims. This is very much to follow a Cynic line. Yet the tradition makes the objectors consistently Jewish. Again there would seem no reason for the later tradition, in south Syria or elsewhere, to combine a fictionally Cynic Jesus with an irrelevant Jewish opposition. The only plausible starting point is an actually Cynic Jesus, creating anticipatory pockets of freedom for the oppressed.

Jesus does also express a concern for the rich themselves. They, too, are victims. Unlike one of the sources used here, Seneca, he offers no hope of a spirituality where wealth and integrity may be combined. He simply offers an alternative vision for which it may seem worth abandoning any other, including that of financial prosperity or power or both. He offers no magic formula for possessing wealth without being possessed. In Jewish tradition 'the poor', those who are to a greater or lesser extent dispossessed are often commended, especially for their allegiance to God. Their opponents are often thought to have gained their wealth and power dishonestly, even by violent wickedness. But the wealth itself does not seem to be seen as a danger, and the poor do not ask to be preserved from it. Rather is there the hope that it may come to them, as the more deserving. Jesus maintains a Cynic disparagement of wealth itself – though he gives it a Jewish name, mammon.

The programme Jesus announces runs the risk of seeming absurdly unrealistic, even in the still relatively under-populated and fertile areas of the east Mediterranean. He invites people to live at home in God's world now, expecting every real need for a full life to be met. Isn't that how any father would treat his children? What many readers discern as an 'inaugurated eschatology' in Jesus' proclamation is a summons to live 'as if' God's rule were already fully effective. Other Jewish seers tended to be more realistic. When God has achieved his purposes, the fact will be entirely obvious. There'll be no 'as if': *Sibylline Oracles*; Philo, *de praemiis et poenis*; *Psalms of Solomon*, etc. Jesus urges the kind of 'as if' practised by Cynics, by those who doggedly insisted on living 'as if in the age of Cronos', the Golden Age. Yet, again, his terminology is Jewish, but what Jesus presses is an absurd Cynic trust in the possibility of living fully now.

(c) *The Love of Enemies*

The changed values and revised hopes that Jesus is shown proclaiming to all and sundry could not hope to be particularly popular. It was obvious that he would offend the wealthy and the powerful, as well as any others content to conform. He and any who followed him could certainly expect enmity from established leaders. That was clear from the fate of earlier Jewish prophets (Elijah, Micaiah, Amos, Jeremiah: Luke 13.34, Q; cf. 13.33). Josephus has many accounts of prophetic figures killed by the established leaders of the day;[18] John Baptist was only the most recent. But Jesus is also said to have expected rejection by 'his own people' and his own family, and to have promised that level and kind of unpopularity to his followers. It is Cynics, with their brash disturbance not only of the comfort of the rich but also of the subservient apathy of the poor, who court and expect such general hostility.

Towards those who display hostility Jesus, like the Cynics, tells his followers to display a generous love. In the Matthaean form of his teaching this is contrasted both with traditional Jewish and with pagan attitudes (Matt. 5.43–47; whether and how far such contrasts were justified is not here at issue). In Luke the only contrast is with what 'sinners' do, and a specifically Jewish setting for the Cynic-seeming attitude is not particularly obvious.

More distinctively like the Cynics, Jesus is further said to have taught that any obligation, any debt that the sinner might be thought to have incurred, was to be forgiven him, and there is no reference here to prior repentance. Contemporary Judaism, as we have already noted, quite clearly accepted that the repentant were to be forgiven their sins, including wrongs done to oneself. But to ignore repentance and the restitution that must accompany it is to condone wrongdoings, and is itself wicked (as it was for most pagans). It is only likely to encourage more wickedness. To condone is to share the guilt. Society as we know it could not hope to survive too much forgiveness of 'debts' of any kind incurred within it. (It diminishes the difference between the professional thief who cannot be thought to deserve forgiveness of what he has done and the exploiter who must not be thought to need it.) It is Cynics who are willing to assault the structures of society by indiscriminate forgiveness; and Jesus appears to agree. Yet where this affirmation of forgiveness occurs in Jesus' teaching on prayer (Luke 11.2–4; Matt. 6.9–15) the general context presupposed in the other clauses of the prayer is again clearly Jewish.

(d) *God as Father*

The God that Jesus in the gospel sources serves, trust and prays to is clearly the one Lord who has Israel as his covenant people (Mark 12, passim; Luke 11.2–4, 'Q', as above; Matt. 17.24–27; Luke 19.1–10; etc.). In the 'Q' tradition Jesus both addresses and refers to this God as 'Father' quite often. In Matthew (but most likely not in his other source-material) Jesus still more frequently speaks of 'my father' and 'your father'; Luke has such additional references concentrated in his Passion narrative. Mark has far fewer, but they include the twin '*Abba, patēr*' of 14.36, which seems to reappear in Paul (Gal. 4.6; Rom. 8.15).

It would not seem to have been unusual for Jews in the Galilee and Judaea of Jesus' day to talk of and to God as the father of his people, and the usage was already there in Jewish scripture. It is much harder to find God addressed in prayer as the individual's 'father'; harder, but, as Geza Vermes has shown, not impossible. The frequency and pervasiveness of the Christian usage is nonetheless distinctive, over against what we find in the Jewish material; and where Vermes finds individual charismatic rabbis said to have addressed God as '*abba*', the Christian sources assure all that they may.[19]

Such a frequent and general usage is otherwise only to be found among Cynics. Even if it should turn out that the way the word was being used was different (a possibility allowed for but not adopted in the previous chapter), superficially the practice is Cynic: and, yet once more, Cynic in a clearly Jewish context.

Though Jesus in the tradition encourages others to address God as 'Father', his own status is clearly distinctive. 'No one knows the Father save the Son' (Matt. 11.27); 'if anyone is ashamed of me and mine . . . the Son of Man will be ashamed of him when he comes in the glory of his Father and of the holy angels' (Mark 8.38). In Jewish revelatory literature around this time there are many human figures granted some special insight. Among them Enoch (in the Similitudes of *I Enoch*, perhaps end of the first century CE) apparently finds himself as judge with the appellation 'Son of Man'. Only with the Master of the Qumran hymns, however, do we find anything quite like the direct claim that Jesus is said to have made: 'I the Master know you, O my God . . . I have faithfully listened to your marvellous counsel . . .' (IQH 12). In IQH 9 God's parental care is celebrated; but he is not addressed as Father. (Suggested pagan parallels, from Celsus' second-century polemic, or from the *Hermetica* are doubtfully apposite as well as being too late to be significant on their own.)

It is only among the Cynics with their 'parresia', their bold confidence in the friendship of the gods and their high status as sons of Zeus, that we find pervasively and in quantity claims to insight, filial status and judicial function that would sound at all similar to the kinds of things we find Jesus claiming.[20]

(Talk of a teacher as 'saving', 'liberating' is more readily found in Cynic than in Jewish writing; but it is found in other schools, too. Lucretius makes just such a claim for Epicurus! We have noticed already the critical question, Would such a teacher ever be brought to a cross? and have already answered, Yes, in the Cynic tradition, it might well be expected.)[21]

From the early Christian material in the previous chapter we have assembled a number of strands which seem most nearly akin to Cynic thought of anything from the period available to us, yet these strands come with a clear Jewish colouring. We have been suggesting that good sense can be made of this phenomenon only if this matter at least comes from a single source, set in early first-century Palestine, but already influenced by the work of wandering Cynics: and this source can really only have been Jesus himself.

To imagine that an entirely non-Cynic Jesus had followers who after his death and in different areas of the movement built-in this and much more Cynic-sounding material is very difficult. Not only do they create a new Cynic figure, but they take the trouble to trick him out in alienating Galilaean Jewish dress. As has been allowed, difficult does not mean impossible. But until a coherent hypothesis along such lines has been elaborated, and then tested in detail against the evidence, the account proposed here must surely hold the field. To recapitulate:

1. A great deal of the early material relating to Jesus would have sounded Cynic to its first hearers. Much of this is set out in the previous chapter, and even more evidence is available in my *The Christ and the Cynics*. The closeness of the parallels is indisputable, and we must assume those who preserved and used this matter were content that it should be so. Only if as much or more from other apposite sources were adduced, or detailed examination were to show the material time and again to have been in fact and against present appearance deliberately distinguished from the Cynic parallels assembled, would the foundation of the present study begin to look at all insecure.

2. So, these early Christians, with their Christ, proposed a variant of Cynic social subversion, as discussed in the previous chapter.

3. Then, either they effectively conspired to change a non-

Cynic Jesus into one who would be consistently Cynic in ethos while remaining (unaccountably) Palestinian Jewish in appearance, or there actually was such a Jesus. The latter seems much the more likely.

We must then conclude that the only 'historical Jesus' available to us is this Jewish-Cynic teacher. If the Cynic material is removed (by some arbitrary 'criterion of dissimilarity' for instance), there is practically nothing left.

On the other hand, if no other explanation is forthcoming for the Cynic ethos of the Jewish-looking early Christian material, the historical authenticity of this Jewish-Cynic Jesus seems very firmly established. If there is no historically plausible alternative account of how the early Christian material reached this hybrid form so consistently in so many areas of the new movement's membership, and so soon, we have to accept that the core material along with much if not all of the remainder of the synoptic tradition in something very close to its present Cynic-sounding form, must stem from Jesus himself, and must have meant what has been here suggested, or something very close to it. It will have been re-shaped in oral use, and re-shaped again by the evangelists. But the basic impetus is from Jesus, as is the particular selection of Cynic concerns and attitudes, and the particular mix with strands from contemporary Judaism. Every Cynic teacher from whom we have at all extensive material creates his own characteristic selection and emphases. This one comes from Jesus of Nazareth.[22]

(Some lesser elements of the tradition, as just noted, and as is widely accepted, do, however, almost certainly stem from the individual evangelists. In addition to stylistic idiosyncrasies (such às Matthew's 'kingdom of heaven') there is Luke's insistence on 'repentance', and on prayer, for example. Matthew's stress on 'interiority' in chapter 5 still fits within the range of Cynic approaches for which we have evidence, but could well be a later development; and so on.)

The final chapter of this book is based on the conviction that most of the teaching surveyed in Chapter III as used and lived by early Christians is also to be read as stemming from Jesus himself. It coheres with the core of Cynic-style teaching in Jewish dress which it has been argued here is distinctively his. It could have been added later, but there is no telling. If it is made up of later expansions, it coheres so well that it remains entirely in character. All in all it is to be taken as expressing his concerns and conveying his attitudes.

If his attitude to questions of authority has been correctly discerned, then the affirmation that the teaching is his still leaves any who would count themselves his followers with the responsibility of deciding for themselves how to respond to it.

There are other Christianities, some of them almost as old as this one, and we must consider them, briefly, and try to see how this one relates to them. Among them we shall consider the kind that became normative, in which Jesus is seen as God incarnate.

There are many other accounts of Christian origins, most of which largely ignore the Cynic material assembled here as a basis for the 'paradigm shift' proposed. We shall glance at one or two of these alternatives.

But the only original Christianity (for anyone who wants it out of historical curiosity, or for living, or whatever) is a Cynic one, one that is political, and is socially subversive. It threatens anyone who considers it with freedom. The freedom it proposes even threatens those of us who are rich, and prefer the other freedoms we probably at present enjoy.

The practicalities of that threat and promise will concern us in the last part of the book. But first, some other reconstructions, and then some other early Christianities.

4. *Other Readings of the Evidence*

In a book I wrote some twenty years ago, *The Church and Jesus* (1968), I urged the importance of noting as much as possible of the wider context in any account of the life of the early church (or churches). However, I had been led not to expect much help from any first-century 'philosophical' texts, and in general I did not expect any fresh light from any currently available source to fall on those early Christian communities whose traditions of Jesus helped form our gospels. At the time, although I had read quite widely, I don't think the Cynics had even been brought to my attention. Among New Testament scholars they seem now in retrospect to have drifted out of favour sometime after W. R. Halliday's *The Pagan Background of Early Christianity* (1925), though prior to that their relevance had seemed entirely obvious to S. Dill, *Roman Society from Nero to Marcus Aurelius* (1905), III ii, 'The Philosophic Missionary'.

It is only slowly, and while pursuing other interests, that the implications of the Cynic material as here displayed have been borne in on me. Whether or not the argument holds, others will have to judge for themselves. But for what the confession is worth, this picture has surprised me, contradicting my own earlier expectations. We do seem to have available indications of popular thinking of the time, the Cynic material does afford relevant 'controls' to help us to interpret the implications of the gospel traditions. And once a clearer picture emerges of the early Christian communities in question, a clearer picture than ever seemed likely, then in addition a clearer picture of any preceding stimulus, from Jesus himself, is now discernible.[23]

The logic of the argument is very much the one I tried to tease out twenty years ago. What is 'new' (to me, and largely to the post-war debate about Jesus and the church and the churches' records of him) is the extra, Cynic, evidence.

Citing that book of mine (among many others) E. P. Sanders has argued, however, in his recent *Jesus and Judaism*, that it is useless trying to start any historical investigation into the life of Jesus on the basis of the sayings material. Sayings can be far too readily re-shaped to suit later needs. Their exegesis by different scholars can produce widely different results, as he shows in an introductory survey, and again in a chapter on 'The Sayings': 'We never have absolute certainty of authenticity, and we probably have the original context of any given saying seldom if ever.' Rather should we start with events, for there we have (effectively) indubitable 'facts'.[24]

Sanders lists some 'almost indisputable facts', eight in all:

1. Jesus was baptized by John the Baptist.
2. Jesus was a Galilaean who preached and healed . . .

5. Jesus engaged in controversy about the temple . . .

(and there were twelve disciples, in a ministry confined to Israel; Jesus was crucified by the Romans outside Jerusalem, an identifiable movement followed, suffering some Jewish persecution). Later, in summary, Sanders lists some interpretative corollaries. The first is 'Jesus shared the world-view that I have called Jewish restoration eschatology'. Some sayings have been drawn into his account, once his basic 'facts' have each been established. But the remainder are simply left on one side, to be dealt with by someone else, by anyone who happens to want to write a history of the synoptic tradition.[25]

There are massive inconsistencies in this programme, (though, as I have already acknowledged, there is much in Sanders' account of issues such as repentance and forgiveness in first-century Judaism where I confess myself largely convinced).

First, one cannot claim to be dealing with 'the facts' if one simply files away the great bulk of what purports to be the evidence as simply inconvenient. It just will not do merely to assert that the burden of proof lies with those who affirm the authenticity of sayings ascribed to Jesus. There is a burden of proof (well, at least of consistent hypothesizing) on those who would put sayings ascribed to Jesus anywhere at all. And that includes those who think there are good reasons for leaving any unapportioned. Of course it is going to be impossible to do everything in one study. But there must be at least an outline sketch of how it came about that evidence which is accepted got preserved in usable form among other again that is ambiguous, perhaps, and other which relates only to various later users of the material. 'The facts' of the history of the tradition have to be considered if any part of the tradition is to be used in any 'factual' historical reconstruction.[26]

As I argued (in slightly different words) in *The Church and Jesus*, there must always be a reconnoitering of what lies ahead as part of demonstrating the validity of any reconstruction. (There will be one in a few pages' time for the case argued here.) How poor or irrelevant evidence got into the records must be argued at least in outline.[27]

But there is a still more serious inconsistency in Sanders' division between 'sayings' and 'facts'. Quite simply, if Jesus said something, that is a fact (and an event), and as much a fact (and event) as his supposed entering the temple in Jerusalem on any occasion.

And there is more still to the issue than that. Actions are all 'intentional'. If that is not precisely tautological in everyone's usage, it certainly seems to be in Sanders' own. Actions are all intentional in the sense that if there was no intention it was not in that sense an 'action' at all. An avalanche is not an action by the snow.

Sanders is sure that Jesus performed actions (in an intentional sense) in the temple. Indeed, he is so sure that he feels he knows that turning over tables must have been an indication of a destruction that was to precede rebuilding, and so for all the other 'facts'.[28] I am in turn certain these are rightly treated as actions, and so intentional. But this entails that issues of meaning and interpretation of meaning are just as pressing as in any other part of the tradition. Since these accounts were always bearers of meaning, they were always as liable as any saying to be given a different context and a different nuance of meaning, without any sure guarantee that the original 'intentional action' would be left in any way discernible. Whether we have 'facts' or not depends on how the tales of the supposed events were treated by those whose 'sayings' these tales were. They can only be shown to be 'facts' within a wider and well demonstrated hypothesis which explains how they were preserved as factually valid. Such an hypothesis demands an account of the community or communities that told the tales, and is not even provisionally complete until that work is at least sketched out, on the basis of the whole corpus of tradition relating to those communities.

Such an embracing hypothesis, inevitably, belongs within a still wider one, even more likely to be implicit, and so on. It would not be possible to have a world history even sketched usefully in every historical essay. But the greater the tally of connections proposed, the more objective is the resulting reconstruction. It is often easy to fit one piece of a jig-saw puzzle into the wrong place, or even half-a-dozen. The larger the number of available surrounding pieces involved, the more likely one is to avoid making or being accused of mistakes. So Professor Sanders rightly follows his story of Jesus through into the 'determinate community' that claims Jesus as its origin. But the history of the evidence is also an essential part of the story, an integral section of the jig-saw. Telling the story of the evidence involves accounting for all that the witnesses thought of as evidence, and giving as clear an account as possible of the story of the witnesses on whom it depends.[29]

It is, necessary instead, and by contrast to start where this study has, with the beliefs and attitudes of those early Christians who purportedly told stories about, and repeated the teaching of Jesus, and it is necessary to attempt to fit all that into the intentional world of their day. There is no historically valid short-cut into tales of 'non-verbal' events as 'facts', and no way back to the figure of Jesus that by-passes the verbal events, the sayings, attributed to him.

Setting the synoptic material in the wider context of contemporary Cynicism does not even pretend to take the issue beyond dispute. What it does do is suggest a fairly coherent 'control' outside of the material itself for that material's interpretation; and then the argument of this study unfolds. That the Cynic material is relevant is entirely vulnerable to criticism, on the basis of some still wider hypothesis, which might be forthcoming, showing (perhaps) that Cynics had agreed never to enter Jewish territory, or that there would have been obvious markers in the Christian material distinguishing it at once from what may to a twentieth-century Westerner such as myself look very similar. (It is not, of course, just a matter of spinning such an hypothesis. I can do that. It is a matter of elaborating it coherently and supporting it with evidence.)

Other writers do take much more note of the sayings material. As Professor Sanders points out, they come to very different conclusions. This is true even of those who have made a special effort to situate the sayings material in a wider context, writers such as J. Jeremias, G. Vermes, A. E. Harvey, J. Riches, for example. I have myself in the past found them all very well worth considering, and on many detailed issues, persuasive. But they simply have too little contextual material to go on, too few pieces of the jig-saw to be able to do more than propose yet one more re-arrangement. It is entirely possible to suggest some fresh small-scale hypothesis, and on its terms divide the synoptic material between Jesus and the early Christians, and then fit that Jesus into some reconstruction of contemporary Judaism. Within any such restricted hypothesis the apportionment will look entirely objective, and, for instance, the much discussed 'criterion of dissimilarity' can operate. Even Professor Sanders uses it: The church's later embarassment at the story of Jesus being baptized by John presents a picture too unlike later belief to have been invented.[30] Within Sanders' tacitly presupposed picture of the (uniform?) development of early Christian thinking, the argument is sound. Yet one only has to frame an alternative hypothesis which also has some contemporary fit, for a quite different conclusion to be demanded.

It would be quite reasonable to suggest an hypothesis that included a stage in the life of the tradition where Jesus, like every first-century teacher, had to be found a predecessor (there is plenty of evidence for such a demand being likely to be felt). John is the sole available contemporary candidate (see Josephus), despite the contrast in their views acknowledged in the tradition. Only a little later does this become embarassing (with which compare the unease of Cynic tradition at Diogenes' connection with Antisthenes, itself very likely originally an invention . . .). In this construction, the baptism story begins as a conventional fiction.[31]

As I argued in my *The Church and Jesus*, if we have no 'external' controls that allow us to apportion the synoptic material 'objectively', we are bound to be left without any way to judge between competing constructions. And one must still allow that even framing an hypothesis involving more, hitherto 'external' evidence, only shifts the argument on to another level, it does not conclude it. But it remains the case that the more the evidence, the fewer 'compossible' hypotheses it is likely to fit.

I have suggested that the Cynic material is similar enough to that in the synoptic tradition to demand attention; once attended to, a possible relevance can be spelled out in detail, first for the communities who used the tradition, and then for its antecedents. There I must leave it, hoping that the case will not be ignored, allowing that some equivalent or better alternative hypothesis may well be forthcoming.

I hope that the relevance of this discussion of ways of reading the evidence does not itself need to be argued. Issues of truth and of integrity intertwine, and the freedom to pursue historical truth is itself important as a part of eschewing any hypocritical pretence. But much more positively, Jesus himself is important, as the embodiment of the teaching ascribed to him. In the kind of teaching discerned here, the teacher is the first 'fruit' that allows us to appraise the tree.

5. *Checking the Sequel*

Some of Jesus' immediate followers were sure that the figure of Jesus was still more important than that. Those who seem to have responded to him as a fresh kind of Cynic were among those who were convinced that God had raised him to glory. Jesus the teacher had been especially chosen by God, he was God's anointed. Jesus himself might just possibly have allowed this term 'messiah', in a very general sense, to be used of him. He had, anyway, talked of being in a filial relationship with God, God's son; and such talk now remembered took on still more significance.

In the community whose tradition Mark inherited, Jesus' self-effacing talk of himself as son of man, the humble figure who nonetheless had a role in the forthcoming judgment, was now read in the light of Daniel chapter 7 and all its splendour. By the time Mark was writing up a selection of his community's traditions in the early seventies, the grandeur of the status now accorded to Jesus had been read back into some of the episodes of the tradition, and some of the designations used for Jesus there; and what God had done through Jesus 'for' humankind was now seen in cosmic and metaphysical terms.[32] As determined by God, Jesus had acted 'for us' (even 'in us', maybe); but perhaps rather less 'through us'. Jesus' Jewish-Cynic incitement to a new vision for human living is still there, but now much more as an 'interim ethic' of the acceptance of suffering discipleship, rather than as a challenge to live already the life of the end time. There is less social subversion, a greater readiness to accept things for the moment as they are, because more has been done by God and more still waits to be done by him; and the rest has much less significance.

The 'Q' material comes into written form in the fifties or sixties, and by then less theological development had taken place, though the way the group preserving it treats its tradition would suggest it saw Jesus as a living Lord, rather than as a nobly dead teacher. In its written form this material gathered considerable prestige by the eighties and nineties when it is treated with great respect by Matthew and later still by Luke, so that the Cynic motifs remain clear, even in Luke, despite his 'conformist' portrayal of the church in Acts.

It is difficult to date the Epistle of James, but it affords very significant evidence for a continuing Cynic strand among Christians. There is considerable overlap with the synoptic sayings tradition, but also a proper Cynic willingness to think out the implications of the tradition independently. Cynic opposition to riches and the rich is powerfully stated (and much the same may be said of the 'Two Ways' section of the Didache – whenever that is to be dated). After the first verse of James there is no reference to Jesus as Lord; there is none at all to Jesus as raised, or as redeemer. But issues of freedom are important. (If the arguments for the attribution to James the brother of Jesus were thought persuasive, then the Epistle of James would be even more impressive evidence for the availability in Galilee and Judaea of Cynic discourse! But probably the kind of Greek used precludes this otherwise attractive suggestion.)

The Paul of Acts does not look at all Cynic, and Luke's sketch has encouraged writers such as E. A. Judge to picture Paul adopting the role of sophist, dependent on wealthy 'patrons', male or female. This on its own would not exclude a Cynic connection: as wealthy a patron as Seneca could have a Cynic 'chaplain', Demetrius. However, R. F. Hock (in *The Social Context of Paul's Ministry*) has argued cogently for a very different picture, based on Paul's own writing; and A. J. Malherbe in particular has picked out a number of passages in Paul where he seems to be defining himself quite specifically in terms of Cynic debates about role and ethos. That this is relevant both to Paul and to those he addresses seems to be taken for granted by both.[33]

Paul, too, of course, is also convinced that in Jesus God did not simply send a teacher. In the resurrection to glory of the one who had been crucified God had changed the human situation in a way that showed that nothing that went before had been adequate for God's over-riding intentions for humankind. The law had not been sufficient and clearly Jesus' own teaching could not have been. A totally new situation had had to be created through Jesus' crucifixion and resurrection to glory. Even more than in Mark is there the feeling of an interim ethic (cf. I Cor. 7).

The way is prepared for the much more 'conservative', 'conformist' approach of the 'deutero-Paulines' (Colossians, Ephesians, I and II Timothy and Titus, I Peter, I Clement, Ignatius). Here we find Stoic-style 'submission codes' adopted, and respect for the emperor firmly and unconditionally inculcated. In his Gospel Luke includes much of the material of 'Q' and Mark (by now very authoritative), but he balances it with his over-all picture of the Christian's conformity to Jewish tradition, and their acceptability among those in authority (the latter especially in Acts). Respectful respectability becomes the dominant ethos among Christians long before Constantine and Eusebius of Caesarea.[34]

However, alongside the way of social conformity and quietism of the later New Testament writings (and noting the rather different but penetrating and incisive social critique of the Revelation to John), the possibility of a Christian Cynicism continues to remain open. Whereas Luke effectively neutralizes the Cynic material he includes, and never encourages even a suspicion that that is how Paul may have seen his role (he never in fact shows the Cynic teaching of Jesus in 'Q' being put into practice in the early church!), Matthew, on the other hand actually added further material with a strongly Cynic flavour to what he earlier took from 'Q' and from Mark.[35]

This is how Lucian sees Christians in his picture of the career of Peregrinus, in the next century. That Cynics can readily be mistaken for Christians is presupposed in Justin's polemic against the Cynic Crescens: he was only persecuting Christians to distance himself from them. There are many favourable references to Cynics in some of the later Fathers; and the secondary sources refer to more that I have not been able to verify (including comments by the emperor Julian, and an intriguing story of a certain Maximus coming to be consecrated bishop of Constantinople still wearing his Cynic cloak). In conversation it has also been suggested to me that the '*contemptus mundi*' of the early eremites and especially the stylites may owe much to an ongoing tradition of Christian Cynicism. But that (for me) remains only a question. What I would hope the foregoing has done is sketch the sort of 'follow through', the 'trajectory' I have urged it is necessary to trace if any argument about Jesus and the early Christians is to gain at least initial credibility. I am not suggesting Cynic roots that suddenly disappeared. I am arguing that a Cynic understanding of Christianity can be seen to have been strong enough and obvious enough to carry through into the succeeding centuries.[36]

6. *Other Christs, Other Christianities*

as allowed, non-Cynic Christianities quickly emerged, with their non-Cynic Christs (such as the very religious and metaphysically powerful Christs of Hebrews and of the Fourth Gospel). These often enable the wealthy to be nice and wealthy and pious, and enjoy being nice and pious and wealthy, which is, on balance very likely better than being nasty and wealthy (whether pious or not) – and enjoying that. Such variants have encouraged the poor to be nice and pious and poor – indeed, nice enough not to disturb the rich. That, however, may well on balance be worse than being nasty and impious and effectively liberating the rich; save, of course, for the likelihood of doing no more than substituting some newly rich for those now dispossessed.

On the other hand, many of those who over the last one hundred and fifty years have given us their pictures of Jesus as teacher have included the entailment, 'and no more than that'. 'A very great teacher', 'one of the greatest', 'the greatest of all times' – that kind of thing. It is entirely open to anyone at all persuaded by this study to respond in that way. It would not be inappropriate to the man I have been suggesting started it all off, simply (but perseveringly) to concentrate on his teaching and example.

My own faith, for what it and its expression are worth, is actually other, as may be my readers'. I retain the long traditional Christian language of 'incarnation'. I trust that God made his own the life of this Cynic Jesus. God accepted his experience of trying to share this Jewish-Cynic vision, and his dying. The measure but also the actuality of God's self-involving and vulnerable love is his identification of himself with this Jesus. All of Jesus' experience was God's experience. God – God the Son – was 'in' every move and thought and impulse and sensation of Jesus from conception to death – and new life. His life was lived as anyone's may be, in response to God's Holy Spirit. But his life was owned, in a way others' are not, by God, as his own. However, this is in a very important sense, another story. It is a second story that may be told, if one wishes, when one feels the first story, the story of Jesus, has been told as best may be, with the historian's tools available.[37] The first story shapes the second, the second does not affect the telling of the first at any point. The Jewish-Cynic Jesus I have been sketching did not think he was God incarnate; it cannot be imagined that such a thought ever crossed his mind.

But when God accepted the conditions of a human life, these Jewish-Cynic ideals were the ones he lived and tried to share.

I also have to accept, following from what stands at the start of this section, that telling this second story may endanger the first. It may always be that it neutralizes the possible effect of the vision Jesus tried to share. I would myself hope that the telling of the second story would empower the living of the vision of the one of whom it is told. But it must sadly be admitted that it can have quite the contrary result.

Versions of the second story are celebrated in liturgy. Our hope should be that this will always be a focus for a renewed dedication to costly discipleship, and a renewed empowering for it. If acts of worship do afford occasions for opening ourselves up to the God and father whom Jesus trusted, they should allow us to renew our appreciation of Jesus' vision, and our willingness and ability to live it. Yet, again, there is the accompanying danger. Expressions of fealty in bad verse, offerings of cultic homage, may readily be alternatives to real obedience.

It is, though, very odd, that it can be those most keen to defend the privileged metaphysical status of Jesus as God who are least willing to let him change the world they are saying is his. He's in his heaven, and all's well with the world. Now that is blasphemy: that is to call him Lord and treat him as a fool.

V

Jesus and the Threat of Freedom

The only Jesus we have any historical access to is the Jesus of the tradition preserved in use by the early Christian communities. I have brought forward evidence to show that that Jesus of the early communities stands in the Cynic tradition, albeit with a strong Jewish colouring. I have also argued that we may have considerable confidence in taking the main lines of our picture of that Jewish-Cynic Jesus of the early communities as also indicating the actual Jesus of Galilee and Judaea.

The only Jesus we have is a threatening Cynic figure. The freedoms he challenges us to accept preclude a great many of the liberties that those most likely to notice this book most dearly enjoy. Christianity has evolved, in Weber's phrase, as a 'theodicy of success'. The more strong-minded can afford to ignore it altogether (they need no justification for what they succeed in doing); unless perhaps they turn it into the cult of a tribal war-god ('in God we trust'). The more sensitive among the possessors can use it to fortify and decorate their enjoyment of disproportionate privilege: Jesus as fairy godfather. The more timid among the dispossessed can use Christian faith to explain their toleration of injustice for others as well as for themselves: Jesus as perpetual Cinderella. The Jesus of this study rebels insistently against any such captivity.

If Chapter III of this book has been at all persuasive (perhaps with the support of the further material in *The Christ and the Cynics*); and even more if the fourth chapter has, then the reader might well – might better – write this concluding chapter for her or himself. The theoretical implications for the present-day situations of North America, Britain, France, and the whole 'Western' world outlined in Chapter II are probably clear enough not to need much statement, and urgent enough not to need much persuasion.

However, it may be that a sketch of the consequences that the present writer sees in the material here assembled may afford the reader some further basis for critical appraisal.

First it must be insisted that there will be no attempt even to outline an economic policy or system that could be guaranteed to 'work' on the basis of Jesus' Cynic teaching as here understood. Systems are not favoured in the teaching itself, and I do not pretend to be much good at using the technical vocabulary in which systems and critiques of systems are currently articulated. No detailed attempt will be made to fend off any free-market capitalist who may want to dismiss this study as just another left-wing attempt to capture Christ for Marxism; nor, 'on the other side', to prevent the present findings from being dismissed as just another bourgeois liberal flight of fancy. There is no overt alignment either with a 'Weberian' view that ideas must be capable of changing economic and social reality, nor with a Marxist view that economic praxis determines ideological response.

There is nothing in the teaching of Jesus as understood in the earliest days of the church or in the days of Jesus himself to give comfort to any kind of system that subordinates people to capital and to markets. Neither state, worker, nor 'free enterprise' capitalism can draw any valid support from this Jesus. Apologists for such systems (all we have at present) would claim that their particular form of capitalism is simply a means to a greater human flourishing. Perhaps ours is not yet free enough, or controlled enough, or participatory enough or responsive enough. But given a little more liberty to exploit, or a little more programming, or consultation, or market research, or advertising, and all will be well.

The response from the Jesus tradition is one of total incredulity. When elephants grow wings and fly, or when camels dance through the eyes of needles, then these promises will come true.

But the two-millimetre camel (or three metre hole for the thread) is not just factually improbable. (It is irrelevant that fourteenth-century guides to wealthy tourists could find reassuring postern gates to allow suitably amenable camels to pass.) The impossibility of a Jesus-style human flourishing being found where wealth is the controlling motive in society is an impossibility in logic. The best result imaginable by 'mammonic' criteria would always preclude the kind of flourishing to which the Jesus tradition points. It is simply other. Even if the results actually obtained under various forms of capitalism were not always as miserable for most as seems most likely, its successes could only be failures for followers of the Cynic Christ.

It could be the case that the most appropriate response today is still to 'drop out' ostentatiously, living an alternative life-style that dramatically puts in question the values of the wider society. Over recent years in Britain, around mid-summer, a very small group of 'hippies' (original and recent) have attracted considerable attention from the news-entertainment media for their determined efforts to camp around the very ancient Stonehenge. A few hundred people are made to present an even greater threat to accepted civilized values and to the very life of the nation than the fall-out from the still recent nuclear accident at Chernobyl (or the refusal of Americans to risk Gadafy's vengeance by holidaying in Britain). It may be that nothing less obviously 'offensive' will have any impact at all, and that the over-reaction of the press may bring others to ask how it is that their own preferred life-styles can look so unattractive.[1]

There is not much sign of any such effect in Britain over recent years; and Michael Harrington's account of similar phenomena in the United States would suggest a like lack of impact. It is indeed probably significant that he sees people 'confined' to battered mobile homes only as victims, not as pointers to any kind of viable alternative life-style. However, the fact that the hippie kind of protest, past and recent, has not more effectively challenged popular consumer orthodoxy is not in itself enough to exclude it from serious Christian consideration. Jesus himself was not very effective, nor (despite Lucian's fears) were the pagan Cynics. The attempt to persuade (rather than guarantee results) is essential to any life-style focussed on Jesus. His is not the Epicurean way of safeguarding one's own integrity among brothers, and to hell with the rest. Christians and Cynics have a divine mission to all. But it is a mission to persuasion (as opposed to manipulation or to sheer force), and persuasion always runs the risk of failure; and failure to persuade cannot invalidate the attempt. Jesus' kind of freedom can only be offered freely, and the offer is always open to refusal. The hippie kind of independence parade could be a proper, even the only true way to offer Jesus' freedom.

There does, however, seem to be a much more serious failure than the inherent danger of failing to persuade, in any of the hippie protests noticed by the present writer (dependant on other informants). They have seemed too radical in appearance and not radical enough in ethos. The appearance is too readily discerned – or at least, portrayed – as a pose, a shallow disguise for just another version of the same kind of consumer hedonism in which the rest of us indulge. These ragged travellers just happen to have their own preferred ways of reducing their lives to easily enjoyable proportions. The rest of us have ours. Their ways are parasitic on ours: they want commercial drugs, commercial music, commercial vehicles, the cast-offs of the commercial world. They want the ordinary world to continue, so it can support them in their harmless self-indulgence. They expect to exploit the natural world as commerce does, without ill-effects accruing.

It is a sign of the insecurity of British society that it picks on such ineffectual 'enemies', hiding itself from more real threats to its environment. But there is in hippie-style protest no Christian or Cynic incisiveness – even if there is often still less in the kind of good manners that passes for discipleship among most Christians.

Any properly Christian critique of society has to be much more openly honest about our continuing involvement in the system we criticize and seek to change. Uninvolved, we have small chance of effecting anything; accepting involvement, we shall not easily avoid the appearance of hypocrisy, and of that we need to be aware.

It probably has to be accepted that there is no possibility of effecting instant change in any way that would not make things worse. Even were the wealthy exploitative nations to wipe themselves out in some manner that did not contaminate the rest (perhaps with one of the latest nerve-gases), there is enough wrong in the remainder of the world to ensure the continuation of misery there. If the South American debt were to destroy the Western banking system, it would be the rich and powerful who would still eat well while the rest lost their crumbs. In the unlikely event of enough people being persuaded (by Christians or by anyone else) to abandon consumerism overnight, the effects would be even more catastrophic for those already marginalized than for the recent expropriators. And it is very unlikely that a handful of followers of the Cynic Christ could achieve anything on that scale, even if it did seem appropriate to try.[2]

As long as the system continues there is no way of really 'dropping out' while at the same time retaining any effective chance of changing the system. Though this can easily look like a soft option chosen for its softness, it does seem the least likely to remain ineffective. In a way the issue echoes the divisions between John Baptist (ascetic, in the wilderness) and Jesus (involved, among the villages). And that is perhaps not unlike the division among pagan Cynics between the uncompromising harshness attributed to Diogenes and the gentle approach ascribed to Antisthenes. Wealthy and exploitative though 'Western Society' is, it would still seem to be appropriate to respond to the Cynic teaching of the Jew Jesus by remaining within that society, but adopting a life-style that is as cheap as possible and as 'personally' rich and as generous and as visibly and vocally subversive as possible, 'in the world but not of it'.[3]

This final chapter is no place to discuss in any more detail the likely effectiveness of various means to the kind of freedom and flourishing with which Jesus entices and threatens us. (And, as said, even if others usefully could, I make no such pretence.) It would be irresponsible, however, not to raise again the issue of 'violence' and 'force'. The words are as slippery as many others. We have (in Matthew) the insistence that we should not resist assaults against ourselves; we have the example of Jesus' own refusal of the way of armed rebellion. But do these outweigh the wickedness of our passive complicity in the violence done to the lives of millions of our fellow humans for the sake of maintaining our standard of consumption? Should our love for those in power outweigh our love for the victims? It seems to me that the only properly Christian consideration is the one avoided here, but about which I have written elsewhere. Only if we are sure that it would make matters worse for the victims are we justified in refusing to use force against the oppressors. In love for the oppressors themselves – ourselves– we should take whatever are the most effective means to end the oppression.[4]

Rather than attempt a sort of casuistry of Christian-Cynic freedom it seems better to sketch a few imaginary case-studies of people finding themselves threatened by the kinds of freedom offered by the Jesus of the early tradition.

(a) *Jo-Meg*

Jo-Meg is thirty-six, graduate, teacher of English literature, mother of two children, happily married to Richard (who is happily married to her). Jo-Meg is an elder of her local church, which the family attends together, and they are close friends of the present minister. His brother is a State senator, and ambitious. Richard is a company lawyer for a medium sized corporation with varied manufacturing and retail interests mainly in the east of the United States. The children, Jonathan and Lena, are both at school, and Jo-Meg has been promised a teaching post at the local high-school next Fall. The extra money will allow them to move house to a better part of town, and make it easier for Richard to entertain business associates. The children's friends from church mainly live over there, and the children are becoming rather embarassed at the tiny pool in the garden and Jo-Meg's old Volkswagen. Jo-Meg's closest friend from college days is Angie, Catholic, divorced, mother of three, maths teacher in the poorest of the town's high-schools, activist in Chicano causes, and Jo-Meg has been helping her on the sidelines. Richard's main work-load at present is to create barriers against the unionization of the corporation's agricultural workers, and putting together minimal interpretations of the safety at work legislation in the various states where the farms are situated. There is a move in the company to abandon local holdings and concentrate in Costa Rica, where the labour costs are so much lower. The transfer would hit their town badly. If Richard can help make staying put look more financially attractive, he will be very popular among business colleagues where they live.

The Jesus of the early gospel tradition, however, seems to be inviting Jo-Meg and Richard and their children to see all this promising future as a captivity. The feasible alternatives would not bring his perfect freedom, either. But they would afford substantial steps in his direction. And they are very menacing.

Jo-Meg can probably pass the teaching post to another single-parent friend. That will mean they do not move their home. They stay, and continue to offer open house to many of the ill-disciplined neighbourhood kids. It may well put Jo-Meg's relationship with Richard under strain, though she will have more time and energy to share with him and the children, and he could see that as a real bonus. But she will also be urging a suggestion he made as a joke: he could try to reassure the financial managers with what would turn out to be very flimsy anti-union protection, until the risk of a transfer to Costa Rica was over. The peasants there would remain in possession of their land, which would still be feeding them all, rather than raising cash crops and employing less than a third of them. Richard himself had also thought of leaking corporation safety guidelines to the various state officers concerned. Pressing Richard to take seriously what he only suggested as jokes will strain their relationship, as will Jo-Meg's continuing support for Angie, as well as her efforts to get their own wealthy church involved in a development project in Indonesia, with its spin-off in political education among the congregation.

Almost every aspect of this will demand a simpler life-style, not least the temptation to save against Richard losing his job altogether. They are used to holidaying very cheaply (so Angie and her children feel free to come too) and enjoying the simplicity. Somehow neither they nor the children sustain it when the vacation is over. Playing being (relatively) 'poor' for three weeks in the year is one thing; a full fifty-two would be something else.

They are actually being invited to enjoy a much fuller freedom for each other, and for friends around them, and for enjoying the world where they live, as well as more time for openness for God. They may also be able to help to enable a much greater measure of freedom for many others now and in the future.

But it is much easier to see the promises as threats and the gains as losses, and if I were Jo-Meg, I'd play safe. I think. But I'd not have much time for regrets, not when I was teaching, and looking after the big new house, and ferrying the children to friends and being entertained by senior executives and talking about holidays in Venice and Sri Lanka, and planning the next move across three states, and how to tell the children, and wondering what I'd do at home in a strange city, especially if I couldn't get a job, and would Richard's salary increase be enough on its own . . .?

(b) *Monique*

Monique is twenty-two, and works as a secretary in a bank. She has been a practising Catholic for some three years, coming to the church from a home background completely indifferent to any faith, and largely indifferent to her. Her introduction was through a friend in a Young Christian Worker (JOC) group who'd been very supportive after Monique's first, brief and painful affair with a boy who'd ditched her when she thought she was pregnant (but, as it turned out, wasn't).

A regular Wednesday mid-day mass and common meal has brought Etienne into her life, a very serious young man from a very traditional Catholic family. Etienne laughs at some of his parents' views when he is with her – but not when he is with them. They would have preferred to find him a girl from their own background, but have to accept that not many young people of good family are practising Catholics these days. It was only later that she realized how carefully they had checked that she had no Jewish ancestry. They do not approve of that Le Pen; but they would be glad to see the back of 'the blacks'.

When she is with Etienne Monique finds an incredible new richness to life. They share music, theatre, walks, meetings of their town's botanical society (where they are the highly prized 'young people'), poetry, novels. She had never thought to try for

University; he had, and had used the time well, and is now finding his aesthetic awareness still further enhanced in the sharing of it. They find each other physically very attractive, though she has to keep telling herself that two gentle kisses on meeting and on parting express a real affection, not coldness, nor shyness. He will almost certainly ask her to marry him. They will have lots of children.

Her friend in the JOC is Camerounian by birth, and entirely French in her outlook. Monique has mentioned the JOC to Etienne, but not to his parents; she has not mentioned Stephanie to either, though Stephanie is beginning to wonder why she has never met Etienne. The group continues with its support for *Medecins sans Frontieres*, and for political prisoners in Chile. Returning from a meeting with Stephanie and her boy cousin all three have been harrassed by the police. She knows the commissioner of police, he banks where she is a secretary, and she could probably register an effective complaint. But the story might travel.

The Jesus of the early gospel tradition might be thought to have blessed Monique of late with freedoms she would not have thought existed. Now he is insisting that she follows where they lead, at the risk of losing Etienne, who brought many of them to her. She must risk losing him by pressing him to choose between the Christianly valid freedoms he enjoys and is so good at sharing, and those aspects of his upbringing which conflict. She must risk sharing her political engagement with him, as well as allowing him to share his aesthetic awareness with her. For what he could contribute as well as for his own sake, she must risk asking him to risk a break with his family. She must introduce him to her JOC group, to Stephanie and her cousin, and to the realities of police treatment of blacks. She must also find some way of letting him know of her one past affair, for which she never felt guilt; and for which any guilt there might have been had long been removed. Etienne should believe that, as a good Catholic. But what buried repugnance might an admission of past 'unchastity' allow to surface? All in all she must risk putting more of herself into their relationship, not simply responding to him – even though that itself might just possibly frighten him away, be for now too 'unfeminine'.

It would be much easier to relax into the very mildly charismatic pietism of the church they both attend, leaving Etienne to propose marriage in his own good time, and forget the JOC group, and Stephanie, and the poor and the political prisoners, and the police. After all, she can tell herself, if Etienne's parents met an African or a Jew injured in the streets, they'd take the injured person to hospital. They know their Christian duty. They would never show callousness, let alone be deliberately unpleasant to someone's face. That would not be right.

The more Monique is aware of the Jesus of the gospel tradition, the more he threatens her peace and her happiness by the peace and the happiness and the freedom he insists on trying to draw her to.

(c) *Fred*

Fred is in his late seventies, and a widower, living alone in a council bungalow. He has his own garden, and he lives in a part of the town where the only threat is from the neighbours' cats and from slugs. He grows vegetables and flowers and he has some fruit trees. He also has his health, and lives quite comfortably on his state pension and a small one from the railways. He'd worked for one of the old companies, and then for the state owned British Rail, and for more than fifty years. He still has concessionary travel rights.

He is a good talker and an even better listener. But he has so much in his own head and eyes and ears and nose, and his arms and his legs, he feels no great loneliness if he's seen no one else for days on end. He goes walking in the hills around the northern town where he has always lived. He knows the rocks and the soil and the plants and the birds and the small mammals and the insects, and he looks out for them at the times when they should be there, and he greets them like old friends. Newcomers he welcomes with intrigued interest, lost species he laments. Just occasionally he permits himself a sentimental reverie, back to a three-year courtship in some of the same hills. But then they wed, and hard times were soon on them, and the children, and Emmy died young, they never walked the hills again together. He's been used to loneliness since the children went their ways. He can enjoy the visits, and the grandchildren . . . great grandchildren now, one lass has come to show him. But he's just as happy, no more, no less, on his own. The evenings are fine, with a book from the public library, or the wireless, or his gramophone (that's what he still calls them). He's never bothered with television.

He's never much bothered with church, either, hasn't Fred. He was in the choir as a boy – all his friends were. They pulled that church down fifteen years ago. Emmy and he got wed in church. The children were Christened. He had Emmy taken into church when she died with the fifth little one. He made friends with one or two parsons, nice lads, really, doing their best. But the music in church wasn't up to much.

And then that play came on the wireless, and the Jesus of the sermons he'd dreamed through as a boy upset the calm of his evening days. Shouldn't he share a bit more of all he'd got? If he had the strength to go walking after he'd repainted his own house, he'd got the strength to do a bit of painting for the widow up the road. If he could enjoy the hills, so could those three lads round the corner, if he could get them decent boots from some of the family, and anoraks from a jumble sale and take the boys out one Sunday. If he could enjoy a peaceful evening with his own radio, perhaps he could sit in for that young couple who never seemed to get out together for want of a baby-sitter. And if his garden looked tidy enough, he could leave it be and take a spade out for that couple across the way, younger than him, but house-fast with rheumatism.

And that got him caught up with a group of neighbours who were trying to organize that sort of caring, and he found himself on a simple counselling course, and, yes, it turned out he was good at listening. But one thing leads to another, and now he's taken to badgering his local councillor about things the Town Hall should be doing. He'd been a party member, years back, Labour party, and a good union man. But you leave that to the young ones. Only not so many seem interested. Perhaps he could help the secretary, write some of the letters when people came with problems. He'd even had a letter of his own read on the wireless, when some daft chap in Parliament said things could hardly be better.

Young Jack (young Jack? he's past fifty) comes to sort his dad out. Tells him he'll wear himself out. Nigh on eighty, he can't go running round the way he used to when Jack and his brothers were young. Anyway, there's others paid to do that sort of thing. They'll take advantage of him. They could afford to hire someone, just too mean to have the house painted. When did he last take a good train ride . . .? He'll get himself mugged, going out at nights. It'll be nuclear disarmament next, he says. Then wishes he hadn't.

Fred has taken to talking to this Jesus he imagines, like he just sometimes talks to Emmy. 'Jack's quite right, y' know. I've mebbe ten good year left, if A'm careful, and the hills get better 'n better now the smoke's stopped pourin'; out o't' chimneys. But y've got me cawght, y' knows. I can't lay off now. I were in a snug shell. But I'm not fer going back in. And as fer them bombs . . .' You don't have to be young to be free with the freedoms Jesus summons you to.

And Fred is people I know.

However, the actual social, political and economic power of those willing to live the freedom to which Jesus invites us in this way will be quite small. It is as a token, as an experiment in living for others to see, and perhaps for future generations (if there are any) to note and be attracted by, that this sort of discipleship could be important. In countries where there are Christian communities, but where the whole of society has not been sucked fully into the insistence on having more to consume next year than last, such basic communities already flourish, one is assured. For our own societies, corrupted by galloping consumption, such a life lived among traditional or untraditional Christians, 'in the world but not of it', could at least be ready to offer an escape ready for others to adopt when the contraditions of consumer capitalism finally triumph, if the climax is not totally destructive.

In countries which swap their oligarchies by the vote of the people as directed by the advertisers, even small minorities can be quite important. One or two percent of the population can swing an election in the United States as in the United Kingdom. Such a group committing a sizable part of its disposable income to appropriate development in the poorer and most exploited parts of the globe could be a very influential pressure group. Just a small part of that money going into educating others might (in Britain at least) quickly match the education budgets available to the political parties.

The bulk of the money donated could itself make a real difference in enabling fellow human beings elsewhere to grow food, make clothes, build houses, find water, so they too may live and enjoy the same range of inexpensive experience in each other's company. Within their own countries, the more that economic power shifts to the majority, the less vulnerable is their group or the nation as a whole to exploitation from outside. The less luxury 'we' demand, the less the pressure to turn some peasant off her land or drag her daughter into a factory. The more a richly enjoyable pattern of social life at a sustainable level engages more people, the less are available resources channelled into consumer inessentials, or inessentials now judged necessary. The next technological advance is worth avoiding, and radio at a level that can be truly local, 'of the people', is, for instance, a good stage with which to rest satisfied.

It would be very important for our followers of Jesus in the countries of the rich to be very well informed about their world, and aware of what their fellow citizens were thinking. They would need to be able to seduce or goad them into rethinking their attitudes, rethinking their understanding of the world around, attempting at least to match the power of Jesus (or of the pagan Cynics, for that matter) to sting people into a responsible freedom, taking charge of their own lives in community.[3]

In this context Christians (and any allies) would be able to harry any political party (left, right or centre) that was wedded to the heresy that you are the things you consume, by being always better informed, and able to spread the information. There is no guarantee that the powers that be would accept this kind of challenge without a struggle. Reactions to the American Catholic Bishops on issues of social concern (say, *The Challenge of Peace*, 1983, on nuclear deterrence) or the Church of England's report, *Faith in the City*, both very balanced, neither pressing at all hard for radical change, suggest that active repression might soon emerge, to match the experience of the church in America's El Salvador or South Korea, or Britain's naughty nephew, South Africa. The followers of the crucified Christ are not offered a guaranteed easy passage. People can be very evil, and power is still delightfully corrupting, especially, as Jesus pointed out, when it is exercised against us for our good.

There will still be plenty of offences to forgive people, plenty of opportunities for refraining from condemnatory judgment, living the redemption that at least some Christians will go on trusting Christ's life and death and living again have powerfully enabled: the kind of freedom with which he entices or threatens us.[5]

Appendix: the Sources

The most important sources for this book as a whole are the first three gospels in the New Testament collection, and then perhaps the letter of James. Dates for their composition are disputed among scholars, but all may be plausibly dated to the last third of the first century, and only with some difficulty much earlier or much later.

The next most important sources for the study as a whole are those that claim to be 'Cynic' or are seen as such by scholars today (or as 'Stoic-Cynic'). Among them are works by Dio of Prusa, notes of lectures by Epictetus, the so-called '*Cynic Epistles*', and the collection of popular Cynic traditions in Diogenes Laertius book VI. There are other items, especially some pieces from Lucian of Samosata, and asides in other writers, notably Plutarch. (References for the brief accounts that follow are in the notes.)

Dio was born in Prusa,[1] in Bithynia (in modern Turkey,) about AD 40, living until as late as 120. After an early career as a 'sophist' (intellectual entertainer) he was converted to a strongly Cynic form of Stoicism, perhaps by Musonius Rufus (another author on our list). Sent into exile away from Italy and his homeland by Domitian for his public criticisms of the Emperor, he wandered the eastern empire, and beyond its borders, as a Cynic preacher, modelling himself on Diogenes. Restored to full rights under Nerva and the later Antonine emperors, he seems to have maintained many of the concerns and Cynic disciplines of his exile. He still travelled, now as semi-official representative of Trajan. He seems to have maintained a genuine rapport with popular audiences, who listened, and remembered, and even bought pirated copies of his speeches, to his pride (and amusement). Dio tells us often that there were many other Cynic preachers like him.

Epictetus came from Hierapolis in Phrygia (again, modern Turkey), a slave, born of a slave mother. His dates are still less secure, but he was also a pupil of Musonius Rufus, and he was also banished from Rome by Domitian (along with many others). The initial impression gained from the notes taken of his lectures by one of his pupils (Arrian)[2] is that his classes would have been made up of the sons of ethically sensitive aristocrats. But many of his illustrations presuppose a very mixed audience, from people with slave attendants for the children, to those who would have to share child-care with their wives. Epictetus' Greek (as it appears in Arrian's notes) is some of the closest we have to that in the New Testament. Again we seem justified in taking what he is recorded as saying as indicative of ideas in general circulation.

The Cynic Epistles[3] are imagined letters of early Cynic teachers (and others, including Socrates, a Cynic hero though himself pre-dating the start of the Cynic way). The letters seem to come from a spread of dates, some from pre-Christian times, some contemporary with the beginnings of Christianity, and others from as late as the second century. By and large they represent a radical, severe and less literary, so perhaps more 'populist' strand of Cynicism. Some at least seem to have had quite a wide circulation, being quoted by other authors (including Diogenes Laertius, next in the list).

Diogenes Laertius[4] is the latest of our authors, and may himself have written in the early third century AD, or even later. But the anecdotes and sayings he collects seem to represent popular impressions over the centuries, and many of them already appear in our other writers, as well as in earlier ones. They would seem to afford a valid source for ongoing popular impressions of the Cynics (and it is such popular impressions that concern us here).

Lucian of Samosata[5] wrote around the middle of the second century. He gives us an attractive selection of stories about the Cynic philosopher Demonax, a contemporary of Dio's, and other indications of popular Cynicism and its continuing appeal among poorer people, as well as our first clear indications of links with Christians. He, too, was well travelled, and a popular if sceptical communicator.

So much for our main sources for Cynic teaching. There are further indications in the other sources that have been used earlier in chapter II to build the picture of general concerns and attitudes at the time.

From the last third of the century and on into the next come the works of Plutarch,[6] a prolific and eclectic popularizer, fairly closely contemporary with Dio, and again a man well travelled. Much less is taken from the 'intentional' history writings of other near contemporaries, Tacitus and Suetonius. The 'rhetorician' Quintilian's[7] discussion of the kind of education needed to enable a young man to plead at law contains lots of incidental information on ideas taken for granted not just in his highly educated circle, but in the courts where his advice was meant to be used. Pliny senior collected conscientiously (though not in fact uncritically) popular views on almost everything; his nephew and adopted heir, Pliny junior,[8] quotes with approval the tag that nothing human is alien to him, and is also used to addressing popular audiences. The renegade Jewish general turned historian, Flavius Josephus,[9] provides first hand information about Palestine in his own lifetime (he was about 30 when the rebellion broke out in 66CE) as well as from other sources; but also and incidentally makes us aware of attitudes that his gentile readers will take for granted, as well as ones they will find strange.

Earlier than these, and contemporary with Paul is Nero's adviser and would-be 'spiritual director', the multi-millionaire Seneca,[10] who nonetheless kept his own Cynic 'chaplain', Demetrius. In his letters Seneca often seems to echo the concerns we find in more obviously Cynic sources, as well as providing us with the insights of a man concerned to develop his own sensitivity to human life around him. From just a little earlier still we have Philo,[11] the learned (and also wealthy) Jewish scholar from Alexandria, devoted to explaining in terms of popular Greek philosophy the Jewish traditions to which he owed his loyalty. Philo also quotes Cynic ideas and anecdotes (among much else). Earlier than both, but still very relevant, because still popular and influential are Cicero, and Dionysius of Halicarnassus, who wrote a history of Rome used both by Josephus and by Plutarch.

From Christians whose works were not accepted into the New Testament 'canon', but who wrote around the same time material that was valued and preserved, we have the first letter of Clement to the Christians of Corinth (around 95 CE). We have the letters of 'bishop' Ignatius of Antioch, to churches in the province of Asia, around 110. Much harder to date, there are the Didache, (the 'Teaching of the Twelve Apostles') and the closely related Epistle of Barnabas. From the church in Rome there is the rather wordy '*Shepherd*' of one Hermas, perhaps around 130;[12] and, a little later, the more philosophical and expository writings of Justin, a native of Samaria.[13] These for the most part reinforce the arguments for the picture so far presented (for which, again, see my *Strangely Familiar*).

Some scholars would also use 'Gnostic' writings from the third-century Nag Hammadi library, and other sectarian Christian groups to fill out their picture of the kinds of thinking likely to have been shared by early Christians.[14] However, what emerges as 'mainstream' first- and early-second-century Christianity is clearly much more closely akin to mainstream pagan society as evidenced in the writings here cited, than it is to this later sectarianism. (Dio, in particular, is important, as showing how Cynic preaching could find a ready audience in town and country, within and outside the Empire.)

In my *Strangely Familiar* there is further displayed something of the extent to which apparently more distinctively Jewish material from Qumran, from the 'apocalyptic', 'revelatory' writings, and from later Rabbinic traditions in the *Mishnah* and *Midrash Rabbah (Genesis)* support the general picture sketched here, of attitudes to life in the eastern Mediterranean in the first Christian century. Specifically Cynic views that often seem mostly closely akin to our early Christian material are quoted extensively here in Chapter III. Many more appear in my *The Christ and the Cynics*, and references are given to the relevant sections of that work.

These constitute our main sources of information for

approaches to living at the time, in the areas and in the strata of society where Christianity first spread. There is some corroboration in Egyptian papyri, in inscriptions and in graffiti. But the subtleties of people's hopes and fears and aspirations only come effectively to expression in the literary material. Some initial justification for taking this material as relevant for the levels of society of the first Greek-speaking Christians has already been given. The cumulative weight of the parallels displayed in my *Strangely Familiar* is also relevant. The main defence in this study rests with the detailed quotations and references in Chapter III.

The translations from Greek and Latin are my own.

Notes

Introduction

1. That freedoms conflict, and that there is no 'absolute' freedom are commonplaces. For useful discussions of senses of 'free': Paul Spicker, 'Why Freedom Implies Equality', *JAP* 2:2, 1985, 205–216; Jan Srzednicki, 'Freedom and Capacity', *Philosophy* 59 (229) July 1984, 343–348; Andreas Eshete, 'Character, Virtue and Freedom', *Philosophy* 57 (222) Oct. 1982, 495–513; R.A.Sharpe, 'Freud and the Freedom of the Sane', *Philosophy* 55 (214) Oct. 1980, 485–496; S. Hook (ed.) *Determinism and Freedom*, Collier 1961; I.T.Ramsey, *Freedom and Immortality*, SCM Press 1960.

2. First-century concerns about freedom will be illustrated in the next two chapters; but see also F.G.Downing, *Strangely Familiar*, pub. Downing, 44 Cleveland Road, Manchester M8 6QU, 1985, especially sections II and VII; and Ramsey Macmullen, *Enemies of the Roman Order*, Harvard 1966, especially ch. 2, 'Philosophers'; and Klaus Wengst, *Pax Romana*, SCM Press 1987.

3. Much more detail is to follow; but see R. Macmullen, *Enemies*, again, and e.g., D.B.Dudley, *A History of Cynicism*, London 1937, reprinted Hildersheim 1967; A.J.Malherbe (ed.) *The Cynic Epistles*, Scholars Press 1977; and among other writing by A.J.Malherbe, including his 'Self Definition among Epicureans and Cynics', in B.E. Meyer and E.P.Sanders (eds), *Jewish and Christian Self-definition*, Vol. 3, SCM Press 1982, 46–59; and now his *Moral Exhortation, a Greco-Roman Source Book*, Westminster 1986; and F.G.Downing, 'The Politics of Jesus', *Modern Churchman* NS XXV, 1982, 19–27; and 'Cynics and Christians', *NTS* 30, 1984, 384–393.

I Freedom in the First Century

1. For a fuller discussion of these issues, see my 'Interpretation and

the "Culture Gap"', *SJT* 1987 [forthcoming], and 'Our Access to other Cultures', *Modern Churchman* XXI, 1977, 28–42; J. Barton, 'Cultural Relativism', I and II, *Theology* LXXXII 1979, 103–109 and 191–199; B. Wilson (ed.) *Rationality*, Blackwell 1970; M. Hollis and S. Lukes, *Rationality and Relativism*, Blackwell 1982; J. Skorpski, 'Relativity, Realism and Consensus', *Philosophy* 60, 1985, 341–358.

2. Our access back through time is discussed in my *The Church and Jesus*, SCM Press 1968, and *The Past is All we have*, SCM Press 1975; and 'Philosophy off History and Historical Research', *Philosophy* XLIV, 1969 33–45; C.A.J.Coady, 'Collingwood and Historical Fact', *Philosophy* L, 1975 409–424; John Tosh, *The Pursuit of History*, Longman, 1984.

3. The sources used for this sketch of first-century life are discussed in the *Appendix*, pp 175–179. The passages referred to and many more are collected in my *Strangely Familiar*, noted above (Introduction). References will be given to the relevant sections of that collection, in most of the remaining notes to this chapter. For this paragraph, see *Strangely Familiar (SF)* II i.

4. *SF* I iii, IV Appendix i; and Plutarch, *de amicorum, moralia* 94B.

5. *SF* III ii; and G.H.R.Horsley (ed.), *New Documents Illustrating Early Christianity*, II, Macquarie University 1982; Cicero, *de senectute* 5–46; A.D.Nock, various items in his essays collected by Zeph Stewart (ed.), *Essays on Religion and the Ancient World*, Harvard 1972.

6. Gillian Clark, 'The Women at Corinth', *Theology*, LXXXV, 1982, 256–262.

7. See e.g., A.S.Hunt and C.C.Edgar, *Select Papyri* I and II, Harvard (Loeb) 1932; Horsley, *New Documents* I, II and III; S.Dill, *Roman Society from Nero to Marcus Aurelius*, London 1905, II i and ii; *SF* I i and Appendix.

8. Dio 7.76–80.

9. Musonius Rufus 13 and 14 in C.E.Lutz, *Musonius Rufus*, Yale 1947.

10. Plutarch, *coniugalia praecepta, moralia* 141A–142E.

11. Referring to Hunt and Edgar, Horsley, and Dill, as above; and to Dio 38.15, and Seneca, *epistulae morales* 104.5.

12. *SF* IV i; Horsley, *New Documents* II 16; Pliny jr, *Letters* IV 19.

13. *SF* I; Pliny jr *Letters* VIII 10, 11, V 16; Musonius 4; *Genesis Midrash* XVIII 1.

14. *SF* I ii; Epictetus II 24.18, I 23.8–9, Plutarch, *consolatio ad uxorem, moralia* 608CD; Cicero, *de finibus* V 15.42.

15. Epictetus III 22.70–76; Luke 11.11–13; Dionysius of Halicarnassus, *Roman Antiquities (RA)* VIII 51.3–4.

16. *SF* IV i; Cicero, *de finibus* V 48; Quintilian, *Institutes* I 1.20; Epictetus IV 11.35, II 21.13–14; Philo, *de mutatione nominum* 270.

17. *SF* IV i, again; Dionysius *RA* XI 28.3; ps. Plutarch, *de liberis educandis, moralia* 8E, Epictetus II 20.29–31.

18. Quintilian, *Institutes* III, especially III 8; Dio 11.6, 42.4–5, 57.10–12; and see my 'Ears to Hear' in A.E.Harvey (ed.) *Alternative Approaches to New Testament Study*, SPCK 1985, 97–101.

19. Dio 33.3–6, Pliny jr, *Letters* VI 16; Quintilian, *Institutes* I, *Preface* 16; Epictetus II 20.29–31, as above.

20. Plutarch, *platonicae quaestiones, moralia* 1000E.

21. *SF* VI iii; Dio 15.26, and 32; Philo, *quod omnis probus liber sit*, 79; Pliny sr, *Natural History* VI 89–91; Seneca, *epistulae morales* 47.10, and all of 90 on the 'Golden Age' (but see also chapter III, below); Pliny jr, *Letters* VIII 16; *Mishnah, Berakoth* 1.7;

22. Dio 62.2; Josephus, *Antiquities* 4.262–265.

23. *SF* VII, and especially Dionysius *RA* VI 86.4.

24. *SF* VII iii; Dio 7.97–126, 3.124–126; Dionysius *RA* VI–VIII, passim; Cicero, *de officiis*, 2.72; Seneca, *epistulae morales* 88.12; Matt. 20.1–15.

25. Cicero, *de officiis* 2.74, 60; Philo, *de virtute* 91, *de specialibus legibus* 2.107; and see my 'Philo and Wealth and the Rights of the Poor', *JSNT* 24, 1985, 116–118, and other references there.

26. Dio 34.21–23; compare J.H.Elliott, *A Home for the Homeless*, Fortress Press and SCM Press 1981; Donysius *RA* VI 36.1.

27. *SF* VI ii; Diogenes Laertius 6.63; 'Anarcharsis' in Malherbe, *Cynic Epistles*.

28. *SF* VII, especially ii, and X.

29. *SF* VII i; Philo, *quod omnis probus liber sit*, 141; Pliny jr. *Letters* VIII 24; Dio 14.1.

30. *SF* VII i, again; Cicero, *de officiis* 1.34; Lucian, *Demonax* 57.

31. *SF* XV iv, v.

32. *SF* XIII ii; Plutarch, *de superstitione, moralia* 164E–171F; Epictetus III 13.14–15, *et passim*; and see Chapter III, below.

33. Plutarch, *de iside et osiride, moralia* 351C–384C; Dio 30 and 36.

34. Plutarch, *de superstitione*, again; Cicero, *de divinatione* 2.148–149.

35. *SF* XV ii, X ii; Philo, *de virtute* 153; Dio 32, 34, 46; Pliny jr, *Letters* X 34.

36. R. Macmullen, *Paganism in the Roman Empire*, Yale University Press 1981, 57 and note; *SF* XV iv and v again.

37. *SF* IV iii; Epictetus III 10.13, 15; Philo, *quod deus immutabilis sit*, 65; Pliny sr, *Natural History* XXIX 2.

38. Plutarch, *moralia* 963E.

39. Pliny jr, *Letters*, X 17A, 37, 39, 98, 99; Epictetus IV 13.5.

40. J. Dunn, *The Politics of Socialism*, Cambridge University Press

1984, 84; Pliny jr, *Letters* X 109, 111; Cicero, *de officiis* 2.72, again; Philo, *de specialibus legibus* 1.121, *de mutatione nominum* 104; Quintilian *Institutes* XII 7.8–12.

41. *SF* VII iii, again. See also K. Wengst, *Pax Romana*.

42. *SF* VI; Cicero, *de officiis* 2.72, yet again; Philo, *de specialibus legibus* 3.156–159; Josephus, *Antiquities* 18.274: the loss of a harvest leaves 'banditry' as the only resource; Dio 7.104–106; R. Macmullen, *Enemies of the Roman Order*, 180. On the ease with which a criticism of wealth becomes a rich man's affectation, see T.E. Schmidt, 'Hostility to Wealth in Philo of Alexandria', *JSNT* 19, 1983, 258–264, and a forthcoming monograph of his. But, as I argued in my 'Philo on Wealth', illustrated in *SF*, and am arguing again here, such sentiments do sometimes seem to be put into practice, in the first century (as in our own).

43. *SF* VI iii; Philo, *Quod omnis probus liber sit* 79, 154–155; Ignatius to Polycarp 4.

44. Epictetus, *Encheiridion* 40.

45. Plutarch, *coniugalia praecepta*. Compare past issues of the British Medical Association booklets, *Getting Married*.

46. R. Macmullen, *Enemies of the Roman Order*, II, 'Philosophers'.

II   Freedom under Threat in the late Twentieth Century

1. The 'witnesses' are J. Ardagh, in *The New France* (3), Penguin 1977, and *France in the 1980s*, Penguin and Secker 1982; M. Harrington, *The New American Poverty*, US 1984, Fircthorn 1985; J. Seabrook, *Landscapes of Poverty*, Blackwell 1985 (and see also his *What went Wrong?* Gollancz 1978); the Archbishop of Canterbury's Commission, *Faith in the City*, Church House Publishing 1985; R.D.N.Dickinson, *Poor Yet making Many rich*, WCC 1983; the journal, *New Internationalist* (Oxford, England); the British newspaper *The Guardian*, Manchester and London. The *Journal of Applied Philosophy* (1984–) also has a number of relevant articles. I shall be sparing with specific page references in the present chapter.

2. As reported in the national papers the next day. One may note the most recent British Census returns (as reported in *The Guardian*, 8 January 1987), and the annual Social Trends, (*The Guardian*, 20 January 1987), on the spread of poverty in Britain; compare the Department of Health Economics report, published 24 March 1987, despite official disapproval. The US Census Bureau, (*The Guardian*, 28 August 1986) reported some slight improvement in 1985, instancing a 2.5% fall in the number of black families with incomes below the official poverty line – down to 31.3%. In all, still 14% of Americans were below that poverty line – thirty-three million people.

3. John Ardagh's recent study, *France in the 80s*, presents a more optimistic view than his earlier one, concentrating now on 'happier' topics.

4. Harrington, *New American Poverty*, 40.

5. Referring to M. Hollis, 'Positional Goods', in A. Phillips Griffiths (ed.), *Philosophy and Practice*, Cambridge University Press 1985, 97–110.

6. For a useful summary of the economic history of the Third World since 1945, Kai Nielsen, 'Global Justice, Capitalism and the Third World', *JAP*, 1:2, 1984, 175–186; but compare also K. Wengst, *Pax Romana*.

III Christian and Cynic Radicalism

1. In this chapter, references beyond those given in the next text will mostly be to the relevant sections of the 'companion' volume, *The Christ and the Cynics*, Sheffield AP 1988; to list all the relevant passages collected there would make these notes unwieldy. So, for this paragraph note *The Christ and the Cynics (TCC)* §151.

2. *TCC* 40; but compare especially ps. Diogenes ep. 26, 30; Epictetus III 22.50; Lucian, *Peregrinus* 15. G. Theissen, '*Wanderradikalismus* . . .' *ZTK* 70 (1973), 245–271 rightly notes the divergencies between these Christian and Cynic passages, but seems not to note the Cynic variations that approach the Christian injunctions more closely, as I go on to suggest in the next paragraph. Note L. Vaage, 'Q: The Ethos and Ethics of an Itinerant Intelligence', 1987.

3. Compare ps. Diogenes ep. 38; Dio 9.10–12; Lucian, *Peregrinus* 17, 20.

4. *TCC* 8; cf. 180, 181.

5. *TCC* 30.

6. *TCC* 173.

7. Compare Musonius III; a woman, too, should be able to withstand someone in authority.

8. Compare A.Ehrhardt, 'Jesus Christ and Alexander the Great', in A. Ehrhardt, *The Framework of the New Testament Stories*, Manchester University Press 1964, 37–43.

9. *TCC* 145(b).

10. *TCC* 127, 145(b), again.

11. *TCC* 185

12. *TCC* 173(a), again.

13. *TCC Introduction* (D), and 7, 23, 24, 210

14. See Ch. I, and R. Macmullen, *Enemies of the Roman Order*, ch. 2, 'Philosophers'.

15. *TCC* 159

16. *TCC* 54, 112.
17. *TCC* 1.
18. *TCC* 36–39, 155.
19. *TCC* 164
20. See especially E. Linnemann, *Parables of Jesus*, SPCK 1966; R. Funk, *Parables and Presence*, Fortress 1982; and a useful survey in H. Hendrickx, *The Parables of Jesus* (2) Chapman/Harper & Row 1986.
21. *TCC* 122.
22. *TCC* 184.
23. W.G.Morrice, 'The Parable of the Tenants and the Gospel of Thomas', *ExpT* 98.4, 1987, 104–107, following J.D.Crossan, 'The Parable of the Wicked Husbandmen', *JBL* 90, 1971, 451–465, suggests this is a parable of prompt response to crisis, as with the Steward of Luke 16.1–8. The possibility is intriguing; but murder as a model for appropriate action would probably be too bizarre to afford any effective challenge to the hearers.
24. *TCC* 2,3.
25. *TCC* 54, 145.
26. *TCC Introduction* (A).
27. *TCC* 176.
28. *TCC* 36, 38, 39, *Introduction* (B).
29. *TCC* 68, 163.
30. *TCC* 36(c), 165.
31. *TCC* 162.
32. *TCC* 16.
33. *TCC* 68, 171. E.P.Sanders, *Jesus and Judaism*, SCM Press 1985, insists that teaching could not have led to death, let alone crucifixion. Cynics would not seem to have thought so. See Ch. IV.
34. *TCC* 18.
35. *TCC* 46(1), 76, 129.
36. *TCC* 21.
37. *TCC* 19.
38. *TCC* 20.
39. *TCC* 147, 214; Matt. 25.31–46.
40. *TCC* 187, 217.
41. *TCC* 20(a).
42. *TCC* 10(a), 14, 178, 204, 216.
43. *TCC* 59.
44. *TCC* 58, 206.
45. *TCC* 46(k), 46(B)
46. *TCC* 206, 214.
47. *TCC* 14, 187.

48. See note (42) to Chapter I.
49. *TCC* 225.
50. *TCC* 59, 77, 78.
51. *TCC* 227.
52. *TCC* 178
53. *TCC* 6, 68, 163. 'Leave the dead to bury their own dead', (Luke 9.59–60) betokens a similar break with all inheritance: *TCC* 36(c).
54. *TCC* 59, 171, 229, 260.
55. *TCC* 46, 46(B), 201, 226.
56. See for instance, H.W. Attridge, *First Century Cynicism in the Epistles of Heraclitus*, Scholars Press 1976, ch. II, 'The Religious Critique of the Fourth Epistle'; and A.J. Malherbe, 'Pseudo Heraclitus, Epistle 4: the Divinisation of the Divine Man', *JAC* 21 (1978), 42–64; and *TCC* 46.
57. *TCC* 46(b).
58. *TCC* 46(B).
59. *TCC* 187(b).
60. *TCC* 46(a).
61. *TCC* 173(c).
62. *TCC* 46(f).
63. *TCC* 46(g)
64. *TCC* 9, 27.
65. *TCC* 52(b)
66. *TCC* 83 (and 4, 7).
67. *TCC* 173(c), again.
68. *TCC* 29, 118.
69. *TCC* 47.
70. *TCC* 11, 48–51.
71. *TCC* 57, 152.
72. *TCC* 10, 153.
73. *TCC* 54, 145
74. *TCC* 161.
75. *TCC* 181; Mark 11.15–18.
76. *TCC* 119.
77. *TCC* 32.
78. *TCC* 29, 50.
79. *TCC* 4, 9, 17, 35, 45, 54, 65, 78, 230.
80. *TCC Introduction* (A).
81. *TCC* 176.
82. *TCC* 175.
83. *TCC Introduction* (C).
84. Compare the argument of R.F. Hock, *The Social Context of Paul's Ministry*, Fortress Press 1980, with the case made by E.A. Judge.

The Social Pattern of Christian Groups in the First Century, Tyndale, 1960; 'The Early Christians as a Scholastic Community', *JRH* 1960, 4–15, 125–137, and 'St. Paul and Classical Society', *JAC* 15, 1972, 19–36; W. Meeks, 'The Social Context of Pauline Theology', *Int.* 37, 1982, 266–277.

85. The Zealot connection was most thoroughly argued by S.G.F. Brandon, *The Fall of Jerusalem and the Christian Church*, Manchester University Press 1961, and *Jesus and the Zealots*, Manchester University Press 1967. Too much has to be excised as 'apologetic disguise' from the conciliatory passages of the synoptic tradition for the case to be persuasive; and there is the deafening silence of Josephus, eager to tar the Zealots with any handy brush. See, e.g. J.L. Segundo, *The Historical Jesus of the Synoptics*, Orbis and Sheed & Ward 1985, ch. V; G. Vermes, *Jesus the Jew*, Collins 1973; reissued SCM Press 1983, ch 2; A.E. Harvey, *Jesus and the Constraints of History*, Duckworth 1982, ch. 2; J. Riches, *Jesus and the Transformation of Judaism*, Darton, Longman & Todd 1980, ch. 5; and further, note (13) to Ch. IV.

86. R. Macmullen, *Enemies of the Roman Order*, especially 60–66, and notes.

87. R. Macmullen, *Enemies of the Roman Order*, chs. 5 and 6.

IV   Jesus as Cynic

1. This study presupposed the analysis of the synoptic material into 'Q' material (matter closely similar in Matthew and Luke, but not present in Mark, suggesting a coherent 'source' used independently by each of the former writers), Mark itself, and other material used just by Matthew or just by Luke. Though that analysis does not persuade all scholars, it is the only one that matches first-century methods of literary composition: see my 'Compositional Conventions and the Synoptic Problem', *JBL*, forthcoming; but also *The Christ and the Cynics*.

2. M. Hengel, *Jews Greeks and Barbarians* (ET) SCM Press 1980, 125; cf. also his *Judaism and Hellenism*, (ET) SCM Press 1974; and *The Charismatic Leader and his Followers*, (ET) T. & T. Clark 1981, 6.

3. Malherbe, *Cynic Epistles*, 35–51; Diogenes Laertius 1.101–105.

4. See e.g., the books listed at note (85) for Chapter III; and also E.P. Sanders, *Jesus and Judaism*.

5. E.g. J.B. Tyson, 'The Two-Source Hypothesis: a Critical Appraisal', in A.J. Bellinzoni (ed.), *The Two-Source Hypothesis*, Mercer 1985, 449 (citing B.H. Streeter); cf. my own *The Church and Jesus*, SCM Press 1968, 122–123, with the same reference.

6. It is even harder to construct any plausible 'hypocritical' reason for such a merger of traditions, to match the kind of motive Lucian suspects

obtains among many Cynics.

7. For the conjectural 'communities' behind the 'sources' listed at note 1. above, see e.g. I Havener, *Q: The Sayings of Jesus*, Glazier 1987; H.C. Kee, *The Community of the New Age* [Mark], SCM Press 1977; K. Stendahl, *The School of Saint Matthew*, Gleerup 1968; also R.E. Brown, *The Community of the Beloved Disciple*, Chapman 1979. Here it is communities as users and preservers and adapters (as in form and redaction analyses) that are in question.

8. See e.g., S. Freyne, *Galilee from Alexander the Great to Hadrian*, Glazier/Notre Dame 1980; G. Theissen, *The First Followers of Jesus*, (ET) SCM Press 1978 (= *Sociology of Early Palestinian Christianity*, Fortress 1978).

9. G. Theissen, *First Followers*, insists, for instance, 'In the case of the synoptic gospels we have to remove material which is of Hellenistic origin', 3.

10. A. Wifstrand, *L'Église ancienne et la Culture grecque*, Editions du Cerf 1957 (though he thinks there was no contact), 7–9; M. Hengel, *Judaism and Hellenism*, I 83–88; and especially, H.A. Fischel, *Essays in Greco-Roman and related Talmudic Literature*, Ktav 1977, and his 'Studies in Cynicism' in J. Neusner (ed.), *Religions in Antiquity*, Brill 1968; and also S. Liebermann, in Fischel, *Essays*.

11. See my 'The Social Contexts of Jesus the Teacher', *NTS* 33, 1987, (forthcoming).

12. V.K. Robbins, *Jesus the Teacher*, Fortress 1984; R. Riesner, *Jesus als Lehrer* (2), Mohr 1984.

13. Other roles are much less likely still. For discussions, see, e.g., R.A. Horsley, 'Popular prophetic Movements at the Time of Jesus', *JSNT* 26, 1986, 3–27; and his 'Menahem in Jerusalem', *NovT* 4, 1985, 335–348, taking issue both with S.G.F. Brandon and M. Hengel on their respective views of the supposed character and relevance of 'Zealotism' for our understanding of Jesus. On this latter issue see also E. Bammel and C.F.D. Moule (eds), *Jesus and the Politics of His Day*, Cambridge University Press 1984; though I myself pointed out in my 'The Politics of Jesus', a much wider definition of 'politics' is needed than that deployed in this latter volume, as Macmullen, for instance, makes clear in *Enemies of the Roman Order*. B.L. Malina, 'Jesus as Charismatic Leader', *Bib. Theol. Bull.* XIV, April 1984, 55–63, usefully criticizes the Weberian category of the 'charismatic' (as too demagogic-authoritarian to fit the synoptic evidence), and allows for a variety of possible influences, though not for other 'non-establishment' figures. Instead he simply imposes an alternative sociological typology on the data. See also note 85 to Chapter III. J.H. Yoder, *The Politics of Jesus*, Eerdmans 1972, does not take enough note of the contemporary context.

14. I am here deploying a 'criterion of dissimilarity', whose uncritical use I have myself deplored, in my *The Church and Jesus*, 111–116. What I would strongly urge here is that it may properly be used within any given hypothesis, as part of its internal structuring, but not as though it could stand 'outside' to determine what data may be admitted for consideration. See further below, and also my 'The Social Contexts of Jesus the Teacher'. Used here the criterion seems to show that the alternative hypotheses considered would be internally coherent; whereas my own does not seem to suffer in that way. However, some fresh rival hypothesis might deal just as well or better with the data. As yet none such suggests itself.

15. Josephus, *Jewish War* 2.215–217; Philo, *quod omnis probus liber sit*, 77–78; L. Vaage, op cit.

16. *The Community Rule* (IQS): *The Damascus Rule* (CD), especially 12–13.

17. Sanders, e.g., in *Jesus and Judaism*, 106–113, 174–211.

18. R.A. Horsley, 'Popular Prophetic Movements . . .'

19. G. Vermes, *Jesus the Jew*, 210-213.

20. According to Origen, Celsus asserted that claims to be 'God, Son of God, Divine Spirit', able to save or to condemn, were commonplace in Phoenicia and Palestine in his day (*contra celsum* 7.9). Origen notes that Celsus offers no precise evidence. Earlier he hints that Celsus may well have made up the idea of others being prompted to such claims by Old Testament prophecies, without any evidence that such claims had actually been made, simply to detract from the idea of Jesus uniquely fulfilling such promises (1.1, 57). Neither this nor still later Hermetic literature is relevant to our first-century Jewish and Cynic contexts.

21. E.P. Sanders, *Jesus and Judaism*, 33–58, 223, insists that no interpretation of the teaching ascribed to Jesus adequately explains why he was executed. See above, note (33) to Chapter III.

22. On the loose connection between finding what is 'characteristic' and what is 'distinctive', see my *The Church and Jesus*, 116.

23. *The Church and Jesus*, e.g., 86–92.

24. E.P. Sanders, *Jesus and Judaism*, 156; and e.g., 5, 118, 307, 329.

25. *Jesus and Judaism*, 11, 13, 326–327.

26. Compare *Jesus and Judaism*, 13.

27. *The Church and Jesus*, 70–73.

28. *Jesus and Judaism*, 69–70. On 'action' and 'intention'.

29. See note (14) above; and *Jesus and Judaism* 91–92 and note.

30. Ibid., 91f and note.

31. Diogenes Laertius 6.21; ps. Crates 6; ps. Diogenes 37; Dio 8.5, 72.16; *TCC* 2; A.J. Malherbe, 'Antisthenes and Odysseus and Paul at War', *HTR* 76, 1983, 143–173.

32. On 'Son of Man' I am persuaded over-all by B. Lindars, *Jesus, Son of Man*, SPCK 1983 (but note the suggestions of R. Bauckham, 'The Son of Man; "A Man in my Position" or "Someone"', *JSNT* 23, 1985, 23–33, and R. Casey, '"Son of Man" – General, Generic and Indefinite', *JSNT* 29, 1987, 21–56. In general, on the remainder of the development of christology, I am content to remain within the terms of the discussion represented by J.D.G. Dunn, *Christology in the Making*, SCM Press 1981, (though I think the idea of pre-existence came on the scene with Paul, and so earlier than Dunn allows); compare also I.H. Marshall, *The Origins of New Testament Christology*, IVP 1976; R.H. Fuller, *Foundations of New Testament Christology*, Lutterworth 1965.

33. See note (84) to Chapter III; and also A.J. Malherbe, 'The Beasts at Ephesus', *JBL* 87, 1968, 71–80; 'Exhortation in First Thessalonians', *NovT* XXV, 1983; 'Antisthenes and Odysseus and Paul at War'.

34. See my 'Law and Custom in Luke-Acts and in late Hellenism' in B. Lindars (ed.), *Law and Religion in the Bible* [or some such], (forthcoming), and other essays in the collection; more briefly, my 'Freedom from the Law in Luke-Acts', *JSNT* 26, 1986, 49–52.

35. *TCC* 101-150.

36. Justin, *Apology* II.3. Justin himself clearly wants to be distinguished from Cynics, in line with the quietist and conformist strand in early Christianity noted in the previous paragraph but one; cf. *Apology* I.17; and note A.J. Malherbe, 'Justin and Crescens' in E. Ferguson (ed.), *Christian Teaching: Studies in honour of Lemoine G. Lewis*, Abilene 1981. For other references, see my 'Christians and Cynics', note (34); see K. Surin, '*Contemptus Mundi*', *JAAR* LIII. 3, 385–410.

37. See my *A Man for Us and a God for Us*, Epworth 1968. For the relevance (still at a theoretical level) of linking a 'liberation' theology with an incarnational christology based in a critical historical assessment of Jesus' human ordinariness, see J. Moltmann, *The Crucified God*, (ET) SCM Press 1974; J. Sobrino, *Christology at the Crossroads*, (ET) Orbis and SCM Press 1978; J.L. Segundo, *The Historical Jesus of the Synoptists*, (ET) Orbis and Sheed & Ward 1985. E. Kasemann's *Der Ruf der Freiheit*, Mohr 1968 (ET, *Jesus Means Freedom*, SCM Press 1969) is powerful, but stays at the level of religious individual and church.

V Jesus and the Threat of Freedom

1. Though the following are not likely to be available to every reader of this book, I note various responses to the 'peace convoy' of 1986, in *The Guardian*: Polly Toynbee, 9 June 1986, an editorial comment, 10 June 1986, one of many reader's letters, from R.L.

Turner, Department of Politics, University of Warwick, 11 June 1986. The British Home Secretary, D. Hurd, likened the hippies to 'mediaeval brigands' and 'robber barons'. The extravagance of the remarks would suggest they had some considerable power, even at a distance, to disturb the heirs of those really effective pillagers and enslavers. Polly Toynbee's interviews suggest a motif of gentle self-pleasing, with still more concern for the people and places affected by the intrusion. R.L. Turner is willing to see the hippies' life-style as a genuinely incisive critique of our society. I would want to allow that my own assessment (two paragraphs below) may be as flawed as Lucian's jaundiced view of artisan Cynics in the second century probably was.

2. The day after I drafted the following sketches, the journal *New Internationalist* 160 (June 1986) arrived, dedicated to 'Radical Lifestyles', and insisting on the relevance of this approach; especially Amanda Root, in her 'Keynote', 4–6. The writers, though perhaps less insulated from harsh realities than I, seem more optimistic than I am as to the likely practical impact of such action.

3. I note especially writing by Charles Elliott, and most recently his *Comfortable Compassion?* Hodder 1987; Jim Wallis, *Agenda for Biblical People* (2), Harper & Row 1984 and SPCK 1986; and Horace Dammers, *A Christian Life Style*, Hodder 1986. Also worth noting at the theoretical level are R.J. Ackermann, *Religion as Critique*, University of Massachusetts 1985, and A. Kee, *Domination or Liberation*, SCM Press 1986; P.J. Wogaman, *Economics and Ethics*, SCM Press 1986.

4. See my 'The Politics of Jesus', art. cit. (n. 3, p. 180 above).

5. Mark 10.42; Luke 22.25.

Appendix: The Sources

1. Dio (Chrysostom) of Prusa; see the *Loeb* edition, Harvard 1932, trans. J.W. Cohoon and H.L. Crosby.

2. Epictetus (Arrian's Discourses of Epictetus), *Loeb*, Harvard 1925, trans. W.A. Oldfather.

3. A.J. Malherbe (ed.), *The Cynic Epistles*, Scholars Press 1977.

4. Diogenes Laertius, *Lives of Eminent Philosophers* (esp. book VI) *Loeb*, Harvard 1925, trans. R.D. Hicks; (references to Diogenes of Sinope, Antisthenes, etc., in this collection are given thus – VI 5, 24 . . .)

5. Lucian of Samosata, *Loeb*, Harvard 1932, trans. A.M. Harmon.

6. Plutarch, *Moralia, Loeb*, Harvard 1927, trans. F.C. Babbitt and others.

7. Quintilian, *Institutes, Loeb*, Harvard 1920, trans. H.E. Butler.

8. Pliny junior, *Letters and Panegyricus, Loeb*, Harvard 1969, trans. B. Radice.

9. Josephus, *Loeb*, Harvard 1926, trans. H. St.J. Thackeray and others.

10. Seneca, *Loeb*, Harvard 1917, trans. R.H. Gummere.

11. Philo, *Loeb*, Harvard 1929, trans. F.H. Colson and others.

12. *Apostolic Fathers, Loeb*, Harvard 1926, trans. K. Lake; I have used the older edition, J.B. Lightfoot, Macmillan 1898.

13. Justin Martyr, *Apologies I & II*, in A.C. Cox, *The Apostolic Fathers*, reprinted Eerdmans 1979.

14. J.M. Robinson (ed.), *The Nag Hammadi Library*, Brill 1977; for discussions of the relevance of the material see e.g., E. Yamauchi, *Pre-Christian Gnosticism*, Tyndale 1973; and A.H.B. Logan and A.J.M. Wedderburn (eds), *The New Testament and Gnosis*, T. & T. Clark 1983.

Select Bibliography: Modern Authors

This list includes a few items which were published or came to attention too late to discuss in the text or the notes. The ancient sources are described briefly in the *Appendix*, pp. 175–179, and convenient editions of texts and translation (mostly *Loeb Classical Library*) are noted there.

Ackermann, R. J., *Religion as Critique*, Amherst, University of Massachusetts Press 1985.

Archbishop of Canterbury's Commission, *Faith in the City*, London, Church House Publishing 1985.

Ardagh. J., *The New France* (3), Harmondsworth, Penguin 1977.

—*France in the 1980's*, London, Secker & Warburg, and Harmondsworth, Penguin 1982.

Attridge, H. W., *First Century Cynicism in the Epistles of Heraclitus*, Missoula, Scholars Press 1976.

Bammel, E. and Moule, C. F. D., (eds), *Jesus and the Politics of his Day*, Cambridge, CUP 1984.

Brandon, S. G. F., *The Fall of Jerusalem and the Christian Church*, Manchester, Manchester University Press 1961.

—*Jesus and the Zealots*, Manchester, Manchester University Press 1967.

Dickinson, R. D. N., *Poor, yet making Many rich*, Geneva, WCC 1983.

Dill, S., *Roman Society from Nero to Marcus Aurelius*, London 1905.

Downing, F. G., *Strangely Familiar*, Manchester, Downing 1985.

—*The Christ and the Cynics*, Sheffield Academic Press 1988.

Dudley, D. B., *A History of Cynicism*, London 1937, reprinted Hildersheim 1967.

Elliott, C., *Comfortable Compassion?* London, Hodder 1987.

Freyne, S., *Galilee from Alexander the Great to Hadrian*, Wilmington, Glazier, and Notre Dame 1980.

Funk, R., *Parables and Presence*, Philadelphia, Fortress 1982.

Girard, R., *Des Choses cachées depuis la Fondation du Monde*, Paris, Grasset, Livre de Poche 1978.

—*Le Bouc Emissaire*, Paris, Grasset, Livre de Poche 1982

Halliday, W. R., *The pagan Background of early Christianity*, London 1925.

Harrington, M., *The New American Poverty*, [US, 1984] London, Firethorn 1985.

Hendrickx, H., *The Parables of Jesus* (2), London, Chapman/ New York, Harper & Row 1986.

Hengel, M., *Judaism and Hellenism*, (ET) London, SCM Press 1974.

—*Jews, Greeks and Barbarians*, (ET) London, SCM Press 1980.

Hock, R. F., *The Social Context of Paul's Ministry*, Philadelphia, Fortress 1980.

Hollis, M., 'Positional Goods' in A. P. Griffiths, (ed), *Philosophy and Practice*, Cambridge, CUP 1985, 97–110.

Hollis, M. and Lukes, S., (eds), *Rationality and Relativism*, Oxford, Blackwell 1982.

Kloppenborg, J. S., *The Formation of Q: Trajectories in Ancient Wisdom Collections*, Philadelphia, Fortress 1987.

Lascaris, A., 'Economics and human Desire': see Girard, R., *New Blackfriars* 68:803 (March 1987) 115–125.

MacMullen, R., *Enemies of the Roman Order*, Cambridge, Mass., Harvard Univerisity Press 1966.

—*Paganism in the Roman Empire*, New Haven, Yale University Press 1981.

Malherbe, A. J., *The Cynic Epistles*, Missoula, Scholars Press 1977.

—*Social Aspects of early Christianity* (2), Philadelphia, Fortress 1983.

—*Moral Exhortation*, Philadelphia, Westminster University Press 1986.

—[many articles listed in the notes here]

Meeks, W., *The First Urban Christians*, New Haven, Yale University Press 1983.

—*The Moral World of the first Christians*, Philadelphia, Westminster/ London, SPCK 1986.

Sanders, E. P., *Jesus and Judaism*, London, SCM Press 1985.

Seabrook, J., *Landscape of Poverty*, Oxford, Blackwell, 1985.

Segundo, J. L., *The historical Jesus of the Synoptics*, New York, Orbis/ London, Sheed & Ward 1985.

Stambaugh, J. and Balch, D., *The Social World of the First Christians*, Philadelphia, Westminster/ London, SPCK 1986.

Timberlake, L., *Only One Earth*, London, BBC/ Earthscan 1987.

Tosh, J., *The Pursuit of History*, London, Longman 1984.

Vaage, L., 'Q: The Ethos and Ethics of an Itinerant Intelligence', Diss., Claremont 1987.

Wallis, J., *Agenda for Biblical People* (2), New York, Harper & Row 1984.

Wengst, K., *Pax Romana*, (ET) London, SCM Press 1987.

Wogaman, J. P., *Economics and Ethics*, London, SCM Press 1986.

Index of Ancient Writings

3. Ancient 'Pagan' Writings

4. Ancient Christian Writings, in the Canon of Scriptures

5.Other Ancient Christian Writings

Index of Subjects and Modern Authors